Revolutionizing Repertoires

Revolutionizing Repertoires

The Rise of Populist Mobilization in Peru

ROBERT S. JANSEN

The University of Chicago Press
Chicago and London

The University of Chicago Press, Chicago 60637
The University of Chicago Press, Ltd., London
© 2017 by The University of Chicago
All rights reserved. No part of this book may be used or reproduced in any manner whatsoever without written permission, except in the case of brief quotations in critical articles and reviews. For more information, contact the University of Chicago Press, 1427 E. 60th St., Chicago, IL 60637.
Published 2017
Printed in the United States of America

26 25 24 23 22 21 20 19 18 17   1 2 3 4 5

ISBN-13: 978-0-226-48730-4 (cloth)
ISBN-13: 978-0-226-48744-1 (paper)
ISBN-13: 978-0-226-48758-8 (e-book)
DOI: 10.7208/chicago/9780226487588.001.0001

Library of Congress Cataloging-in-Publication Data

Names: Jansen, Robert S., 1977– author.
Title: Revolutionizing repertoires : the rise of populist mobilization in Peru / Robert S. Jansen.
Description: Chicago : The University of Chicago Press, 2017. | Includes bibliographical references and index.
Identifiers: LCCN 2016058028 | ISBN 9780226487304 (cloth : alk. paper) | ISBN 9780226487441 (pbk. : alk. paper) | ISBN 9780226487588 (e-book)
Subjects: LCSH: Presidents—Peru—Election—1931. | Peru—Politics and government—1919–1968. | Politics, Practical—Peru—History—20th century. | Populism—Peru—History—20th century. | Political participation—Peru—History—20th century.
Classification: LCC JL3492.J36 2017 | DDC 320.56/620985—dc23 LC record available at https://lccn.loc.gov/2016058028

♾ This paper meets the requirements of ANSI/NISO Z39.48–1992 (Permanence of Paper).

For Rogers Brubaker

Contents

Preface ix
Abbreviations and Terms xvii

Introduction 1

1 Who Did What? Establishing Outcomes 27

2 The Social Context of Action: Economy, Infrastructure, and Social Organization 58

3 The Political Context of Action: Collective Actor Formation in a Dynamic Political Field 79

4 The Sources of Political Innovation: Habit, Experience, and Deliberation 121

5 Practicing Populist Mobilization: Experimentation, Imitation, and Excitation 153

6 The Routinization of Political Innovation: Resonance, Recognition, and Repetition 191

Conclusion 204

Appendix A: Chronology 217
Appendix B: Population, Suffrage, and Exclusion 221
References 227
Index 243

Preface

The question of political practice is, or at least should be, central to the study of politics. The things that politicians, and collective political actors like parties and social movements, *do* in the course of pursuing and maintaining political power are just as important as their social origins, identities, motives, ideologies, or organizational characteristics. But while political practice matters a great deal, the scope of what political actors are likely to find themselves doing at any given time and place tends to be quite limited. When political actors act, they usually do so in fairly habitual ways. They follow routine procedures, recycle tried-and-true strategies and tactics, draw on models from the past, and mimic others in the present. Contemporary social movements in the United States boycott companies, march on Washington, and engage in acts of nonviolent civil disobedience; contemporary U.S. political parties hold voter registration drives, produce television ads, and host expensive fundraising dinners. In rare and surprising moments, however, something new comes along. Indeed, none of the practices just noted were common a hundred years ago. If the landscape of political practice at any given time and place tends to be relatively stable, where do new practices come from? Under what conditions, and by what processes, do political actors make a break with their old habits and develop new lines of action? When new practices are elaborated, what shapes their characteristics? And what does it take for new practices to get assimilated into the toolkit of routine go-to options? This book—which is, in the end, a sociological study of the sources of political innovation—seeks answers to these questions.

I argue that explaining the rise of novel political practices requires three analytical steps. First, it is necessary to attend to changes in the terrain of social-structural realities, as these can afford opportunities to political actors who are seeking new practical alternatives. This terrain constitutes the *social* context of action in which political actors are situated. Second, it is necessary to understand the characteristics and unfolding dynamics of the *political* context of action—the local political field in which actors are vying for position—because these contribute to the formation of collective actors with specific endowments, set in relation to one another in particular ways, facing unique sets of opportunities and constraints. Third, it is necessary to attend to the political actors' experimental engagement with new practices as this unfolds over time, with a clear comprehension of the social experience and perspectives available to them as they evaluate practices and judge how they match up with the changing social and political context. I will develop this argument in the introductory chapter and return to it in the conclusion. But for now, suffice it to say that this approach implies the need for attention to macro-historical social and political contexts, but also to meso- and micro-level relationships, interactions, and processes; that it suggests we attend to institutional structures and material realities, but also to cultural resources and situated perception; and that it asks us to consider not only actors' social locations and organizational positions, but also their experiential trajectories and personal habits of thought and action. Most of all, explaining political innovation demands a serious engagement with the problem of human creativity.

I develop this argument through the sustained consideration of a particular historical case—Peru's 1931 presidential election—in which the candidates of two opposing parties, along with their party leadership, elaborated a new modality of political practice that I identify as a distinctively Latin American style of *populist mobilization*. Prior to 1931, nothing like populist mobilization had been practiced in Peru. Indeed, this case represents the first example of large-scale, election-oriented populist mobilization in Latin American history, predating Perón's and Vargas's reliance on the practice by nearly a decade and a half. Over the course of this critical election, outsider political actors—facing a unique political situation, set against a backdrop of changing social conditions—developed and implemented a new set of political ideas, strategies, and tactics. And once populist mobilization had been enacted, its example revolutionized the set of practices that future politicians would have on hand as they attempted to secure or maintain legitimacy and power. Explaining this historical shift is the substantive agenda of this book.

I did not set out initially, however, to study political innovation. When I began this project, I believed that I was embarking on an investigation into the thorny but fascinating topic of populism. Populism has long been a prominent feature of the Latin American political landscape, and a renewal of pop-

PREFACE   xi

ulist activity in the 1990s underlined its continued importance. Neo-populism became a topic of fierce debate amongst scholars, journalists, and members of the interested public. In the early 2000s, the talk in Latin Americanist circles was of Peru's Alberto Fujimori and Venezuela's Hugo Chávez, among others. With their charismatic personalities, flamboyant styles, heated rhetoric, and controversial policies, figures like Fujimori and Chávez had engendered strong loyalties and catalyzed intense opposition. In many respects, they bore a striking resemblance to the populist figures of an earlier generation—people like Argentina's Juan Domingo Perón and Brazil's Getúlio Vargas—whose images have come to define a romanticized stereotype of Latin American political culture. To this young student of contentious politics, the topic seemed both endlessly puzzling and imminently pressing—an impression that rings even more true today than it did then.

It was my engagement with the interdisciplinary populism literature that led me to Peru. As I began to review this literature, I found that much of the recent scholarship was having a hard time making sense of the contemporary Latin American cases. Previous generations of populism scholars, who had focused on the cases of the 1940s and 1950s, had associated populism with a historically specific developmental stage. Accordingly, many observers—having largely relegated populism to the dustbin of history—were caught off guard by its resurgence in the wake of democratization. To me, the difficulties posed by the new cases suggested a need to reassess the existing populism theories, and even to reconsider some of the classic cases on which these were largely based. My search for the most puzzling of the earlier cases led me to the events of Peru's 1931 election. The stark differences between the two populist candidates competing head-to-head in this election—in terms of their social origins, institutional positions, and ideological orientations—seemed to throw a monkey wrench into standard definitions, conceptualizations, and typologies of populism. At the same time, for reasons that will be discussed in chapter 2, the case appeared anomalous vis-à-vis what were otherwise compelling explanatory theories. I found that the solution to the conceptual problem was to take a practice-oriented view to the phenomenon, shifting the focus from populism to "populist mobilization," and understanding this as a versatile mode of practice that could be undertaken by actors of various stripes—in power or seeking it—in pursuit of a wide range of social, political, and economic agendas. The solution to the explanatory problem followed from this practical reorientation, in conjunction with an appreciation of the fact that this was a *new* practice for the Latin American context. As has already been noted, Peru's populist mobilization was precocious; and it was precisely for reasons deriving from this preciousness that the existing populism theories had such a hard time accounting for it. Explaining the rise of populist mobilization in Peru would thus mean explaining an instance of political innovation—hence my ultimate theoretical orientation and explanatory agenda.

The realization that this would be a book about political innovation, not populism (at least not directly), shaped its writing in a few notable respects. I have focused the discussion in the introductory chapter on sociological theories of contentious politics and creative social action, rather than on theories of populism. In an effort to avoid distraction, I have located my brief comments on what scholars of populism might take away from this study in the concluding chapter. And to underscore the fact that I am not here making claims about populism qua populism—especially given the fact that my definition of "populist mobilization" does not overlap neatly with reigning folk or scholarly conceptions of "populism"—I have made every effort to be precise in my language. Except when discussing the literature, I refer to "populist mobilization," to "populist rhetoric," and to "pop*ular* mobilization" (all of which I define in chapter 1), but never, generically, to "populism."

This project would not have been possible without generous financial and institutional support. The archival research in Peru was funded by the Andrew W. Mellon Foundation, the Fulbright IIE fellowship program, UCLA's Latin American Institute, and the University of Michigan's Sociology Department. Further support was provided by the University of Michigan's Society of Fellows, its Office of Research, and its College of Literature, Science, and the Arts. In Lima, the Instituto de Estudios Peruanos (IEP) provided a wonderful intellectual home from which to launch my excursions into the archives. I am exceedingly grateful to the staff of all the archives and libraries at which I worked: the Sala de Colecciónes Especiales of the Centro de Documentación (CEDOC) at the Pontificia Universidad Católica del Perú; the Sala Pedro de Peralta y Barnuevo at the Archivo General de la Nación (AGN); the library of the IEP; the Hemeroteca of the Biblioteca Central of the Universidad Nacional Mayor de San Marcos; the Sala de Investigaciones and the Sala de Hemerográficas at the Biblioteca Nacional del Perú; and the Hemeroteca of the Instituto Riva-Agüero. I owe a special debt to Ana María Arróspide of CEDOC, to César Durán Ybañez of the AGN, and to Virginia García of the IEP. I would also like to thank the Peruvian Fulbright Commission for its hospitality. Portions of this text come from articles published in *Sociological Theory* (vol. 29, no. 2 [2011], 75–96) and *Theory and Society* (vol. 45, no. 4 [2016], 319–60). I thank Springer for granting permission to reprint material from the latter, as well as the anonymous reviewers who provided very

PREFACE   xiii

useful comments on both. The map appearing in the front matter was expertly produced by Rachel Trudell-Jones of the University of Michigan's GIS Consulting Service (with reference to historical information provided in Delaune and Dumas-Vorxet 1930 and República del Perú 1933). At the University of Chicago Press, Doug Mitchell's enthusiasm for this project at a critical turning point encouraged me to press forward, Kyle Wagner kept the process running smoothly, and Adeetje Bouma designed a great cover.

I am very fortunate to have been trained as a sociologist at UCLA. There, an unbeatable team of mentors, colleagues, and friends patiently taught me how to do the work that I do and supported me as I stumbled my way through it. Among them, Leisy Abrego, Rene Almeling, Josh Bloom, Rogers Brubaker, David Cook-Martín, Andrew Deener, Rebecca Emigh, David FitzGerald, Jon Fox, Kurtuluş Gemici, Wes Hiers, Angela Jamison, Jack Katz, Jaeeun Kim, David Lopez, Mara Loveman, Michael Mann, José Moya, Zeynep Ozgen, Dylan Riley, Dan Rounds, Bill Roy, Kristin Surak, Iddo Tavory, Andreas Wimmer, and Maurice Zeitlin deserve special mention, as do all of the participants in the department's legendary Comparative Social Analysis Seminar. At the Michigan Society of Fellows, where I began work on this book in earnest, I am particularly grateful to Don Lopez for facilitating such a vibrant site of conviviality and interdisciplinary exchange. I cannot imagine a more pleasant or intellectually rewarding way to transition from one professional stage to the next. All of my colleagues there were tremendous, but I must single out Sara McClelland and Jeff Knight for their ongoing friendship and support. In the Sociology Department at the University of Michigan, I have been exceedingly fortunate to find such a hospitable environment for pursuing a project like this one. I find myself surrounded here by colleagues who want only to see me succeed in my scholarly endeavors. In particular, I want to thank Elizabeth Armstrong, Rachel Best, Deirdre Bloome, Jaeeun Kim, and Alex Murphy for their unflagging moral support in the final stages of this project.

I am burdened by the knowledge that I have received so many useful suggestions over the years that I have not been able to incorporate into this text, so many incisive criticisms that remain inadequately addressed. Nevertheless, I hope at least that everyone who generously shared their thoughts can recognize some mark of their influence on this work. I benefited greatly from feedback from audiences at the Universities of British Columbia, Michigan, Oregon, Toronto, Washington, and Wisconsin, as well as California at Davis, Irvine, and Los Angeles, Grand Valley State University, and Yale. José Bortoluci, Demetrio Laurente Eslava, Luis Flores, and Simeon Newman provided invaluable research assistance, but also wonderful suggestions for and companionship in this project at formative moments. For their comments on individual chapters, related articles, or developing ideas, I want very warmly to thank Julia Adams, Elizabeth Armstrong, Chris Bail, Josh Bloom, Craig Calhoun, Carlos de la Torre, Kurtuluş Gemici, Neil Gross, Wes Hiers, Angela Jamison, Victoria Johnson, James Mahoney, Eric Schneiderhan, Jason Owen-Smith, Matthias vom Hau, Ed Walker, Andreas Wimmer, and Geneviève Zubrzycki. For their feedback on the entire manuscript, I am particularly indebted to Barbara Anderson, Luis Flores, Müge Göçek, Howard Kimeldorf, Greta Krippner, Karin Martin, Alex Murphy, Simeon Newman, Iddo Tavory, and three anonymous reviewers. For providing endlessly generative responses to my written work back when this was still a project about populism, I thank Rogers Brubaker, David Lopez, José Moya, and Andreas Wimmer. Without their guidance in its early stages, this project would not have been possible. My greatest intellectual debt is to Rogers Brubaker, whose commitment to analytical precision, intellectual integrity, and rigorous yet unfailingly generous and humble criticism has set for me an unattainably high, yet eminently estimable, standard.

Finally, Angela Jamison deserves a special note of recognition. Our years together have done more than anything else to shape me both as a scholar and a human being. Angela has supported this project from its inception with unconditional enthusiasm and confidence. But more than that: her energy, joyousness, deep generosity, and radiant spirit have provided me with a constant source of inspiration and renewal. I simply cannot thank her enough.

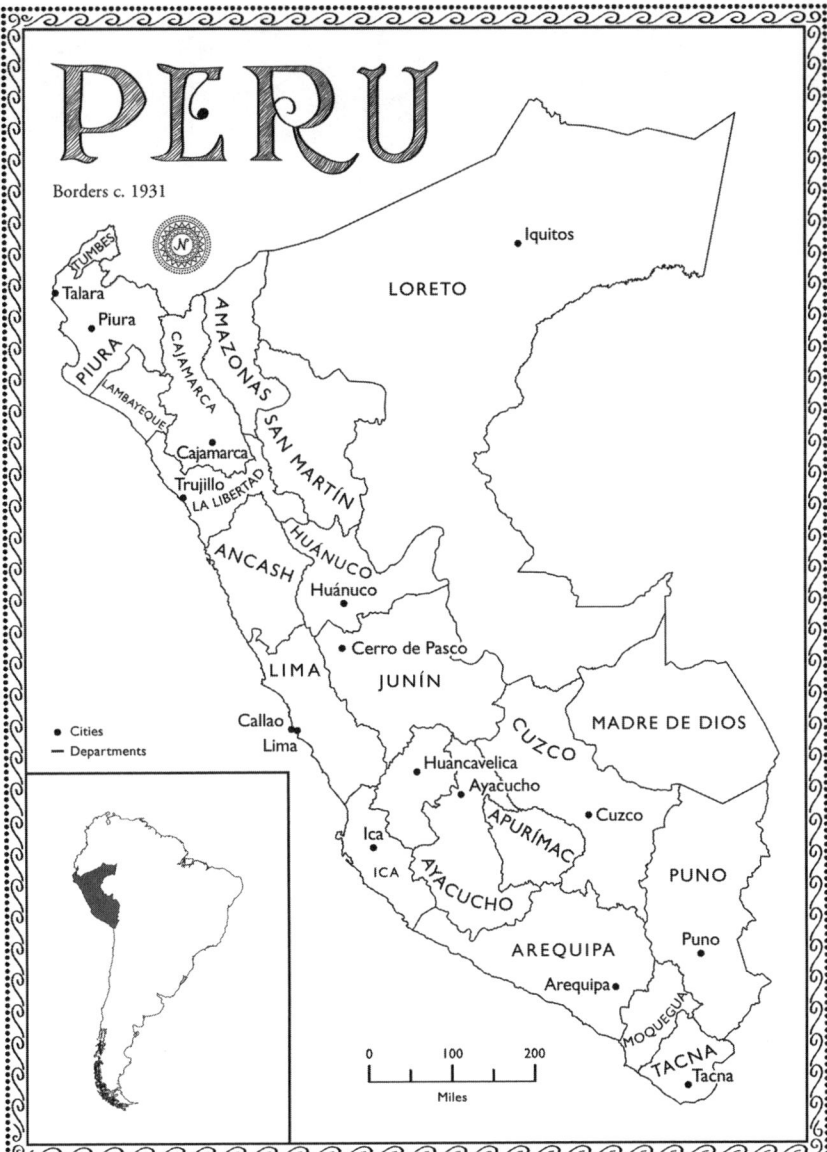

MAP 1

Abbreviations and Terms

Abbreviations

- APRA   Alianza Popular Revolucionaria Americana (Popular Revolutionary Alliance of America)
- CGTP   Confederación General de Trabajadores del Perú (General Confederation of Peruvian Workers)
- CN   Concentración Nacional (National Unity)
- FEP   Federación de Estudiantes del Perú (Federation of Peruvian Students)
- PAP   Partido Aprista Peruano (Peruvian Aprista Party)
- PCP   Partido Comunista del Perú (Peruvian Communist Party)
- PSP   Partido Socialista del Perú (Peruvian Socialist Party)
- UPGP   Universidades Populares González Prada (González Prada Popular Universities)
- UR   Unión Revolucionaria (Revolutionary Union)

Key Terms

Aprista: supporter of, or pertaining to, APRA.

Aristocratic Republic: period of elite civilian rule, 1895–1919.

capitulero: intermediary between party leaders and followers.

caudillo: military or political strongman.

Civilista: supporter of the Partido Civil; later, a broad epithet for anyone associated with the elite politics of the Aristocratic Republic period (left uncapitalized for this usage).

Comité de Saneamiento y Consolidación Revolucionaria (Committee for Healing and Revolutionary Consolidation): commission established by Sánchez Cerro in the wake of his Revolution of Arequipa to punish former members of Leguía's government.

Conscripción Vial (Highways Conscription Act): law enacted by Leguía to compel obligatory labor on national road projects.

Estatuto Electoral (Electoral Statute): electoral reforms promulgated by the Samanez Ocampo junta that expanded the electorate, protected against electoral corruption, and provided for elections in 1931.
Guardia Civil (Civil Guard): national police force accountable to the head of state.
hacienda: landed estate.
indigenista: pertaining to the valorization of indigenous peoples and cultures.
junta: council of military officers that governs a country after seizing power by force.
Leguiísta: supporter of, or pertaining to, Leguía.
Oncenio: eleven-year period of Leguía's rule (1919–1930).
Partido Civil (Civilist Party): dominant elite party during the Aristocratic Republic period, founded on the principle of civilian rule.
Revolution of Arequipa: Sánchez Cerro's coup of August 1930, which unseated Leguía.
Sánchezcerrista: supporter of, or pertaining to, Sánchez Cerro.
War of the Pacific: war fought between Chile and Peru-Bolivia between 1879 and 1883 (won by Chile).

INTRODUCTION

On the morning of Saturday, August 22, 1931, the residents of Lima, Peru, unfolded their morning newspapers to find the entire front page of the city's most prominent daily devoted to an announcement calling them into political action. The bolded text invited "all patriotic citizens to a great demonstration taking place today . . . the first anniversary of the Revolution of Arequipa, in honor of Comandante Luis M. Sánchez Cerro."[1] Although the event was pitched as a nonpartisan, patriotic celebration of the coup d'état that had brought down the long-standing dictatorship of Augusto B. Leguía one year before, readers understood that in effect it was a campaign rally for the architect of that coup, who was now expecting popular gratitude for his heroic deeds to catapult him into the highest office in the land.[2]

The next morning, following what had indeed been a hugely successful pro-Sánchez Cerro event the day before, supporters of the other main presidential contender, Víctor Raúl Haya de la Torre, awoke knowing that they would have to put on an even greater show. Haya de la Torre's APRA party had a big day planned. As the party's newspaper had declared in its own front page announcement on Saturday (in overt competition with Sánchez Cerro's call to action): "On Sunday, August 23, in the Plaza de Acho [Lima's historic

   1. *El Comercio*, August 22 (morning edition), 1931, 1.
   2. Sánchez Cerro had overthrown the Leguía dictatorship in August 1930. This coup had been widely popular, and many Peruvians thought that its principal leader should be rewarded with the presidency for his actions. One year after the coup, Sánchez Cerro—now running as a candidate in a legitimate presidential election—hoped to cash in on this sentiment. But this hope was left implicit in the announcement for the rally of August 22, which mentioned neither Sánchez Cerro's candidacy nor his political party.

bullring] . . . the head of the Peruvian Aprista Party will give his first lecture on doctrine, explaining the theory and aims of the Aprista movement."[3] The lack of a clearly articulated political platform had so far been a liability for the party.[4] The bullring speech promised to change that and, at the same time, to energize supporters with a renewed conviction before sending them out to parade through central Lima.

Thus the two major candidates in Peru's hotly contested 1931 presidential election squared off in the streets of the capital city. Tensions were high on this weekend of competing rallies and marches, given that the opposing camps had clashed violently in the past. But the crowds largely maintained order as tens of thousands of partisans and sympathizers converged on the colonial core, and thousands more looked on from the sidelines and down from the balconies above. The events were well orchestrated, the products of deliberate and sustained political mobilization efforts by the candidates and their parties. Many in attendance had been gearing up for weeks, in party-affiliated political organizations with names like the "First Pro-Sánchez Cerro Political Club of the Artisans and Workers of [the neighborhood of] Barranco" (Club Político Artesanos y Obreros de Barranco Candidatura Pro Sánchez Cerro No. 1) and the "Aprista Civil Construction Workers' Union" (Agrupación Aprista de Construcciones Civiles). While the prospect of taking part in the collective production of spectacle would have no doubt been exciting in its own right, the main draw was the opportunity to hear the equally charismatic candidates speak to the concerns of the historically marginalized and excluded. And the candidates did not disappoint. Each provided a vision of national renewal that promised to help ordinary Peruvians while protecting them from the parasitic elite.[5]

---

3. *La Tribuna*, August 22, 1931, 1.

4. The APRA leadership had been urging Haya de la Torre to release the party's official platform since at least December 1930 (see Luis Alberto Sánchez's letter to Haya de la Torre, dated December 21, 1930, reprinted in Haya de la Torre and Sánchez 1982, 27–30). The lack of a platform had allowed APRA's opponents—especially Sánchez Cerro, but also conservative elites and opponents to APRA's left—to misrepresent the party in a number of ways, knowing that Aprista propagandists had no established grounds for rebuttal. While he would not release the actual platform for another month, Haya spelled out the party program in a lengthy speech on August 23, in an effort to compete with Sánchez Cerro's self-promoting commemorative event on the twenty-second.

5. For accounts of Saturday's events, see *El Comercio*, August 22 (evening edition), 1931; *El Comercio*, August 23 (morning edition), 1931; and *West Coast Leader*, August 25, 1931, 19. For Sunday's events, see *La Tribuna*, August 24, 1931.

The events of this weekend illustrate well the sorts of strategies and tactics that both Haya de la Torre and Sánchez Cerro developed over the course of their presidential campaigns. Both candidates mobilized groups of Peruvians who had been socially marginalized or excluded from the political process in the past; they organized these groups at the local level and staged coordinated public displays of strength; and they infused their private organizing practices and public demonstrations with rhetoric that stressed the common plight and moral virtues of ordinary Peruvians vis-à-vis what they identified as a self-interested, antinational, oligarchical elite. But one would be wrong to imagine that such practices were commonplace in Peru in the first decades of the twentieth century. In fact, this election was the first time in Peruvian history—indeed, in Latin American history—that politicians had practiced what this book will call *populist mobilization* on a national scale to seek elected office. In a context in which politics had historically been characterized by elite machinations, punctuated by the occasional rebellion or coup, Haya de la Torre and Sánchez Cerro each broke with established routine to develop a truly novel mode of political practice.

This occurrence is puzzling from the perspective of structuralist theories of Latin American populism because the social, economic, and political realities that obtained in Peru in 1931 fell far short of what these theories have taken to be necessary conditions for populist politics. These theories, which have their roots in either modernization theory or structuralist Marxism, have tended to focus largely on the paradigmatic cases of Argentina and Brazil in the 1940s and 1950s; and as will be discussed in more detail in chapter 2, they see Latin American populism as resulting from a structural shift in class relations that occurred in the context of peripheral late development. But these conditions were significantly less developed in Peru in 1931 than they would be in Argentina and Brazil nearly a decade and a half later. Peru in 1931 was considerably less industrialized than were either Argentina or Brazil in the mid-1940s, its working class was much less developed, and its dynamics of elite conflict differed considerably. That is, from the perspective of the structuralist theories, conditions in Peru were decidedly *un*ripe for populist mobilization in 1931.

The problem with these theories vis-à-vis the Peruvian case runs deeper than a simple failure to identify correctly the structural predictors of populist mobilization. Rather, it is that structuralist modes of historical and comparative analysis are inadequate for explaining an outcome of this type. This outcome—the historical emergence of a new mode of political practice—involved the exercise of creative human capacities; and creative action is arguably impossible to predict using the tools of structuralist explanation. Even more difficult is to predict creative action that results in something that works and is picked up by others; and more difficult still is to predict the *content* of that creative action. The instruments provided by structuralist analysis are simply too blunt for the job. Whether they mean to or not, structuralist theories tend to proceed as if change in political practice follows in some kind of natural way from big and slow-moving historical transformations. But creative action entails responding in unprecedented ways to situations that have not prompted similar responses from others—that is, it involves acting in ways that contextual conditions do not automatically imply. Further, structuralist theories tend to focus attention away from the actions of individuals or small groups and to neglect the cultural elements of a social context that may condition individual and small-group action—two things that arguably should be at the center of any explanation of creative action. And structuralist theories of social movements suffer from similar problems. While political opportunity theories, for example, are good at predicting when political actors will mobilize and who they will target when they do, they do not provide many tools for explaining the development of *new* political practices, for understanding where these new practices come from, or for explaining what forms these will take (given the range of possible practices that might be devised in response to any given set of social, economic, political, and cultural realities). Thus, explaining the outcome at hand requires somewhat different tools.

In the pages that follow, I will outline an approach to explaining change in political practice that responds to these concerns and can be used to account for the rise of populist mobilization in Peru. While still informed by the substantive contributions of structuralist theories, this approach will foreground processes of political innovation by organized political actors as they confront and move through concrete yet dynamically unfolding problem situations, making it possible to explain why populist mobilization emerged in Peru in 1931 *despite* the seeming unripeness of conditions. Ultimately, I will make the case that this outcome occurred because organized outsider political actors—constituted as such and contingently empowered by the changing dynamics of the political field—had the socially and experientially conditioned understanding, vision, and capacities to recognize the limitations of routine political practice and to modify, transpose, invent, and recombine practices in a way that took advantage of new opportunities afforded by the changing social and political context of action. But before elaborating my argument further, it is first necessary to spell out the historical and theoretical questions in more detail.

The Rise of Populist Mobilization in Peru

To specify the historical questions that this book seeks to answer—and to establish the significance of these to both Peruvian and Latin American history—I must say a bit more about the case and then situate it in the flow of Peruvian political history. On October 11, 1931, Peruvian citizens went to the polls to vote in their county's first legitimate presidential election in over a decade. For eleven years they had suffered under the often dictatorial rule of Augusto B. Leguía, a member of the political elite gone rogue, whose accomplishments in modernizing Peru's economy and infrastructure were rivaled only by his successes at repressing any and all political opponents. When Leguía was finally overthrown in August 1930, it appeared as though a new day might be dawning for the Peruvian people. After an eight-month transitional period of provisional military rule, elections were declared and a new set of laws issued that were designed to expand suffrage and curb electoral corruption. The democratic contest that followed was unlike anything that had been seen before in the country's 110-year history as an independent republic.

Over the course of six months, candidates and their supporters confronted one another in the streets and in the press. They did so not only in the capital city of Lima, but in the far-flung provinces of the north and the south, along the Pacific coast, and in the Andean highlands. In this time of profound uncertainty, some candidates began campaigning weeks before elections were officially declared; and political organizations and clubs continued to form, dissolve, and reconfigure themselves right up until the bitter end. As the candidates and their parties campaigned, political loyalties, alliances, and oppositions were in a state of near-constant flux. Some powerful actors even attempted to outflank the electoral process altogether. On the right, various social and political elites tried to orchestrate backroom deals to shut down the whole affair; and on the left, having been excluded from participation, the Communists supported strikes and criticized the election as a bourgeois sham.

But the initiatives of both the traditional right and the Communist left were overshadowed, and ultimately rendered moot, by the exploits of two quite different—yet equally unconventional—contenders. Víctor Raúl Haya de la Torre was an intellectual born into a downwardly mobile aristocratic family. In keeping with this social background, he was noticeably light-skinned and had European features. Having risen through the ranks of the student and labor movements, he was now a prominent figure of the radical left. Luis M. Sánchez Cerro, the son of a middle-class notary, was dark-skinned with indigenous features. An army officer who had begun his service as a lowly private, he was a career military man with right-wing nationalist sentiments (and right-wing political allies to accompany these).

But while differing in their social origins, institutional positions, and ideological orientations, both of these unlikely presidential aspirants shared in the fact that they came from outside the social and political mainstream. Both hailed from peripheral north-coast provinces, rather than from metropolitan Lima, and neither had kinship ties to dominant social or political elites. Despite such clear outsider status, however, by mid-1931 each had forced his way into the national spotlight, while cultivating powerful movements of loyal supporters. Highly charismatic and sitting at the helms of their own recently formed personalistic parties, these two figures quickly came to dominate the political contest. Each tried to upstage the other in his appeals to newly enfranchised voters and in painting himself as the best alternative to the political exclusions and corruptions of the past. Along the way, the two converged in developing a new mode of political practice that would soon become commonplace in Peru and throughout Latin America.[6]

The two candidates and their parties fixed their crosshairs on more or less the same groups of potential supporters. In the cities and towns, and especially in Lima, they competed for the loyalties of skilled and unskilled laborers, small merchants, street vendors, middle-class professionals, white-collar workers, and students—the ranks of all of which had swelled notably in the 1920s under Leguía. In the countryside, the politicians courted both small landholders and newly proletarianized plantation workers, while proclaiming their sympathies for the plight of the highland indigenous population. Most of the targeted groups had previously been the victims of social stigma and either de jure or de facto political exclusion. Regarded as politically irrelevant, most had never before been seriously courted by national-level politicians. In a dramatic reversal of this trend—a reversal that was as strategically

---

6. Emphasizing the similarities between the two candidates will be controversial in some circles. Haya de la Torre's agenda was more radical, whereas Sánchez Cerro was interested in maintaining the status quo by restoring the national social and political order that had been upended by Leguía. Of the two, Haya is the one most commonly recognized as a "populist." Although he changed his political positions in idiosyncratic ways later in life, he emerged from the left and initially advanced a genuinely transformative agenda meant to break the old oligarchy's stranglehold on political influence. Sánchez Cerro is typically denied the "populist" label, because he lacked a thoroughgoing commitment to social change. Indeed, some historians prefer to call him a fascist (Dobyns and Doughty 1976, 231; Molinari Morales 2006). Needless to say, the disagreement over how these candidates are categorized hinges on definitions and points of emphasis. As this book is focused on the issue of political *practice*, the emphasis on similarity is entirely appropriate. Indeed, it demonstrates the utility of moving beyond stalemated debates about what does and does not count as "populism" (see Jansen 2011).

savvy as it was historic—both Haya de la Torre and Sánchez Cerro validated the identities and concerns of these groups, and made the task of harnessing their political potential a centerpiece of their campaign strategies.

They did so, each knowing that the other was trying to do the same, by devising novel political practices and rhetorical claims that were tailor-made to capture the loyalties of the targeted groups. Each offered his own unique narrative of recent events and definition of the current social and political situation; each outlined his own understanding of the country's social problems; and each presented a particular reading of the nation's past and vision for its future. Their rhetorical claims aligned in valorizing the ordinary, often stigmatized and marginalized, members of Peruvian society as forming the true heart of the nation, and in identifying as the source of these citizens' (and thus the nation's) troubles the continuing political power of an antinational and antipopular oligarchical elite. Of course, since both candidates were making such claims, each strove to identify *himself* with the Peruvian people and his *opponent* with the oligarchy, such that a genuinely popular stance would imply identification with and support for his own political party (and opposition to that of his opponent).

These rhetorical claims animated and were infused into political mobilization projects that grew ever more contentious as the pressure cooker of electoral competition drove each candidate to experiment with increasingly audacious strategies and tactics. Most conspicuously, the candidates and their parties organized unprecedentedly large rallies and marches, often prompting violent responses from opponents and onlookers. While the largest public events took place in Lima, smaller versions were staged in cities and towns throughout the country. These were often held in conjunction with visits by the candidates, as both Haya de la Torre and Sánchez Cerro undertook much more extensive campaigns to the provinces than had ever before been ventured. The candidates' national tours, and the public events that accompanied them, were facilitated by extensive networks of party-affiliated popular organizations. Such organizations—localized political committees, cells, and clubs at the city, neighborhood, and workplace levels—played a critical role in the campaigns by facilitating coordinated participation in party activities (both extraordinary and mundane). Active participation in organizations of this kind politicized ordinary Peruvians, encouraged them to develop new political identities and loyalties, and incorporated them into new structures of social and political solidarity.

In sum, Haya de la Torre and Sánchez Cerro—with the aid of their personalistic parties and party leadership—mobilized previously marginalized social groups into publicly visible political action, while motivating these political efforts with an anti-elite, nationalist rhetoric that valorized ordinary people. That is, they developed a mode of political practice that I call populist mobilization.

These actions might not appear particularly remarkable from the perspective of the present day. Indeed, with the headline-grabbing exploits of contemporary figures like Venezuela's Hugo Chávez and Bolivia's Evo Morales still fresh in recent memory, they might seem like just another example of what we have come to expect from Latin American politicians. That is to say, it is easy to take populist mobilization for granted as intrinsic to the region's political culture if we make the mistake of reading history backwards, according to contemporary understandings of political possibility. But contrary to present-day stereotypes, populist mobilization was far from routine in Latin America—let alone in Peru—prior to the 1940s. Indeed, in the nineteenth and early twentieth centuries, it was not even on the menu of strategic options. Other modes of political practice predominated. Latin American politics had historically been defined by the looming presence of the military in political life; by conflicts between *caudillo* strongmen competing for the spoils of office; and by oligarchical parties organized according to liberal-conservative, rural-urban, and regional rivalries. In the nineteenth century, elite politicians often leveraged their clientelistic networks to marshal private armies and seize the presidency by force. Later, with the rise of electoral politics, they colluded to limit democratic participation, rigged elections, and arranged backroom deals to control electoral outcomes. With a few notable exceptions, bottom-up mobilizations were geographically limited and quickly suppressed. That is, while most countries in the region achieved independence from Spain in the 1820s, their political leaders did not rely on populist mobilization to secure or maintain legitimacy or power.

Peru's 1931 election was thus a critically important moment in the history of Latin American political practice. It produced the region's first example of sustained, national-level, election-oriented populist mobilization. Prior to this moment, never had a candidate for national office so completely flouted traditional channels of political power and so thoroughly staked his political aspirations on the mobilization of support from non-elite segments of the population. In this way, the new practices introduced by Haya de la Torre and Sánchez Cerro represented a radical departure from traditional styles of political action. Explaining this shift in practice is the principal aim of this book.

The events of the 1931 election would change the face of Peruvian politics for generations to come. After this moment, populist mobilization had a track record, as politicians and the general public alike had witnessed it firsthand. More important, they had seen its power to overwhelm the traditional strategies of the political elite. Although populist mobilization was by no means endemic in Peru after the 1931 election—it was certainly not the case that it was practiced continuously thereafter or that it appealed as a strategy to all political actors—the introduction of this mode of practice shifted the terrain of political possibility. Populist mobilization was now a potential go-to strategy; and for all political actors, regardless of whether or not they favored the approach, it became something that they had to anticipate might be used against them. The election was thus a critical turning point in Peru's trajectory of political development. But it was a particular kind of turning point: it was a turning point in the general patterns of the sorts of things that political actors either tended themselves to do or had to anticipate that others might do. It was a turning point in the parameters of political possibility—of what practices were culturally available to political actors. Before this moment, populist mobilization was largely beyond the horizon of the politically "thinkable" (at least by anyone in a position to practice it); after this moment, it was available as a potential strategy. The development of populist mobilization over the course of this high-stakes election thus had profound long-term consequences for Peruvian social and political life.

It also had important consequences for the region as a whole. Once crystalized in the Peruvian context, the set of practices became available to other Latin American politicians—who were very much aware of how events had unfolded in this neighboring country. It would be overstretching to claim that Peru's 1931 election is the lynchpin that explains the rise of populist mobilization across Latin America in the 1940s and 1950s, let alone that accounts for its persistence into the present.[7] But it is quite reasonable to claim that the rise of populist mobilization in Peru played an important role in reshaping the political-cultural environment within which other regional political actors would find themselves operating—and that it would be considerably easier for these actors to draw parallels to the nearby Peruvian case than to other cases more geographically and temporally distant. The election at the center of this book is thus a critical case not only for explaining the historical emergence of populist mobilization in Peru, but also for shedding light on the changing landscape of Latin American politics in the twentieth century.

The primary historical question that this book seeks to answer is the following: Why and how did populist mobilization emerge in Peru in 1931? To answer this question, it will be necessary to confront a series of more concrete empirical puzzles. First, if traditional political routines were so entrenched in

---

7. Explaining the rise, spread, and persistence of populist mobilization throughout Latin America would require much more than this book is able to do.

early twentieth-century Peru, why and how did Haya de la Torre and Sánchez Cerro manage to break with these so dramatically at this particular historical juncture? Second, if something about this moment facilitated a break with political tradition, why did other political actors—of the right and the left—not also change up strategies at this time? Third, if Haya de la Torre and Sánchez Cerro differed so starkly in their social origins, institutional positions, and ideological orientations, why did they end up converging in the sorts of new political practices that they developed? Fourth, why—given what is in theory a wide range of potential options—did this new mode of political practice take on the particular characteristics that it did (i.e., those of what I call populist mobilization)? Fifth, given that this initial practice of populist mobilization was experimental—and vehemently opposed by some powerful actors—why did it ultimately "stick," in the sense of becoming an established go-to strategy for future generations of Peruvian politicians?

Practicing Politics, Changing Repertoires

These historical questions speak to a broader set of theoretical concerns in sociology, history, and political science having to do with political stability and change. Perhaps the most common point of focus for the study of political stability and change is to look at stability and change in political structures. This was a central concern in the political writings of both Karl Marx ([1852] 1969; [1871] 1968) and Max Weber ([1922] 1978). Much of the scholarship on revolutions and social movements is clearly in this vein; but we can also see this emphasis in work on state formation and consolidation, on regime types and transitions, and on the reproduction and transformation of political institutions.[8] Another focus is on the question of stability and change in political identity. The vast literature on party identification and voter realignments would fall under this heading, as would studies of nationalism, the politicization of ethnicity, and other related topics.[9]

---

8. On revolutions, see Goodwin 2001, Skocpol 1979, Wickham-Crowley 1992. On social movements, see Fligstein and McAdam 2011, McAdam 1982, Tilly 1978. On state formation, see P. Anderson 1974, Gorski 2003, Tilly 1975. On regime types and transitions, see Huntington 1991, Linz and Stepan 1978, O'Donnell and Schmitter 1986. On political institutional resilience, see Huntington [1968] 1996, Michels [1915] 1999, Mills 1956. On political institutional change, see Clemens 1997, Mahoney 2001, Mahoney and Thelen 2010.

9. On party identification and voter realignments, see Campbell et al. 1960, Manza and Brooks 1999, Manza, Hout, and Brooks 1995. On nationalism, see B. Anderson 1991, Brubaker 1996, Gellner 1983. On the politicization of ethnicity, see R. Jenkins 1997, Laitin 1985, Yashar 2005.

But while all of these issues are important and will bear on the argument here in various ways, they are not my primary interest. Rather, this book is concerned first and foremost with explaining changes in how politics is practiced. Over the past couple of decades, political sociologists have focused increasingly on the domain of practice. This is evident in work on political spectacle and performance (Alexander, Giesen, and Mast 2006; Berezin 1997; Tilly 2008), on political violence (Auyero 2007; Brubaker and Laitin 1998; Tilly 2003), on political organizing (Clemens 1997; Morris 1984; Polletta 2002), and on social movement strategies and tactics (Bloom 2015; Ganz 2009; Tarrow 1998; Zald 2000), among other topics.

The issue of political action, or practice, would not be of interest if either one of two opposed statements were true. It would not be interesting if political action were completely predictable—if political action followed automatically from a political actor's social position, material interests, social identity, or ideological orientation. But political action is not epiphenomenal in this way. If choices in modes of political action were determined by the actor's social position or related material interests—if, for example, all working-class movements favored the same political strategies—we would not see the range of political practices that we do, nor the variability in terms of their application. If all political action followed simply from social identity, the same: we would see all women's movements favoring the same practices and all ethnonational separatist movements acting in the same way. If all political actions were simply the result of ideological orientation, we would not see the infighting that we do within ideologically aligned groups over issues of strategy. As has been argued by others, and as this book will demonstrate, political practice simply cannot be read off of social position, interests, identity, or ideology.[10] It is at least relatively autonomous from these things, and thus presents itself as a social scientific problem.

At the same time, however, political practice is not a free-for-all, with everyone reinventing the wheel at every turn. If this were the case—if political action were completely random, or at least unconstrained—then what any given political episode looked like would be as unsurprising as any other. Political practice, while in principle still worth accounting for, would be impossible to explain in any kind of rigorous way. But political practice is not a free-for-all; instead, it tends to be quite patterned, fairly limited in range, and relatively stable at any given time and place. If political practice is neither

---

10. All of the work on political practice cited above usefully problematizes political action in this way.

completely indeterminate nor deterministically epiphenomenal of social conditions, then the question of its stability and change over time warrants investigation in its own right.

What are the sources of stability in political practice, if they are not to be found in prepolitical social realities? In more settled contexts, robust political institutions tend to produce relatively stable rules of the game according to which power is exercised, interests are balanced, and political functions are performed, producing relative stability in practice. At the same time—and critically in cases like Peru in 1931, characterized by social disruption and institutional instability—there is a *cultural* stability to political practice, deriving from shared histories of political experience, notions of acceptable and unacceptable ways of acting, and horizons of what is politically "thinkable." More often than not, politicians do what they themselves or others had done previously, without much deviation, reproducing existing political routines out of habit. Of course, they improvise here and there, because some improvisation is always necessary when adapting available practices to contexts that are never entirely identical in their specifics to previous ones. But in general, the array of political practices is relatively limited, stable, and reproduced over time. All of this means that political practice—whether conventional or contentious—tends to involve only minor improvisation on a relatively limited set of practices that politicians normally enact. In this way, it is constrained as much by culture as it is by institutions.

Political sociology describes this quality of political practice through the metaphor of repertoires (McAdam, Tarrow, and Tilly 2001; Tarrow 1998; Tilly 2008). The repertoire concept has been central to contentious politics research for more than twenty years, but it is most closely associated with the work of sociologist Charles Tilly—who introduced the term in a 1976 article and first made it the subject of sustained treatment in his 1986 book, *The Contentious French*. For Tilly (2006, 34), the concept was meant to "capture some of the recurrent, historically embedded character of contentious politics." It did this by highlighting the existence of scripts for the tactics and practices used in collective claims making, and by pointing out that most political action is some sort of limited improvisation on these scripts (ibid., 34–35). That is, protesting social actors draw on historically and culturally limited repertoires, or "tool kits" (Swidler 1986), of contentious practice when enacting their public claims making. Because they tend to be reproduced with minimal modification, such repertoires come to stabilize the meanings of those practices through which politically opposed groups routinely interact, and thus to circumscribe what is strategically thinkable. In this way, they play a key role in constituting the political culture of a given time and place, lending a measure of stability to political practice.

But even if they are stable most of the time, repertoires can change. Sometimes they change gradually; but in rare moments, the world of political practice is shaken by something dramatically new being done. When this happens—especially if the new practice produces unanticipated success—the game changes in the long run, altering the course of political practice as the repertoire changes. Precisely because political action tends to draw on routine practices in the existing repertoire, moments in which practices deviate from the regular pattern—that is, moments of novelty—become particularly interesting, even puzzling. If political practice is patterned, and if these patterns are generally stable, then the question of what produces *change* becomes important.

This is thus a book about change in political repertoires. The central theoretical question that the book seeks to address is this: If repertoires of political practice are generally stable and reproduced over time, under what conditions and by what processes do they change? Answering this question requires attending to three interrelated subquestions. First, under what conditions, and by what processes, do political actors break from their old habits to develop new practices? Second, what shapes the characteristics of the new practices that they develop? And third, what does it take for these practices to get assimilated into—and thus change—the broader political repertoire?

Given this understanding, we can now recast the historical question in more appropriate theoretical language: what follows is best understood as a sociological study of a historically important shift in the Peruvian political repertoire. Explaining this shift is the principal aim of this book.

Existing Approaches to Repertoire Change

Political repertoires have been the focus of a growing body of culturally inflected scholarship within the social movements literature. A good deal of research has been devoted to mapping the strategic terrain by describing the characteristics of existing repertoires. Some of this work has analyzed the tactical options and practical resources that have been culturally available to specific social movements at particular historical moments (Ennis 1987). Operating with a longer time horizon, other studies have traced the historical trajectories of particular repertoires in specific countries (Steinberg 1995; Traugott 1995). Still others have examined repertoires over time through the lens of their instantiation in broader waves of contentious political activity

(Beissinger 2002; Tarrow 1989, 1995; White 1995). Finally, some have taken a more comparative approach in attempting to describe general historical patterns in repertoires across both time and space (Roehner and Syme 2002). Overall, such scholarship has been valuable, establishing as a phenomenon worth explaining the existence of historically contingent yet relatively stable assemblages of political practices. It shows how political action is constrained and enabled by repertoires, thus lending stability to political practice writ large. But this work has generally focused more on charting the contours of the phenomenon than on explaining *change* in repertoires over time.

Another line of scholarship has attended to the question of why, given a relatively stable repertoire of possibilities, social movement actors choose to implement certain practices, strategies, or tactics rather than others. Some of this work has attempted to explain strategic choices by focusing on factors *internal* to the movements in question. Such factors include a group's culture (Polletta 2002; Wickham-Crowley 1992), its organizational collective identities (Clemens 1997), its ideological commitments (Snow and Benford 1992), its members' "tastes in tactics" (Jasper 1997, 229–50), and the qualities of its leadership (Ganz 2000, 2009). Other work on strategy selection has focused on factors *external* to movements. Such work has argued that movements' understandings of how their strategies will be perceived in a given sociopolitical environment play a role in shaping their activities (Brumley 2010), that the institutional characteristics of the *targets* of protest sometimes drive movements' tactical choices (Walker, Martin, and McCarthy 2008), and that movements' practical options are shaped by the dynamics of the strategic situations in which they find themselves (Jasper 2004). All of this work has attended more closely than the repertoire-mapping studies just described to the decision making of political actors. But because it has focused largely on contemporary social movements operating in contexts of relatively robust repertoire stability, it likewise fails to shed much light on the more historical question of repertoire change.

In the end, Tilly's own historical studies of the development of modern protest repertoires in France and Great Britain provide the most useful jumping-off point for addressing the question at hand (see, e.g., Tilly 1986, 1995, 2008). Tilly's general argument is elaborated most fully in his synoptic 2006 book, *Regimes and Repertoires*. Here, as elsewhere, he focuses on how small changes at the margins of existing repertoires can eventually culminate in their slow transformation over the course of decades. His substantive argument, in summary, is that protest repertoires tend to change in dialogue with changes in the political opportunity structure (see Tilly 1986, 1995). That is, Tilly's explanation for repertoire change foregrounds the importance of changing macro-historical conditions—and especially *political* conditions (in the cases of France and Great Britain, those associated with the development of the modern state)—as they slowly reshape the terrain of contention.

While Tilly's work has much to offer and provides a solid starting point, it is not entirely satisfactory for explaining repertoire change in the Peruvian case. In this regard, it suffers from at least three limitations. The first two have to do with the nature of the outcome—that is, that the type of repertoire change that Tilly studied differed from that found in the Peruvian case. The third limitation concerns how the mode of repertoire change that Tilly studied influenced the sorts of theoretical conclusions that tend to be extrapolated from his work. I will elaborate on each of these points in turn.

First, there is the issue of the *pace* of repertoire change. Tilly chose to focus on cases in which political repertoires changed gradually, over the course of many decades. But while it is indeed true that repertoires often change quite slowly, they sometimes change much more quickly, through dramatic episodes of radical innovation (see Walder 2009). Tilly (2008, 12) granted as much when he noted that, "to be sure, radical innovations sometimes occur suddenly and spread rapidly," offering the explanation that "rapid changes in political contexts offer more stimuli to radical, rapid innovation in performances." This was precisely what happened in Peru in 1931, when the rapid elaboration of a new mode of political practice changed the political repertoire in a very short period of time. But while recognizing the distinction between gradual and rapid repertoire change, Tilly (ibid.) felt that the former was more important to understand, since "most of the time political contexts change incrementally . . . [and] as a result, so do performances." This may or may not be the case. Regardless, however, one would ideally like to be able to explain both.

Second, there is the issue of the *focal breadth* of the process of repertoire change. Tilly studied cases in which the repertoire changed as many social and political collective actors—across a broad ecology of similar actors, located in different places, operating at least somewhat independently of one another—began modifying their practices in similar ways over roughly the same period of time. We might say that the focal breadth of change in such cases is wide, or diffuse. But while repertoire change—especially gradual change—often takes place in this sort of diffuse way, with actors responding independently to similar situations and adjusting their actions over time, it can also emerge out of a much more narrow, or centralized, point of origin. Especially in cases of rapid change, the innovative actions of a smaller number of prominent social or political actors—influential first movers—can have a widespread impact, rippling out to transform the broader repertoire. While Tilly's work concerns diffuse change, the Peruvian case is a clear example of centralized change. Again, this incompatibility between Tilly's work and the Peruvian case does not amount to a criticism of that work per se; but it highlights a gap in its applicability to the full range of cases of repertoire change. And, arguably, an understanding of the dynamics of centralized repertoire change only stands to enhance our understanding of the dynamics of diffuse change.

The third limitation of Tilly's approach, for present purposes, derives from the first two. A focus on gradual and diffuse repertoire change predisposes the researcher to search for slow-moving and macro-level explanations, which inevitably shifts the lens away from localized and eventful interactions and processes to broader structural conditions. This may be perfectly appropriate for the study of gradual and diffuse change, both because of the particular contours of the phenomenon and as a practical response to the demands of data collection. But it can lead the reader of such studies (if not the researcher him- or herself) to forget that macro-structural conditions do not themselves produce repertoire change—*people* do, as they act in specific, structurally constrained contexts. The result can be an overestimation of the adequacy of structuralist theories of repertoire change and a lack of tools for the study of rapid and centralized instances of the phenomenon. While it is still important to attend to the structural context when explaining rapid and centralized repertoire change, it is also necessary to attend to the interactional and iterative social processes by which political actors come to transcend their established routines to elaborate new lines of practice as contextualized situations unfold. While it is clear from Tilly's later work that he appreciated the importance of this task, his work on repertoires provides few tools for undertaking it.[11] An adequate approach to repertoire change must address all three of these limitations before it can build on Tilly's important contributions to historical and political sociology.

Toward a Sociology of Situated Political Innovation

Based on the discussion thus far, an approach to repertoire change that will be capable of explaining the Peruvian case must be tailored to focus on rapid change that originates from a centralized set of political actors, and it must provide tools for identifying the processes producing regular patterns of action at this more localized level. At the same time, given the nature of the case, it must be prepared to accommodate the unpredictability of unsettled times in poorly institutionalized contexts—and the fact that this means that

---

11. See, e.g., McAdam, Tarrow, and Tilly 2001; and cf. Gross 2010.

social rules, roles, collective actors, and organizations may be in a state of flux. What, then, is the best way to proceed? The discussion above has already suggested the inadequacy of approaches implying either a strong structuralism or a radical notion of contingency, but the limitations of these warrant further elaboration here.

Especially in the field of comparative politics—but also in what sociologists Julia Adams, Elisabeth Clemens, and Ann Orloff (2005) have referred to as "second wave" historical sociology—political action has tended to be approached with a form of macro-analytic social or political structuralism. There are a few problems with this approach, at least when it comes to explaining repertoire change. The first is that it tends to treat political practice as epiphenomenal of deeper structures. But as noted above, political practice is at least relatively autonomous from these, and indeed can itself have recursive consequences for social conditions—in that it can result in the reconfiguration of social relationships, solidarities, and cleavages. Structuralist approaches thus fail to appreciate that political actors themselves can play important roles in constituting their own bases of support; and this is particularly important to bear in mind when studying populist mobilization. A second problem follows from the first. As suggested above, repertoire change is ultimately the result of human action, not abstract structural conditions. This means that any explanation pitched solely at the macro-analytic level misses out on an important part of the action driving the process, which takes place at the micro- and meso-analytic levels. Finally, whether implicitly or explicitly, structuralist approaches advance a quasi-deterministic mode of explanation that is entirely inappropriate to the subject of repertoire change. If the notion of political repertoires is premised on the fact that political actors tend to act in fairly routine ways, then for a repertoire to change, some actors must act in ways that their predecessors had not; and, more critically, they must act in ways that their contemporaries—confronted with the same sociopolitical conditions—are not acting. That is, those who drive repertoire change are by definition acting audaciously and creatively; and audacity and creativity cannot be predicted deterministically. At the very least, the centrality of creative action to the outcome in question means that an adequate explanation must go a step beyond the identification of necessary or sufficient structural conditions—traditionally the bread and butter of comparative-historical research (see Cyr and Mahoney 2012). For these reasons and others, traditional structuralist approaches are inappropriate to explaining change in political repertoires.

Critiques of structuralism are nothing new in political and comparative-historical sociology. But some of what has come in the wake of these critiques is equally unsatisfying (albeit for different reasons). For many, the alternative to structuralism has been to embrace a sort of radical contingency. Indeed, contingency has become something of a buzzword for "third wave" historical sociology and the historical turn in the human sciences more generally. As a polemical response to structuralism, this has no doubt been useful; but the utility has diminishing returns. Strong contingency arguments continue to operate according to terms established by structuralist theories, which posit contingency as the negation of structural determination: that is, what cannot be explained by structure is idiosyncratic, unpatterned, unexplainable. Contingency is structural determinism's residual category. But this category is much too expansive, ignoring various other ways in which social life is patterned at the meso and micro levels. The alternative to arguing that an outcome is not wholly determined by macro-structural conditions is not to argue that it is the unpredictable result of radical contingency.

It is also possible to explore other sources of the patterned nature of social action, interaction, and relationships. Given that the mode of repertoire change of interest here is rapid, with its origins in a relatively well-circumscribed social space, it is necessary to develop a set of analytical tools for looking inside structurally conditioned yet eventful political contexts, and explaining how people respond to and interact in the context of micro-level situations as these unfold over time. This requires not only attending to structural conditions, but also, as much as possible, understanding the situation from the perspectives of the actors involved—located as they are in a particular place and time, with a limited spatial and temporal horizon of knowledge and experience. That is, explaining the rise of a new mode of political practice requires stepping into the shoes of conscious and creative historical subjects for whom it *did not yet exist* in the political culture. Because repertoire change involves the introduction of novelty, the actions taking place at the micro level that are of most interest for the outcome in question are expressions of profound creativity. Accordingly, it is necessary to go beyond just attending to institutional rules and social routines—because creative political action breaks these—to rely instead on a theoretical perspective that attends to the often neglected human capacity for creativity.

This book seeks to demonstrate that the key to explaining repertoire change is to understand it as a product of contextually situated innovation by collective political actors. Change in a repertoire means that something has been added to the preexisting set of practical possibilities.[12] That is, political

---

12. This is analogous to the introduction of a new product (to take an example from the economic domain), a new technology (to take an example from the technological domain), a

repertoire change entails innovation, which involves the exercise of human creative capacities to transcend the stability of routine expectations and practice. It is increasingly common in cultural, economic, and organizational sociology to treat innovation as a process of recombination—that is, of the fragmentary transposition, adaptation, and resuturing of existing practical models into something new (Berk and Galvan 2009; Clemens 1997; Faulkner and Becker 2009; Stark 1996; Swidler 2001). *Political* innovation similarly involves the recombination and reshaping of practices from *here* and *there*, from *now* and *then*, into something novel that makes sense for and is useful in the context at hand. But creating something that is successful in this way is easier said than done. Recombinatory possibilities are often limited by experience and constrained by convention; and it is remarkably challenging to stitch together new packages of practices that are both internally coherent and appropriate to given situations—especially when those situations are hard to read, the future is uncertain, and the practices to be newly enacted are untested. Explaining political innovation requires understanding where the innovative impulse comes from, what leads to the translation of that impulse into effective action, and why that action takes the form that it does. Given these powerful constraints, where can explanations of political innovation— and thus ultimately of repertoire change—find traction? The most promising place is in a systematic approach to practice that foregrounds the lived experiences of social actors who are capable of responding creatively to the unpredictable situations in which they find themselves.

Such an approach is provided by the pragmatist theories of social action originally formulated by Charles Sanders Peirce ([1878] 1992), William James (1975), John Dewey (1922, 1925), and George Herbert Mead (1932, 1934), and recently revived in American sociology by Hans Joas, Neil Gross, and others.[13] This perspective departs from the action theories implicit in much political sociology by rejecting means-ends assumptions as teleological (Whitford 2002) and by theorizing explicitly the sources of creative social action (Joas 1996). Rather than assuming that social actors rationally assign means to the achievement of distinct, preformulated ends, pragmatist theories view

---

new theory (to take an example from the intellectual domain), or a new musical form (to take an example from the cultural domain).

13. See Gross 2008, 2009; Joas 1985, 1993, and 1996. Good overviews of classical American pragmatism are available in Gross 2007, Schefler 1974, and Shook and Margolis 2006. More recent works, representative of the new "pragmatist turn" in American sociology, include Bargheer 2011; Biernacki 2005; Dalton 2004; Emirbayer and Goldberg 2005; Emirbayer and Mische 1998; Emirbayer and Schneiderhan 2013; Frye 2012; Mische 2009; Schneiderhan 2011; Silver 2011; Tavory and Timmermans 2014; and Whitford 2002.

humans as developmentally evolving problem solvers who, encountering "practical problems that arise in the course of life" (Gross 2009, 366), are embedded in unfolding situational contexts in which "ends and means develop coterminously" (Emirbayer and Mische 1998, 967–68). Action unfolds in a continuous stream in which "ends" and "means" are constantly shifting in relation to one another; in which "ends" are never *ultimate* ends, but *anticipated* final results (what Dewey [1922, 225–27] called "ends-in-view"); in which anticipated "ends" can thus be understood as "means"; and in which "means" themselves become experienced as short-term "ends" (see Bargheer 2011, 13–14). This makes it necessary "to reconceptualize human agency as a temporally embedded process of social engagement, informed by the past (in its historical aspect), but also oriented toward the future (as a capacity to imagine alternative possibilities) and toward the present (as a capacity to contextualize past habits and future projects within the contingencies of the moment)" (Emirbayer and Mische 1998, 963). The possibility of *creative* social action emerges through this process of experimentation and developmental social learning, in response to the contingent formation of subjectively understood problem situations (Gross 2009, 366; Joas 1996; Schneiderhan 2011, 594–96; see also Dalton 2004) because—although habitual action may be the norm—there is always "the possibility, greater in some circumstances than others, that a novel way of responding to a problem could emerge for any of the actors involved" (Gross 2009, 369).[14] Only when this tenuous process produces success does the result have the potential to become routinized and recognized after the fact as an instance of political innovation (see Dalton 2004).

Accordingly, *situated political innovation* can be understood as a joint product of the careful reading by social actors of historical conditions and of the practical problem situations that these constitute; of the informed assessment of the expectations and strategies of others; of a stock of experience and the ability to recognize practical alternatives; of anticipating the likely outcomes of possible lines of action; of intelligent and savvy experimentation; and of reassessment, self-correction, and redirection—in short, of contextualized learning through trial and error, with only an incomplete comprehension of the immediate reality and a hazily uncertain (if hopeful) view of the future.

---

14. The sociological question, with regard to innovation, is thus not, *who has exceptional levels of innate creativity, and who lacks it?*—as if there were dramatic inequalities in the distribution of this human capacity—but rather, *what triggers creative responses to particular situations?* (given that these are significantly less common than are habitual responses).

Because of the tendency of pragmatist approaches to focus at the individual level, a modest accommodation is required for it to be a useful tool for understanding political processes. In studying the political sphere, it is necessary to attend not only to *individual* actors responding to situations and devising courses of action, but also to *collective* actors (more or less organized)—as it is ultimately these collective actors that develop and enact lines of political action. In attending to collective actors, it is important not to take them for granted as naturally given or to presume internal consistency across their constituent elements (as their members may not all share the same experiences, agendas, habits, and responses). Collective actors are historically and situationally constituted, in ways that could have been otherwise. How they are constituted matters for how they will respond to situations and formulate lines of action; and, ultimately, for whether their actions will be innovative. It is thus necessary to attend to how parties, movements, and other collective actors form, and how their members relate to one another. What stocks of experiences and routines do individual members bring to the collectivity? What is the relative weight of these individuals (and thus of the experiences, dispositions, and capabilities that they bring to the table) vis-à-vis one another? What is the authority structure within the group? How do members share information and their assessments of the situation with one another? How are their strategic decisions—which will ultimately guide their lines of action—made? What is the group's capacity to act? These questions all have their analogues at the individual (even cognitive) level, but become especially important at the collective level. These considerations add a layer of complexity to the analysis, but are not incompatible with pragmatist principles.

In translating pragmatist approaches to the political sphere, it is also important not to neglect the broader context in which political action is situated. Pragmatist approaches emphasize that the problem-solving activities that hold the possibility for creative responses (whether by individuals or collectivities) always play out within a circumscribed context of action. This context is partially constituted by broader patterns of social structural conditions, but also by the field of other social agents interacting over time against the backdrop of these conditions. This means that, while not an automatic or easily predictable product of structural conditions, neither is human creativity somehow independent of these. Rather, it is situationally "anchored" (Joas 1996, 132–33). Political innovation, then—understood as the contingent product of creative recombination through temporally unfolding and problem oriented social interaction—is always *situated* in a particular context of action. This point is critical for the analysis to follow; but unfortunately, pragmatist approaches are often less than satisfying when it comes to specifying how elements of the broader, historically rooted setting impinge on the context of action (in much the same way that macro-structuralist theories often leave the micro level loose and implicit).

In studying repertoire change that originates in the actions of a relatively circumscribed set of collective political actors, one element of the context of action to which it is particularly important to attend is the broader set of relations among these actors—that is, the structure and dynamics of the political field. The context of a political situation is one in which multiple collective actors are oriented toward one another, are aware of how others are acting, and elaborate their own lines of action in response to one another. These actors, competing for similar spoils, confront the same rules of the game. And the political rules—whether formal or informal, explicit or tacit—govern how contention will play out and delimit who can and cannot legitimately act in the field. These rules are not imposed from the outside, but are rather endogenous to the field (whether established by dominant actors or agreed on by all). In unsettled times, this field is not a static thing. The relative positions of actors vis-à-vis one another can change, new actors can come into being, and old actors can be reconfigured or dis-integrate. Thus, the dynamics of the field can play a key role in the constitution of collective political actors, as well as in shaping their actions. At the same time, as the field and its actors can change, so too can the rules. If the goal is to explain the innovative actions of one or more actors within such a field, it is necessary to explain the changes in the structure and dynamics of the field that impacted the actors doing the innovating. All of this might be thought of as the *political* context of action.

At the same time, all of the political actors vying for position in a field are simultaneously confronting and moving through the same society, with its economic conditions, configuration of social relations, and technological and infrastructural endowments. It should be clear from the foregoing discussion that these conditions cannot be relied on to predict political action on their own. At the same time, however, any approach to political action that stops at the level of the individual, collectivity, or political field, and fails to take into account these social conditions, is similarly inadequate. It is necessary to consider how social conditions such as these can enable particular modes of practice, increase their likelihood of success, and thus afford opportunities to astute political actors. At the same time, as actors orient to the context of action, these social realities are as much a part of what they must attend to as the political realities just discussed. This might be thought of as the *social* context of action.

Finally, the development of a novel mode of political practice through situated political innovation does not in itself amount to repertoire change.

The new practice could fall flat, fail to produce noticeable success in the situation, or for other reasons not be taken up by others. If this were to happen, the novel practice would be ephemeral (as so many are) and the repertoire would persist unchanged. For a political repertoire to change over the long run, the new practice must become routinized—it must be used successfully by others in a range of situations until it itself becomes a part of political actors' stocks of experience and habit. For this to happen, the practice must resonate with audiences at the time of its use. This means that it must be appropriate to the social and political context of action and produce some measure of success for the group practicing it. At the same time, the usefulness of the practice must be recognized by other political actors in the field—both contemporary and future—in such a way that its future use becomes something to be considered or anticipated. Finally, for a new practice to become routinized, others must repeat it to the point that the possibility of its use becomes obvious. Characteristics of the social and political context of action figure centrally in whether these things transpire in the wake of innovation; and it is only when this happens that political repertoires are transformed.

Thus, to explain historical change in political repertoires, it is necessary to attend to the nature of the social and political conditions shaping a given context of action and affording possibilities for political innovation; the situational construction of the relevant collective political actors within a changing political field; the formation of the problem situations that these actors confront; the tipping of these actors' practical responses from routine action into political innovation; and the solidification of the new political practice as a "sticky" innovation that is taken up by others.[15] Specified in this way, a pragmatist approach to repertoire change encourages the systematic examination of how, in rare moments, creative political actors translate existing conditions into new forms of political action. Viewing repertoire change as a result of situated political innovation thus remedies some of the limitations of Tilly's approach and facilitates the historical explanation of the case at hand.

The remaining chapters unfold both chronologically and analytically. Chapter 1 circumscribes the outcome theoretically by sketching a definition of "populist mobilization" and clarifying how this differs from other modes of political practice. It then goes on to substantiate the outcome empirically by demonstrating that 1931 did indeed mark a moment of profound transformation in the Peruvian political repertoire. It does this through a survey of how

---

15. This formulation builds on Gross's (2009) lucid distillation of a "pragmatist theory of social mechanisms."

political practice changed in Peru between 1824, when the country achieved independence from Spain, and the second half of the twentieth century.

Chapter 2 establishes the social context of action by providing an overview of the significant social-structural transformations that Peru experienced in the first decades of the twentieth century. It then goes on to consider how the significance of these transformations should be understood. This exercise serves two important purposes for the book's overall argument. First, it demonstrates that the dominant structuralist theories of populism cannot adequately explain the rise of populist mobilization in Peru. Second, it suggests that social-structural conditions matter, but not in the way that traditional structuralists think they do. While changing social conditions did not make populist mobilization inevitable, they did make it newly possible by generating new grievances, making new groups of potential supporters both politically available and logistically reachable, and laying the social groundwork for political organization and mobilization. Just as important, they formed part of the context of action to which politicians of the day were subjectively oriented as they elaborated their lines of political action. The chapter argues, counterintuitively, that populist mobilization emerged in Peru in 1931 not because conditions were ripe (as structuralists might have it), but because changes in what were still unripe conditions (from the perspective of structuralist theories) spurred creative action by contingently empowered political outsiders who were attuned to the possibilities that they afforded.

Chapter 3, which focuses on the political context of action, explains how two collectivities of previously marginalized political actors, with personal and organizational characteristics that would dispose them to creative political action, crystalized and then came to find themselves in unlikely positions of viability on the national stage by May 1931. It argues that this was not an automatic byproduct of the changing social-structural conditions, but rather the result of contingent events and interactions unfolding within a dynamically changing field of political contention. Empirically, the chapter traces shifts in political relationships (both cooperative and antagonistic), as well as the formation and dissolution of collective political actors, across four significant periods of reconfiguration of the political field that took place between 1918 and 1931. The ultimate state of the political field, and the resulting composition and characteristics of the collective actors, set the stage for the forces of Haya de la Torre and Sánchez Cerro—as contingently empowered political outsiders—to take their first steps toward political innovation in May 1931.

Chapter 4 excavates the sources of political innovation in the first few months of electoral campaigning. At this critical moment, collective actors from across the political spectrum faced new challenges and opportunities, but they responded to these differently. Some continued to act in routine ways, while others began to cobble together novel packages of practices. Through comparison of the initial actions of all four major political tendencies (the forces of Haya de la Torre and Sánchez Cerro, but also of the Communist left and the traditionalist right), this chapter explains this variation in response. The explanation centers around an understanding of how these actors' perceptions of the situation and of their practical strategic options were shaped by their previous, socially conditioned experiences, worldviews, and habits of thought—all of which were conditioned by their positions in the political field. Only the leadership of Sánchez Cerro's and Haya de la Torre's embryonic parties experienced the moment as constituting a critical problem situation that required a break with previous routines and a creative turn toward new forms of action. As these leaders began to experiment with new practices, it was their previous experiences—filtered through deliberative environments that facilitated radical departures from the norm—that led their practices to take on the characteristics of what would become a distinctly Latin American style of populist mobilization.

But political innovation is a process that unfolds over time. New practices have to be tested on the ground, in specific situations in which others are also acting. Accordingly, chapter 5 follows the development of populist practices over the course of the last few months of electoral campaigning, paying particular attention to how the political actors adapted their innovative practices to the context at hand, as well as to how these practices were refined over time as the actors assessed their own actions and responded to the actions of their competitors. It argues that the dynamic of competition between the two parties, and their assessments of their own strategic successes—that is, their experiential learning from themselves and from one another—led to a ratcheting up of the practices that they had been enacting since May. Focusing in particular on the parties' grassroots organizing efforts, their practices at mass rallies, and their political rhetoric, it shows how populist mobilization crystalized and gained in coherence between July and October 1931.

Chapter 6 explains how this new practice became routinized in Peru. Just because a political actor does something does not mean that this action will succeed or that it will become a go-to practice for others. For this new practice to enter into the repertoire in a stable way, it has to be repeated by others; and for this to happen, it has to resonate with popular audiences and be recognized as useful by other political actors. Populist mobilization, although new for the context, shared enough similarities with previous ideas and practices to avoid appearing entirely foreign to popular audiences; it produced recognizable successes for its practitioners; and it was subsequently picked up by other Peruvian actors. Furthermore, the fact that politicians in other Latin American countries were aware of these events played an important—though by no means simplistically determinative—role in the development of populist strategies elsewhere in the region. This last substantive chapter demonstrates that this was the case and shows how it happened.

Finally, the concluding chapter summarizes the historical argument, presents a more schematic version of my pragmatist approach to repertoire change, and considers the implications of this approach for scholars of historical change and contentious politics. The chapter closes with a few brief remarks on how the theoretical considerations that have shaped this book might inform continuing research into the problem of populism.

1

Who Did What?
Establishing Outcomes

Peru's 1931 presidential election was a watershed moment in that country's political history. As a result of complex struggles that played out over a relatively short period of time, a new mode of political practice—populist mobilization—was introduced, fundamentally revolutionizing the repertoire of practices available to Peruvian politicians. In the process, structures of social solidarities and antagonisms were reconfigured, new modes of claims making were introduced, and conceptions of social and political reality were altered. Future political action would confront a new landscape of political possibility. It truly was a structure-transforming event, in the sense articulated by William H. Sewell Jr. (1996). In light of this fact, it is remarkable that the case has received so little scholarly attention.

The event is not very well known, even amongst Latin Americanist academics. Indeed, its significance has gone underappreciated in Peruvian historiography. Jorge Basadre, the foremost Peruvian historian of the republican era, did recognize the importance of the election and devoted considerable attention to it (Basadre 1999, 12:3167–69, 13:3177–208). But apart from his work, there has been only one monograph-length study, in English or Spanish, that focuses squarely on the election and treats both contenders—Víctor Raúl Haya de la Torre and Luis M. Sánchez Cerro—equally (Stein 1980). The one scholarly book on Sánchez Cerro and his political party devotes a mere thirty-one pages to the 1930–1931 period (Molinari Morales 2006). The literature on Haya de la Torre tends to focus overwhelmingly on the figure's changing ideology and to skip quickly over the 1931 election, as it represented just one moment—and, as will be discussed below, ultimately a defeat—in a dramatic political career that lasted over sixty years. The best book on the early years of Haya's party focuses on its social origins and devotes just one chapter to the election proper (Klarén 1973). None of these works focus on explaining change in political practice per se.[1] Recognition of the significance of the event among Peruvianists has thus been partial at best.

Because of this lack of attention, it is not enough merely to stipulate the importance of the 1931 election for Peruvian history—this fact must be substantiated. In particular, it is necessary to demonstrate that there was indeed an important shift in the political repertoire at this time. This must be done before any attempt can be made to *explain* the shift—which is the primary goal of the subsequent chapters. The present chapter thus provides a brief tour through Peruvian history that focuses in particular on what political practices looked like before, during, and after the eventful moment that is the focus of the rest of the book. This tour will make it clear that the 1931 election was indeed a fulcrum in Peruvian history—at least in terms of the political repertoire. Prior to embarking on this journey, however, it is useful to start by providing a working definition of populist mobilization—so that we may know it when we see it, and recognize its absence prior to 1931.

Defining Populist Mobilization

Because this book treats populist mobilization as a subtype within the more general domain of political mobilization practices, it is necessary to begin with what is meant by both "political" and "mobilization"—two terms that have a range of possible meanings. Understandings of what counts as *political* action can range from narrow to broad. For the purposes of this study, I am concerned with a relatively narrow band of the political. I consider a practice to be political when it is oriented toward influencing, changing, or reinforcing the authority relations that are crystalized in the organizational apparatus of the state.[2] As for mobilization, I rely on a fairly straightforward

---

[1]. I would be remiss not to acknowledge that, while they pose different explanatory questions than I do, the books by Steve Stein and Peter Klarén are masterful historical studies, in an otherwise mostly deserted historiographical landscape, without repeated recourse to which the present study would have been impossible.

[2]. This understanding follows Max Weber ([1922] 1978, 54–56) in restricting "the political" to relations of domination, maintained through force, threat, and legitimacy, over a given territory. In the modern era, such territorialized authority relations are typically centralized in the organizational apparatus of the nation-state. Given this understanding of the political, "politically oriented" action is action that "aims at exerting influence on the government of a political organization; especially at the appropriation, expropriation, redistribution or allocation of the power of government" (ibid., 54). This can include activities "likely to uphold, to change or overthrow,

understanding based on the idea that, at its core, the term points to a transition from passivity to activity. I define it as the process by which a number of individuals are moved to coordinated action in pursuit of shared aims; and I include under this broader umbrella those activities by which the material and organizational capacity for—and cultural bases of—such coordinated action are generated.[3] It is important in outlining this definition to note that—because the construction of a sense of shared purpose is always an interpretive accomplishment, and because the coordination of activity relies in part on a cultural infrastructure of shared symbols and meanings—the process of mobilization always has an ideational dimension to it. That said, there is nothing intrinsically *political* about it. What makes mobilization political is when this movement from passivity to meaningful collective activity is oriented toward the accomplishment of political ends. This is the conceptual space within which populist mobilization exists. Now, what makes political mobilization *populist*?

---

to hinder or promote" political authority relations, as well as those of more peaceful groups that seek to influence a political organization (ibid., 55).

3. This definition begins from a literalist understanding of the word as meaning *the process of becoming mobile* (or for my purposes, *active*) coupled with a presumption that the word is being used to describe a *sociological* phenomenon (and so there is something *shared* or *coordinated* about the resulting activity). Tilly (1978, 69) captured this essence well when he identified mobilization as "the process by which a group goes from being a passive collection of individuals to an active participant in public life." One problem with this formulation, however, is that it takes the group for granted as the source of mobilization, rather than recognizing that the formation of a solidary collectivity is often the *result*—and sometimes a primary *goal*—of mobilization (Brubaker 2004, Calhoun 1991). So a better understanding would be the process by which a number of passive individuals are moved to coordinated activity. As Anthony Oberschall (1973, 102) has noted, the coordination part of this usually involves some "process of forming crowds, groups, associations, and organizations." But as both the resource mobilization (Jenkins 1983, McCarthy and Zald 1977) and more culturalist (Melucci 1989, Snow et al. 1986) schools of social movements scholarship have emphasized, such coordinated forms of activity require a supportive infrastructure of material and organizational resources to provide people with the means to act collectively, and of cultural ideas (frames, discourses, identities, etc.) to bind people together and motivate them. I thus understand the processes of "mobilization" to include not only the ultimate coordinated activity, but also those practices that build and reinforce the material/organizational and cultural infrastructure that makes this activity possible. (This distinction is inspired by Rogers's [1974, 1425–28] identification of "instrumental resources," which are used directly in attempts at influence, and "infra-resources," which enable and condition the usefulness of instrumental resources.) Finally, coordinating action requires that people be oriented in a similar direction—that is, that their aims be at least somewhat coordinated as well, even if these may change as the mobilization process unfolds.

I define populist mobilization as the mobilization of marginalized social sectors into publicly visible political action, while articulating an anti-elite, nationalist rhetoric that valorizes ordinary people.[4] Put more schematically, what makes populist mobilization distinctive is the way in which it infuses what I call popul*ar* mobilization with popul*ist* rhetoric. The first of these definitional elements points to the mobilizing activities themselves, the second, to the ideas animating those activities. "Populist mobilization" might thus be thought of as a compound concept that requires definitional elaboration across two domains: the practical and the discursive. This distinction is analytically useful, so long as it is remembered that it is also somewhat artificial—as what is done is inseparable from the *meaningfulness* of what is done in any real world situation. With this caveat, let us consider each element of the definition in turn.

Specifying the first half of the equation is relatively straightforward. As suggested above, I understand popular mobilization to be the mobilization of marginalized social sectors into publicly visible political action. This means that it involves mobilizing people who are either socially stigmatized or usually excluded from the sphere of political power and influence. This could include the poor, the unpropertied, members of ethnically marginalized groups, or people who—for these reasons or others—have not been previously mobilized into political action.[5] It also means that popular mobilization involves animating such people into coordinated political activity in a way that is noticeable to others in the public sphere.[6] This can be done by staging political events—like marches, rallies, speeches, and demonstrations—in public space. But such mobilization can also involve the orchestration of more private gatherings or other organizing activities, insofar as these are publicized or otherwise made widely visible. In many settings, visible mobilization of the marginalized is by its very nature a politically contentious act—regardless of how orderly or well-reasoned it may be—because it poses a challenge to dominant sociopolitical conventions, structures, and actors. It is thus often read

---

4. It is important to note that what follows is aimed at circumscribing a particular modality of political mobilization practice, not at providing a definitive definition of populism per se. I have elsewhere discussed the slipperiness of "populism" as a concept and argued in favor of narrowing the focus to the domain of practice (Jansen 2011). For an extended discussion of this perspectival shift and its implications for the interdisciplinary populism literature, see this previous work.

5. See Gamson's (1975, 16–17) rationale for focusing on previously unmobilized supporters.

6. See Tilly's (1984, 306) definition of "social movement" for a similar emphasis on public visibility.

by its opponents as socially disruptive and destabilizing, or even as threatening and confrontational.

The second half of my definition of populist mobilization inhabits the discursive realm. I have suggested above that it involves the articulation of an anti-elite, nationalist rhetoric that valorizes ordinary people. When I use the term rhetoric here, I use it in its broadest sense: to imply sets of ideas and categories, understandings and depictions of reality, ways of elaborating ideas, modes of argumentation and persuasion, and styles of verbal and physical expression—instantiated in public speech, expression, display, or text—that both legitimate and animate action.[7] Populist rhetoric proposes answers to questions like: Who are "the people"? What are their strengths and virtues? How united or divided are they (or should they be)? Who stands outside the boundaries of this category? In what ways do those beyond the boundary threaten the well-being of those within, or the integrity of the whole? And ultimately: With whom does (or should) sovereignty lie? Accordingly, it involves a sort of claims making—although it is important to note that the claims being made are as much about the nature of social and political relations as they are about particular issues or grievances. But all of this requires some elaboration.

The first thing that populist rhetoric does is to posit the natural social unity and inherent virtuousness of "the people"—of the majority of ordinary members of the national community. In characterizing such a broad swath of society, leaders downplay differences and emphasize similarities (or at least propose a vision of unity through functional interdependence). Insofar as it attempts to traverse at least some traditionally politicized social divides (like class, ethnicity, or region)—arguing that the national body and political authority should not be fragmented by party or group—populist rhetoric is holistic and inclusive. Populist leaders may develop arguments that "the people" includes workers, the urban poor, the landed and landless peasantry, and indigenous populations, as well as professionals, the middle class, or even certain segments of the elite (if they can avoid identifying them as such). Along the way, they adopt nationalist ways of speaking and framing situations. At the most fundamental level, populist rhetoric represents an attempt to forge a solidary "people" through its rhetorical invocation.[8]

7. I do not mean an "ideology," if by this we mean an elaborate, coherently structured, and internally coherent system of ideas. Indeed, one of the first criticisms leveled against populists is typically that their ideas are ad hoc, contradictory, and imprecise.

8. This formulation is adapted from Brubaker (2004, 10), who makes a similar point regarding ethnicity. The question of solidarity is of classic sociological concern. In recent decades, scholarship on class (Fantasia 1988; Przeworski 1977; Thompson 1963), on race, ethnicity, and

But at the same time as it works to construct an inclusive and solidary national people, populist rhetoric also constructs the image of an equally solidary—and threatening—opposition to that people. To do this, it paints the picture of an antagonistic vertical relationship, in which some kind of parasitic, antipopular elite (often identified as an economic or political oligarchy) lords over the ordinary people below. This elite is portrayed as having disproportionate and unjustified control over the conditions affecting the rights, well-being, and progress of the virtuous national people. Precisely which social groups get tarred with the elite brush can vary significantly from one case to another. Indeed, this can be a tricky issue for populist leaders, who sometimes themselves hail from the higher social echelons and who often require the support (even if it must be quiet support) of at least some well-placed elites to sustain their political projects. But regardless of how the popular enemy is constructed, this Manichean rhetoric (de la Torre 2000, 12–20) ultimately aims at forging a sense of vertical antagonism at the national level. True virtue and sovereignty rests with the people, below, while immoral elites exercise illegitimate authority from above.

The rhetorical construction of a solidary and immoral elite is, importantly, instrumental to the rhetorical project of elevating the moral worth of—and collapsing competing distinctions within the category of—"the people." The act of circumscribing a "people" necessarily requires the identification of some groups as antipopular; and the act of identifying the popular enemy among the elite facilitates a sense of shared purpose below. Further, if ordinary people are the heart of the nation, then antipopular elites are antinational as well. It is tempting, although overly simplistic, to conclude that populist rhetoric combines a logic of horizontal inclusion with one of vertical exclusion—since it typically maintains some measure of horizontal exclusion (against pariah ethnic groups, for example) and vertical inclusion (of particular elite segments seen as allied to the popular cause). But it is safe to say that the vertical, "people-elite" opposition is portrayed as the primary categorical opposition in a social field otherwise characterized by shared purpose and functional interdependence. In this respect, populist rhetoric is about the variable construction of social solidarities and antipathies at a national level. And, critically, it attempts to position the populist leadership (whether

---

nationhood (Brubaker 2004; Hobsbawm 1983; R. Jenkins 1997), and on political cleavages (Laitin 1985) has (re)problematized the concept, questioning the assumption that solidarity is a natural result of the relations of production, of market position, of rational decision making, or of primordial biology. Rather, solidarities are made through complex processes and are contingent events that happen and fluctuate (Brubaker 1996, 18–22).

individual, movement organization, or party) at the fulcrum of the national struggle. As the people's natural protector and representative, the populist leadership will fight to right the nation's state of moral imbalance, if given the mandate.

It is important to maintain this distinction between popular mobilization and populist rhetoric, because each can be practiced independently of the other. Popular mobilization is not always accompanied by populist rhetoric. It may be motivated by other sorts of ideas (e.g., socialist, fascist, or anarchist), by a less well-articulated sense of injustice (as in food riots), or by clientelistic social obligations. Nineteenth- and early twentieth-century Latin American history contains numerous examples of popular mobilization that was not motivated or justified by populist principles.[9] Without such principles in play, however, these cases do not meet the definition of popul*ist* mobilization advanced here. Furthermore, just as popular mobilization is not always infused with populist rhetoric, neither is populist rhetoric always instantiated in a mobilization project. It is entirely possible, even common, for public figures to articulate populist rhetoric without actively practicing popular mobilization. Latin American history provides numerous examples of this as well.[10] The term "populist mobilization" should be reserved only for those instances of political practice in which popular mobilization and populist rhetoric are co-present and mutually reinforcing. The populist rhetoric animates, specifies the significance of, and justifies the popular mobilization; and the popular mobilization instantiates the populist rhetoric in concrete political activities. While the two planes remain analytically distinct, there is a clear historical correlation. With a sort of elective affinity, each suggests itself to the other from the perspective of those undertaking political projects. Finally, for the purposes of this book, I am only concerned with populist mobilization that is large-scale, election-oriented, and sustained over a period of time.

The definitional work undertaken so far makes it possible to identify populist mobilization and to distinguish it from other modalities of political practice, but it has been pitched at a fairly abstract level. This has been intentional. Because while it is useful to identify commonalities across this general form

---

9. Peru's electoral campaigns of 1871–1872, which will be discussed below, provide just one example (Giesecke 1978; Mücke 2001). In these campaigns, poor and illiterate Peruvians were mobilized through electoral clubs to participate in marches, rallies, and mob actions. But this mobilization relied on clientelism and coercion rather than populist rhetoric.

10. Haya de la Torre, for instance, developed his populist rhetoric through public writing over the course of nearly ten years in exile without engaging in any kind of sustained, large-scale popular mobilizing.

of rhetorically charged mobilization practice, it is important to work from a definition that accommodates the fact that the specifics of the practice have varied historically across time and place. The precise content of populist rhetoric varies across time and place because different regions and localities have their own unique histories of political styles and symbolism, of group representations and narratives, of the boundaries of social identities and their variable salience, and of claims making and issue framing. And the specific sorts of tactics involved in popular mobilization likewise vary, because different places at different times have different economic realities, structures of social relations, political systems, communicative infrastructures, and patterns of public life. That is, even while sharing the formal characteristics outlined above, one instance of populist mobilization may look quite different from another in a different time and place, in terms of the content of the rhetoric and what the mobilization activities look like.

Accordingly, this book does not claim to be explaining the origins of populist mobilization writ large, nor is it advancing the claim that populist mobilization first emerged in Latin America. The world had clearly seen examples of populist mobilization outside of Latin America prior to 1931. Rather, this book is concerned with explaining the historical emergence of the particular set of populist mobilization practices that developed with reference to the realities of this specific regional context—the distinctly Latin American style of populist mobilization. Per the definition outlined above, the Latin American variant of populist mobilization shares baseline formal similarities with populist mobilization practiced elsewhere. At the same time, Latin America's particular history of colonialism, independence, and state formation, its particular economic conditions, its cultural and religious traditions, its particular ethno-demographic composition, and even its geographical realities have contributed to shaping what populist mobilization looks like in the region.[11] Here, populist mobilization has usually involved top-down mobilization by a charismatic leader, drawing on the cultural tropes of a *caudillo*-type persona (which could include a sort of machismo, an impassioned unpredictability, a capacity for violence, and often religious savior-type imagery). It has involved extensive grassroots organizing and efforts to channel supporters into personalistic party structures. It has involved contentious street mobilization and other public displays by the poor, socially marginalized, and politically excluded. It has articulated a popular nationalist vision—often alongside tropes of *indigenismo* or *mestizaje*—that valorizes workers, peasants, and

---

11. Indeed, explaining how such conditions shaped the characteristics of the practical modality is one of the main aims of this book.

sometimes indigenous groups and the middle class (insofar as they exist) as together forming the heart of the nation. And it has constructed as its target the image of a unified and oppressive political or economic oligarchy—whether a political class that can be painted as the agent of past social and political exclusion, or economic elites that can be blamed for poverty and exploitation. This Latin American style of populist mobilization had its origins in Peru's 1931 presidential election. It had never before been practiced in the region on this scale as a way to secure elected national office; and after this critical moment, other examples cropped up in neighboring countries.

Having thus circumscribed the book's outcome of interest theoretically, it is now possible to establish it empirically in the Peruvian case. To do this, the remainder of the chapter will provide the reader with a whirlwind tour of the history of political practice in republican-era Peru. As we will see, there was no populist mobilization in Peru prior to 1931. Rather, this new mode of political practice was developed over the course of that country's 1931 presidential election; and after this critical moment, it had entered into the repertoire of practices available to other Peruvian politicians, such that it recurred time and again throughout the remainder of the twentieth century.

Caudillos and Oligarchs, 1824–1930

Prior to 1931, populist mobilization was not a part of the political repertoire in Peru. A brief tour through Peruvian history, while necessarily schematic, should suffice to substantiate this point (see table 1.1).[12] Along the way, this section will detail the sorts of (nonpopulist) practices on which politicians *did* routinely rely, while also clarifying why a few historical episodes to which the imprecise term "populism" has occasionally been applied were qualitatively different from what came later (and do not meet the standards of the definition of populist mobilization outlined above).

Popular political participation has long been a touchy subject in Peru. At the time of Spanish colonization, the territory that would become the viceroyalty of Peru (in 1542) was home to one of the two largest and most powerful indigenous civilizations in the Americas—the Incan Empire. Late in the colonial period, it would also be the site of one of the largest indigenous rebellions that Spain faced in its American colonies. In 1780, Túpac Amaru II—a mestizo notable who claimed to be a descendant of the last Incan ruler,

---

12. The best English-language introduction to Peruvian social and political history is Klarén 2000.

TABLE 1.1. Political timeline, 1542–1930

Historical Period	Major Political Events	Political Practices
Spanish colonial rule (1542–1824)	**1542** Viceroyalty of Peru established.	Colonial administration, occasional insurrection
	1780–81 Túpac Amaru II leads large but ultimately unsuccessful rebellion against colonial authorities.	
	1824 Peru achieves independence from Spain.	
Age of the *caudillo* (1824–45)	**1824–45** Chronic politico-military conflict between regional strongmen. Politics remains decentralized, fragmented, volatile.	Political militarism, clientelism
	1841 State declares monopoly on guano.	
Guano boom and bust (1845–79)	**1840s–50s** Guano boom contributes to state growth and political centralization, empowers liberal elites.	Political militarism, clientelism, electoral corruption, brief popular mobilization (in campaigns of 1871–72)
	1850s–60s First national-level elite parties form, supported by local political clubs.	
	1872 Election of first civilian president, Manuel Pardo, founder of the Partido Civil.	
War of the Pacific and reconstruction (1879–95)	**1879–83** War of the Pacific fought against Chile, resulting in devastating defeats for Peru and Bolivia.	Political militarism
	1883–95 Social unrest and military rule.	
Aristocratic Republic (1895–1919)	**1895** Second civilian president, Nicolás de Piérola, comes to power by aligning his Partido Demócrata with the Partido Civil.	Elite party deal making, electoral disenfranchisement, brief popular mobilization (under Billinghurst)
	1896 Electoral law of 1896 restricts suffrage. Piérola initiates professionalization of army to protect civilian rule.	
	1912 Former mayor of Lima, Guillermo Billinghurst, mobilizes disenfranchised urban supporters to secure presidency through brokered deal (is deposed by elite-led coup, in which Luis M. Sánchez Cerro participates, eighteen months later).	
Leguía's *Oncenio* (1919–30)	**1919** Augusto B. Leguía installed in presidency by the military. He dismantles the elite parties and maintains power through rigged elections, with support of key military officers.	Political militarism, political repression, electoral corruption, military patronage system
	1930 Sánchez Cerro overthrows Leguía.	

Túpac Amaru (1545–1572)—revolted.[13] For five months, he and his indigenous supporters mounted a fierce campaign of resistance in the mountains and valleys around the former Incan capital of Cuzco. The rebellion was ultimately suppressed, but not before having made a significant mark on colonial life. The event provoked a strong backlash. Colonial administrators responded with harsh measures, breaking up the Incan royal family and making traditional dress and practices illegal. But even with the rebellion curtailed and strict social sanctions in place against the indigenous population, creole elites (those of Spanish descent born in the Americas) had caught a glimpse of the social order inverted and been shown just how precarious was their position at the top of the hierarchy. Any signs of popular unrest or indigenous empowerment refreshed these terrifying images. It was partly for this reason that Peru remained a loyalist holdout in the wars of independence. Whereas creole elites led the charge against Spain elsewhere in the Americas, in Peru, they feared that revolution would spark a new wave of social upheaval and threaten their dominant position vis-à-vis the much larger indigenous population.[14] This fear carried over well into the republican era.

When Peru finally achieved independence in 1824, the creole elites made sure that the rigid social hierarchies of the colonial era remained intact.[15] As these elites were apprehensive of popular political participation, their imaginings of the new Peruvian nation distinctly excluded the indigenous population—contra Benedict Anderson's (1991) famous argument locating the world-historical origins of nationalism in the Americas.[16] And not only was Peruvian social life characterized by sharp vertical status distinctions tied to both class and ethnicity, but it was horizontally segmented as well—by language, kinship, and region. Just as there was no vertically inclusive national

---

13. On the Túpac Amaru rebellion, see C. Walker 2014.

14. Note that the antipopular nature of the independence movements in Latin America made them distinctly different from the nationalist and often pro-popular anticolonial movements of twentieth-century Africa and Asia.

15. See C. Walker 1999 for a good history of the transition from the colonial era to the early republic, as seen from the vantage of Cuzco.

16. While he admits the "social thinness" of the Latin American independence movements, Benedict Anderson (1991, 49–50) nonetheless makes the argument, regarding the "large, oppressed, non-Spanish-speaking populations," that the European-descendent creoles "consciously redefined these populations as fellow-nationals." But historians have since demonstrated that elite imaginings largely excluded the indigenous population (Méndez 1992 and 1996; Thurner 1995, 292). For further critiques of Anderson from the perspective of Latin America, see Itzigsohn and vom Hau 2006 and Lomnitz 2001 (3–34). The notions of citizenship and nationhood inscribed in the early nineteenth-century Peruvian political imagination are a far cry from those that would correspond with the populist mobilization of a century later.

idea at this moment, horizontal bridges were similarly difficult to imagine. As Aljovín de Losada (2005, 72) has argued, neither was there a developed sense of structural injustice or class confrontation during the nineteenth century. Such ideas were only elaborated with any systematicity much later, as new socio-political movements took the stage in the late nineteenth and early twentieth centuries. That is, whereas populist rhetoric relies on a vertically oppositional and horizontally inclusive conception of the national people, such ideas have not been universally available and resonant throughout Peruvian history—they certainly were not in the early nineteenth century.

As in other Latin American countries, the wars of independence in Peru resulted in a decentralization of political authority and produced a generation of locally powerful strongmen—or *caudillos*—supported by their own private armies and clientelistic networks.[17] Fierce competition between these *caudillos* for the spoils of office, at both the regional and national levels, led to a period of profound political instability between 1824 and 1845—a twenty-one-year period in which Peru saw no fewer than twenty-four regime changes (Klarén 2000, 137). At the presidential level, an upstart *caudillo* would first confront the incumbent with force, backed by his own personal army. Then, after staging his coup d'état, he would typically profess that he had done so to save the Republic from the corruption of his predecessor. Finally, he would hold an election—which he would inevitably win—to legitimate his actions retrospectively (Aljovín de Losada 2005, 53, 71). Essentially, electoral victories were granted to those who had already demonstrated military supremacy. This dynamic left the country in a state of permanent military and electoral campaign (ibid., 52).

But while political practice in this unsettled period was fundamentally coercive, elections continued to play an important role in Peruvian political life—although these served similarly to limit non-elite influence on political outcomes. Republican political institutions, modeled on the Spanish Cortes de Cádiz, established a system of indirect, multistage elections.[18] As is typical of indirect electoral systems, suffrage was remarkably inclusive under these rules for much of the nineteenth century, allowing broad participation—including by the indigenous population. This inclusivity, however, was filtered

---

17. On the relative power of regions vis-à-vis the Lima-based government in the first two decades after independence, see C. Walker 1999, 130–31. On *caudillo* politics in Peru, see Aljovín de Losada 2000; Gootenberg 1997; and C. Walker 1999. For more general treatments of *caudillismo* in Latin America, see Lynch 1992 and Wolf and Hanson 1967.

18. On the origins of Peru's nineteenth-century political institutions in the Cortes de Cádiz, see Chiaramonti 2005. On Peru's system of multistage, indirect elections, see Aljovín de Losada 2005. On indirect electoral systems in general, see Romanelli (1998, 16).

through a hierarchical system of electoral processes that restricted non-elite participation to the local level. A first electoral stage, with broad participation, took place at the parish level. Here, local notables were selected as electors—who by law had to be literate (in Spanish) and capable of paying a series of taxes—to represent the parish at provincial-level electoral colleges.[19] The indigenous vote in these elections was largely a corporate one: members voted in the interests of their local patrons (Aljovín de Losada 2005, 40–41). The electors chosen in the first stage process would then participate in elections for national offices. Technically, then, this system involved broad participation; but it channeled this participation through hierarchical, clientelistic structures that curbed popular influence on national outcomes. In the words of historian Eduardo Posada-Carbó (1996), these were "elections before democracy."[20]

Given the weakness of the central state governing from Lima, and in the absence of national parties, politics in Peru remained decentralized and fragmented. The independence of second- from first-stage elections empowered, and provided a significant level of autonomy to, local elites—especially priests and municipal authorities—who became critical mediators between local- and national-level politics. The most consistent political lines drawn were regional ones, between the conservative north and the liberal south (Klarén 2000, 154–55). But this polarization was not underpinned by national-level party organizations. The lack of party organizations was not simply a result of distance, rough geography, or organizational incapacity (although these were all prohibitive factors), but also of a deeply held suspicion of parties. When conservatives used the terms *club* and *partido* in reference to liberals in the 1830s, for example, it was with a clear negative connotation—implying a closed, elite clique, unconcerned with the greater *patria* (C. Walker 1999, 146). In the absence of national parties, church and military officials found themselves in positions of particular advantage, as the Catholic Church and Peruvian military provided the only national-level social networks or sources of political experience.

This dynamic began to change in the middle of the nineteenth century. In the 1840s and 1850s, Peru experienced an economic boom that lifted the

---

19. According to Aljovín de Losada (2005, 40, 73), many indigenous elites were elected in first-round elections—especially in small towns and rural areas—but almost entirely for local charges. It is important to remember that "the indigenous population" was not a homogenous group, but rather stratified by its own status hierarchies. For a good analysis of indigenous-elite relations during this period in the Cuzco region, see C. Walker 1999.

20. This paragraph is based largely on Aljovín de Losada 2005. For electoral politics through 1860, see Chiaramonti 2005.

country out of the doldrums of the post-independence years. Guano deposits hundreds of feet thick, the product of seabirds feasting on the marine life that thrived in the cold Humboldt Current, had been accumulating for centuries on the rocky islands off Peru's central coast.[21] A surge in demand for this high-grade fertilizer—fueled by midcentury European industrialization and the drive for greater efficiency in agricultural production that this occasioned (Stein 1980, 22)—enriched liberal elites. At the same time, guano revenues propelled the growth of the Peruvian state, which declared a government monopoly over the resource in 1841 and cashed in by selling extractive rights to foreign interests.[22] Relying on new communication and transportation technologies, like the telegraph, railroad, and steamship, the burgeoning state undertook projects to expand its reach into the provinces. Such penetration encouraged a degree of centralization and began to erode local autonomy (Aljovín de Losada 2005, 37). All of this, combined with the new financial basis for political activities that the guano boom provided to the growing liberal elite, led to the growth of political organizations—both local political clubs and national parties.

Such organizations provided a new mechanism of elite control over the political process. The first electoral clubs emerged as early as the 1840s and were formed to influence outcomes in local-level, first-stage elections. Throughout the 1850s and 1860s, these were gradually integrated into more expansive networks of political organizations—effectively resulting in the first full-fledged national political parties.[23] Rather than shifting political activities from the local to the national level, however, the growth of national parties actually enhanced the importance of the local clubs—as they became increasingly important for producing favorable outcomes in the first-stage elections that determined the electors who would vote in national elections. The more that national parties could claim responsibility, via their local clubs, for getting electors selected in first-stage contests, the more those electors were beholden to them when it came to national level voting (Aljovín de Losada 2005, 36–37; see also 55–56). A consequence of this dynamic, as political organizations became stronger and more complex, was that local electoral outcomes became

---

21. On the guano boom, see Bonilla 1974; Gootenberg 1989 and 1993; and Hunt 1973.

22. As Klarén (2000, 162) explains, guano-era presidents began "to forge the beginnings of a national state, with working congresses; legal codes and statutes; expanded governmental agencies and ministries; and, for the first time, a national budget."

23. On the growth of political clubs in the nineteenth century, see Forment 2003. On the development of local political clubs into national parties, see Aljovín de Losada 2005.

increasingly determinative of national outcomes—and the independence of the two electoral stages was effectively eroded.[24]

The importance to national organizations of controlling local political outcomes led to a shift in political practice, as the elite-run national parties devised new tools for influencing local elections. Through their clubs, they developed techniques for political propaganda, bribed voters and local officials, and exercised corrupt influence over the voting process. They also staged increasingly large rallies to demonstrate their popularity and potential force. Finally, and critically, they mobilized poor and often illiterate members of the local community to act as shock troops, to violently seize polling places in public plazas on election day (while warding off those mobilized by competing parties to do the same).[25] In some respects, this was a very real shift toward a greater role for popular sectors in politics; but it was one that was channeled by clientelism, compelled by coercion, and carefully controlled through electoral corruption. Parties and their local intermediaries (known as *capituleros*) attempted to control voter registration, and then to control the outcomes of voting through unabashed force—seizing polling places from the opposition in such a way that balloting became a farce. In the end, such actions were more about displays of power than they were about the mechanics of vote tallying, as elites in second-stage elections essentially assigned outcomes in backroom deals based on the extent to which parties had succeeded in the streets. The logic remained strikingly similar to the one by which *caudillos* were granted post-hoc electoral wins on the basis of their demonstrated military might. Such practices reached their height in the contentious campaigns of 1871–1872, which resulted in the election of Manuel Pardo—the first civilian president in Peruvian history. Pardo's Partido Civil—which he had founded—was, as historian Peter Klarén (2000, 172) describes

---

24. While the autonomy traditionally enjoyed by local elites was already being eroded by the increasing infrastructural capacity of the state, the growth of national parties—and the concomitant undermining of the independence of the two electoral stages—furthered this erosion (Aljovín de Losada 2005, 59–70). Aljovín de Losada (2005, 59) identifies the presidential election of 1851, in the middle years of the guano boom, as the turning point at which the rise of political clubs began to erode the autonomy of local elites in the political process. Chiaramonti (2005) places the turning point a decade later, at the promulgation of the 1860 constitution.

25. On electoral politics during the time of the guano boom, see Peloso 1996 and 2001 and Velázquez 2005. On the role of newspapers, see Mücke 2001 and Aljovín de Losada 2005. On the development of public opinion and mass print media in the last two decades of the nineteenth century, see Jacobsen 2005. For a good description of corrupt electoral practices in the second half of the nineteenth century, see Villarán 1918.

it, "the country's first civilian-based political party to challenge the long reign of military rule in the country" and "the political expression of the new [liberal] oligarchy."[26] The election of Pardo drove the last nail into the coffin of the age of the regional military *caudillo*.

The 1871–1872 electoral campaigns were the high water mark in a temporary trend toward greater popular participation in politics through electoral clubs and street violence, representing perhaps the best example from Peru's pre-1930 history of popul*ar* mobilization without popul*ist* rhetoric.[27] After a brief period of restricted suffrage, the new constitution of 1860 had expanded voting eligibility significantly, legally enfranchising most Peruvian men over the age of twenty-one.[28] But politicians can respond to an expansion of suffrage with strategies other than populist mobilization. Political leaders in 1871–1872 mobilized popular sectors via clientelistic ties that operated through the electoral clubs. These were not "popular" clubs such as would appear in 1931, in that they typically included members from a variety of social backgrounds—including local elites. Vertical relationships were thus contained within the clubs themselves, and lower class members participated out of clientelistic obligation. As in the *caudillo* era, ordinary people participated essentially out of obligation to their local patrons, and local patrons out of obligation to their patrons higher up. Popular sectors were not mobilized through practices or rhetoric that courted them *as* "the people." Rather, candidates and their parties plied potential supporters with banquets, gifts, money, food and alcohol, and social recognition, while sometimes intimidating them with threats of violence (Mücke 2001, 318–19, 332, 341). When ordinary Peruvians were mobilized to manifest visible support or seize the electoral machinery, this did *not* imply a valorization of common people *as* common people. To the contrary, it might be taken as evidence of the vulnerability of their social location. Thus, before a national system of elite political parties was fully consolidated, there was some competition for popular

---

26. On the rise of the Partido Civil, see Mücke 2004.

27. On the 1872 election, including the role of political clubs in campaigning, see Giesecke 1978 and Mücke 2001.

28. As historian Ulrich Mücke (2001, 320 [italics in the original]) explains, "The franchise established by article 38 of the constitution of 1860 was very broad. All men over 21 years of age who could read and write *or* paid taxes *or* owned a workshop *or* some land were allowed to vote. Legally, the majority of adult Peruvian men did have the right to vote. Many craftsmen owned a workshop or a piece of land outside the cities and many peasants were landowners as members of Indian communities. However, we do not know how many people actually voted. There is no doubt that the municipal authorities in charge of registering voters did not respect the laws but rather attempted to prevent political opponents from voting and refused to register them."

support. But this competition did not take the form of populist mobilization. After the 1872 election, the War of the Pacific and its militarized aftermath (which were themselves followed by restrictive electoral reforms) dramatically reduced the importance of electoral clubs until 1931.

The arc of Peruvian political history up to this point was violently disrupted by the outbreak of war with Chile. Bound by a secret alliance with Bolivia, Peru found itself in a lopsided military struggle with its much stronger southern neighbor over that country's long-disputed claim to resources in Bolivia's coastal Atacama Desert. In what would become known as the War of the Pacific, which was waged from April 1879 through the end of 1883, Peru suffered a devastating defeat. The postwar period of reconstruction that followed was marked by social unrest and unstable military rule.[29] This period ended in 1895, when leaders of the two most powerful parties—the Partido Civil and the Partido Demócrata—set aside their longstanding rivalries and cooperated to oust the military from power and then support the candidacy of Nicolás de Piérola, founder of the Partido Demócrata. Piérola, who was only Peru's second civilian president, acted promptly to consolidate, reorganize, and professionalize the army in an effort to reduce its power to threaten civilian politics (Klarén 2000, 205).[30]

The 1895 election inaugurated a twenty-four-year period of stable, civilian, elite rule—a golden age for the traditional parties—that Jorge Basadre famously termed the Aristocratic Republic (*República Aristocrática*).[31] One of the first things that the newly cooperating elites did was to change the electoral regulations in a way that would reassert elite control over the political process. The rise of national political parties had eroded the ability of indirect elections to serve as a barrier against popular participation. At the same time, the elite parties had been forced by the indirect system to depend on less than reliable measures (like vote rigging)—as well as popular campaigning, which they rejected on principle (Aljovín de Losada 2005, 70; Stein 1980, 25)—to

---

29. On the political disruptions of the War of the Pacific and the civil conflicts that followed, see Mallon 1995.

30. At the same time that he reduced the overall size of the army and cut its share of the national budget, Piérola worked to make the institution more efficient and subservient to civilian politics. This initiated a thirty-year period of military professionalization, undertaken with the assistance of French advisors. The advisors (who arrived in 1896) promoted "a military code that accepted ultimate civilian control as a cardinal component of professionalization" (Masterson 1991, 26).

31. Key works on the Aristocratic Republic include Basadre 1963 (7:chaps. 131–46, 8:chaps. 147–66); Burga and Flores Galindo 1979; Garavito Amézaga 1989; Gonzales 1984 and 1991; McEvoy 1997; Miller 1982; and Miró Quesada Laos 1961.

secure political victories. In response, they passed a new electoral law in 1896 that shifted the system from an indirect to a direct electoral process, but that also dramatically limited suffrage and centralized election procedures in elite hands.[32] These reforms were implemented under the pretext of modernizing the electoral system and doing away with the irregularities and corruption produced by a decentralized system that gave too much power to local elites. But they ensured elite control over the electoral process by limiting the franchise to propertied and literate men over twenty-one and assigning control of the electoral registries and vote counting activities to a centralized body composed of the country's largest taxpayers. The reform marked the end of broad participation at the local level (Aljovín de Losada 2005, 70).[33] The power-sharing agreement between the Partido Civil and the Partido Demócrata quickly dissolved; but this meant only that the Aristocratic Republic would be governed for twenty-four years almost entirely by Civilistas—as adherents of the indomitable Partido Civil were called—rather than by elite pact.[34]

In this period, the parties undertook no popular mobilization and made no attempt to legitimate their rule or animate their political practices with populist rhetoric. Popular sectors were neither consulted nor courted. Indeed, there was arguably more popular participation in politics in the age of the *caudillo* and the late guano era than there was under the Aristocratic Republic. As historian Steve Stein (1980, 189–90) has put it, the electoral reforms meant that "behind-the-scenes machinations perpetrated by the government replaced mob violence as the dominant means of engineering political succession." Regular elections were held, but suffrage was extremely limited and

---

32. On the 1896 electoral reforms, see Basadre 1980 (52–58); Chiaramonti 1995 and 2000; and Peralta 2005 (77–81). For the law itself, see República del Perú 1901. Aljovín de Losada (2005, 70) attributes this reform to a shift in consciousness among Peruvian elites (to one more wary of popular inclusion) fueled by French positivism, social Darwinism, and the disaster of the War of the Pacific.

33. Aljovín de Losada (2005, 73) poses the intriguing question of why there were not massive protests at the limitation of the franchise embodied in the 1896 electoral reforms. His tentative answer is that the indigenous elites who would have led such protests retained the franchise, as they were literate and propertied, and disenfranchising the illiterate indigenous population served to reinforce intra-ethnic hierarchies in a way that favored elite interests.

34. From 1895 until 1899, there existed the possibility of an alternation of power between the Partido Civil and the Partido Demócrata (Aljovín de Losada and López 2005, 13). The electoral law of 1896 was meant to guarantee a power-sharing pact between the two parties—a "*Unión Cívica*," as Mariano Nicolás Valcárcel called it (Peralta 2005, 79). But after the death of a key leader of the Partido Demócrata, relations broke down and the Civilistas enjoyed an almost total monopoly on power.

outcomes were prearranged in backroom deals made in Lima's elite social clubs.[35] In the end, the Aristocratic Republic was a long period of stable, elite-controlled, pseudo-democracy along the lines of what Stephens (1989, 283) has called "constitutional oligarchy."

The lack of popular political participation in this era makes particularly notable the one exception to the overall pattern: the brief presidency of Guillermo Billinghurst (September 1912—February 1914).[36] Billinghurst, the son of a businessman in the nitrite trade, was from the southern province of Arequipa and his family—which had closer business ties to Santiago, Chile, than to Lima—"stood at the margins of the thirty or forty families who ruled the Aristocratic Republic" (Klarén 2000, 222). Before running for president, Billinghurst had been mayor of Lima, during which time he gained the support of that city's growing working class for having enacted a number of reforms that benefited them. It was by encouraging the supporters he had gained as mayor to demonstrate in the streets on the eve of the elections—even though they were not eligible to vote—that he managed to secure the presidency. The demonstrations were disruptive enough to the balloting that the necessary one-third of eligible votes were not cast. This technicality meant that the decision would pass to a sharply divided Congress; at which point, Billinghurst struck a deal with the incumbent that the fragmented congressional elites were unable to block. This brief flash of popular mobilization in the capital enabled Billinghurst to circumvent an increasingly fragmented traditional elite. Once in power, he continued to organize labor on his own behalf and implemented dramatic reforms; but his tenure would be short. After just eighteen months, disgruntled elites organized a military coup that sent the president into exile and marked a restoration of the dominance of the traditional elite parties.[37] The Billinghurst episode is the single moment in Peru's pre-1930 history that comes the closest to looking like the populist mobilization elaborated in 1931; but the figure's mobilizing practices were limited to the capital city and were not infused with a built-out populist rhetoric.

The Aristocratic Republic finally came to an end in 1919, when infighting amongst the leaders of the traditional parties culminated in a power grab by the head of one faction, Augusto B. Leguía (who had already served a

---

35. On the social clubs as a mechanism of elite cohesion, see Klarén 2000, 171. For further discussion of the social ties that produced cohesion among the Peruvian elite during the Aristocratic Republic, see Stein 1980, 24.

36. On the Billinghurst presidency, see Blanchard 1977, Gonzáles 2005, and Martín 1963.

37. On the 1914 overthrow of Billinghurst, see Basadre 1963 (8:chap. 156) and Gonzáles 2005.

previous term as president between 1908 and 1912).[38] Just as Piérola had acted to disempower the military on assuming office, so Leguía proceeded to dismantle the traditional elite parties and undermine their leadership. With the orchestrated consent of key military figures, he ruled as dictator for eleven years—a period known as the *Oncenio*—until his overthrow in 1930. Elections during this period were a sham, and political practice was authoritarian.

Although the Peruvian political repertoire clearly did not include populist mobilization in this period, other contentious practices and radical ideas occasionally surfaced from the bottom up. While these were not in themselves instances of populist mobilization as defined here, they would provide building blocks down the road. Indigenous rebellions occasionally broke out in the highlands, but these were quickly put down. Perhaps the earliest example of a bottom-up movement that articulated identities and loyalties that valued everyday people and linked these with the broader *national* entity of Peru— although they were likewise promptly repressed by the militarized Peruvian state in the period of postwar reconstruction—were the groups of mobilized indigenous peasants that emerged during the War of the Pacific and developed a sort of proto-nationalism, as they resisted the Chilean occupation (Mallon 1995). Then, in the late nineteenth and early twentieth centuries, the rise of new modes of work, shifting class structures, new forms of social organization, and the general facilitation of the spread of ideas through easier communication and travel led to the rise of new socio-political movements and ideologies. Workers in new urban industries, confronted with poor living and working conditions, discovered anarcho-syndicalist ideas and began to organize (Hirsch 1997; Pareja Pfluker 1978; Tejada 1985). This fed the emergence of an anarcho-syndicalist labor movement, which was supported by a handful of professionals and social elites, most notably, the famous anarchist politician and writer Manuel González Prada.[39] The emergence of a small middle class, greater accessibility to education, and the rise of student radicalism in the early twentieth century led to the development of new *indigenista* (pro-indigenous) and socialist movements by the 1920s, propelled especially by the prominent Peruvian intellectual José Carlos Mariátegui (Davies 1974;

38. See chapter 3 for more detail on Leguía's rise and presidency.

39. Anarcho-syndicalism would be the dominant ideological force among the organized working class until the rise of socialism in the 1920s (Pareja Pfluker 1978). The writings of González Prada would influence Peruvian radicals for years to come. The socialist, and later Aprista, popular universities (discussed in chapter 3) devoted classes to teaching his thought and were, in fact, eventually named after him (the Universidades Populares González Prada). For the writings of González Prada, see González Prada 1966.

Klarén 2000, 245–62; Martínez de la Torre 1947, 1:237–74; and see Mariátegui [1928] 1995 and 2005).[40] While these groups engaged in a modest amount of political organizing, they remained largely intellectual movements. Together, the new political ideologies articulated by bottom-up movements provided a rich body of discursive materials that creative politicians could later work with, elaborate, and recombine into a more clearly populist mode of thought that would have the potential to resonate at a grassroots level in 1931.

It should be clear by this point that the repertoire of practices available to political actors remained fairly limited and profoundly elite-centric between 1824 and 1930. Of course, there was variation in political practice over the years, and some political actions did have a popular flavor. There had been peasant rebellions and workers' strikes; and there had been peasant-nationalist, *indigenista*, anarcho-syndicalist, socialist, and student movements. But none of these currents meet the definition of populist mobilization presented above. Nor did political elites—long fearful that popular involvement in politics would upend the hierarchical social order—undertake anything like populist mobilization. When popular voices were heard before 1930, elites typically responded to them as squeaky wheels rather than understanding their potential as political assets. No elite political leader in this period, for example, attempted to capitalize on the support of unions or workers' organizations in aid of his political party (Basadre 1999, 13:3182). When they did mobilize popular groups, as in the campaigns of 1871–1872, they did so largely through clientelistic obligations, material incentives, and outright coercion, not by articulating populist principles. Many regimes had been unabashedly authoritarian. But even in putatively democratic periods, the electoral system was incredibly effective at preventing the influence of non-elites on national political outcomes. Whether dominated by military *caudillos* or "democratic" oligarchs, Peruvian politics was elite politics. Political outcomes were the result of intra-elite struggles for power; and the political practices that produced them were aimed at swaying the actions of other elites. The political repertoire included executing coups d'état and other forms of overt coercion, activating clientelistic social obligations, making backroom political deals, mounting letter writing campaigns within elite circles, and rigging electoral rules (as well as elections themselves), but not populist mobilization. Regardless of the fact that only rarely was a given political institutional arrangement

---

40. On *indigenismo* in the early twentieth century, see Arroyo Reyes 2005, Castro Pozo 1924, Davies 1971 and 1974, de la Cadena 2000, Deustua and Rénique 1984, Tamayo 1980, and Valcárcel 1927. For the writings of Mariátegui, see Mariátegui [1928] 1995 and 2005.

stable for more than a few years at a time, the repertoire of political practice was firmly entrenched—and populist mobilization remained virtually unimaginable.

Populist Mobilization in the 1931 Election

But the repertoire was about to change.[41] On August 22, 1930, Luis M. Sánchez Cerro—then a junior army officer stationed in the provincial town of Arequipa—toppled Leguía's dictatorship in a much lauded coup d'état. This so-called Revolution of Arequipa precipitated one of the most tumultuous years in Peruvian history. With the overthrow of Leguía, the political landscape was left in a state of disarray. The worldwide Depression had already devastated the Peruvian economy; and Leguía had systematically dismantled the country's traditional political parties, leaving a vacuum on his ouster.

Sánchez Cerro immediately assumed power as head of a specially formed military junta. From this position, he wasted no time in persecuting leftist dissidents and former supporters of the Leguía regime with equal fervor. But however powerful he had become, he remained dissatisfied with the provisional status of his post. By January 1931, it became clear that he intended to install himself in the presidency. This was Sánchez Cerro's first tactical mistake, but it was not a surprising one—given that it represented a standard, *caudillo*-like response to a type of situation that Peru had seen before. But these were in many ways unusual times. Most members of the junta, steeped as they were in an ethos of military professionalism, were displeased at the undemocratic nature of Sánchez Cerro's intentions and favored a return to civilian rule. In response to what has been described as an "epidemic" of at least six different military insurrections against Sánchez Cerro's planned presidential ascension, the junta members forced his resignation and exile in March and, after a brief period of turmoil, reorganized themselves under new leadership (Villanueva Valencia 1962, 65–68). Sánchez Cerro had held the reins of power for just six months.

In March 1931, the reconstituted junta declared that a free and fair presidential election would be held later that year. Although this new junta occasionally clamped down on civil liberties, it enacted official electoral reforms on May 26, 1931. The new rules outlined in these reforms curbed the possibilities for electoral corruption while expanding suffrage. And although the junta tried for a time to impede Sánchez Cerro's return, it ultimately acqui-

---

41. This section provides only a schematic overview of historical events that are covered in more detail in chapters 3, 4, and 5.

esced—allowing the fallen hero of the Revolution of Arequipa to mount an official campaign for the office that he had tried to steal only months before. The upcoming election would be the first legitimate one that the country had seen in eleven years.

The traditional parties had been severely weakened by Leguía's prior persecutions. As a result, while a few elite politicians tried to build viable campaigns, the political field was left uncharacteristically open. It was in this context that Sánchez Cerro and Haya de la Torre, both of whom were already well known and popular in their own ways, set to work on building their personalistic political organizations. Although Víctor Raúl Haya de la Torre had spent the second half of the 1920s in exile, removed by Leguía in 1923 for his leadership of antiregime protests, he was highly regarded by students and workers for his previous radical activities. He technically founded his APRA party (Alianza Popular Revolucionaria Americana, or the Popular Revolutionary Alliance of America) in Mexico in 1924, but the party's official presence in Peru remained negligible until the fall of the Leguía regime. The Peruvian branch of the party, the PAP (Partido Aprista Peruano, or Peruvian Aprista Party), was formed in September 1930 by supporters who remained loyal to Haya, even while the figure himself remained in exile. Haya directed party activities via correspondence as it became increasingly clear that he would be allowed to run in the pending election, and he finally returned to the country in mid-July 1931. Opposing him, Sánchez Cerro remained a force to be reckoned with. Still riding on the swell of popularity that he had enjoyed in the wake of his coup, the figure maintained the loyalties of many ordinary Peruvians, as well as conservative elites who had opposed Leguía's regime. As was the case with Haya, Sánchez Cerro's supporters organized and campaigned on his behalf until his return from exile in early July. With the assistance of his elite allies, Sánchez Cerro formed his own party, Unión Revolucionaria (or the Revolutionary Union party, sometimes abbreviated here as UR), on July 30, 1931, to provide a more organized apparatus for channeling the activities of his supporters.

In uncertain times in which the political field was in a dynamic state of flux, the two candidates and their embryonic parties made a break with routine political practice and began to act in creative new ways. Given their outsider statuses, Haya de la Torre, Sánchez Cerro, and the organized leadership of their APRA and UR parties had accumulated stockpiles of political experience that were unlike those of Peru's traditional elite politicians; and they drew on these as they assessed the situation and devised their strategies. Over the course of seven months, from April to October 1931, the two sides converged in developing remarkably similar sets of practices in their heated struggle for the presidency. As demonstrated by Steve Stein (1980, 195–99), each candidate did have certain social sectors among whom he did particularly well (Haya among organized workers, Sánchez Cerro among unorganized workers). But in general, the APRA and UR parties were competing with one another in their efforts to mobilize more or less the same groups of marginalized common citizens who had been previously excluded from the machinations of elite-dominated politics (see figure 1.1). And the political mobilization practices that they developed to do this aligned with the definition of populist mobilization outlined above.

The candidates and their parties staged unprecedentedly large mass events in Lima and other cities. These were symbolically provocative—and often contentious—affairs designed to capture the attention of the Peruvian public. They typically involved a period of rallying and speechmaking, in which the charismatic candidate (and often others) would address crowds numbering in the thousands—sometimes tens of thousands—at a central plaza. The rally would typically be either preceded or followed (and sometimes both) by a period in which the assembled supporters would parade through the city—shouting, singing, chanting slogans, and waving banners—past crowds that had assembled to watch the spectacle. The events were flush with patriotic as well as partisan symbolism, as supporters attempted to equate the party with the national-popular good. All of this was extremely provocative, given Peru's long history of elite-dominated politics, the elite's inability to mount viable campaigns of their own, and the scramble between the two main candidates to take advantage of this fact. Although especially APRA prided itself on its members' disciplined and orderly comportment, isolated eruptions of violence were not uncommon. In many cases, wealthy elites watched warily from their balconies above as the parade passed along the city's main thoroughfares, while supporters of the opposing candidate clashed with marchers at the margins. On one level, these events served to animate already committed supporters; on another, they were efforts to attract new supporters and to capture constituencies. At the same time, however, these events were also demonstrations of political power to opponents and government authorities. Overall, they were performative events that communicated the candidate and his party's standing in the political field to supporters, bystanders, officials, and opponents alike.

At the same time, Haya de la Torre and Sánchez Cerro staged wide-ranging tours of the country. This was also an unprecedented move, as previous national-level elite politicians had tended to focus their attentions on Lima, rarely making personal appearances elsewhere. Taking advantage of

FIGURE 1.1. Haya de la Torre and Sánchez Cerro battle for control of the Peruvian nation. Source: *Variedades*, October 21, 1931, 4.

an expanding railway infrastructure—and even the recently introduced possibility of air travel—the candidates visited major cities and small villages throughout the coastal and Andean provinces (although largely neglecting the sparsely populated Amazonian region). In these towns—many of which had never received a national-level politician—they met directly with local community leaders and partisan supporters, while also staging yet more rallies, speeches, and marches. The candidates' tours demonstrated their commitment to a genuinely *national* popular project, both to the provincial citizens who they visited, but also (and perhaps more important) to poor and working-class Lima audiences with deep provincial roots.

The parties also relied extensively on local-level, grassroots organizing to build loyalty and solidarity among adherents, to coordinate recruitment efforts, and to turn out bodies to the mass demonstrations. Sánchez Cerro organized over 150 neighborhood clubs throughout the poorer sections of Lima, in an effort to mobilize recent rural migrants living in provincially tied enclaves within the city. Haya de la Torre's APRA party organized a competing set of neighborhood clubs in Lima, while also supporting union organizing throughout the country and founding over one hundred popular universities to educate and organize workers. To a certain extent, these localized political organizations were built on top of the country's expanding civic organizational infrastructure. They held regular meetings, in which they heard speakers, planned recruitment activities, and prepared for rallies and other events. They often coordinated with one another, building horizontal ties of solidarity across locality and employment sector. And, albeit in different ways, these local organizations were integrated into the hierarchical structures of their respective parties. Through such grassroots incorporative organizing efforts, both vertically organized political parties rooted themselves deeper into the soil of Peruvian social life than had ever been attempted, let alone accomplished, before.

Finally, the charismatic candidates each developed his own brand of anti-elite, nationalist rhetoric targeted at ordinary Peruvians. Both candidates sang the praises of Peru's Incan heritage, elevated the indigenous population, valorized workers, and painted an inclusive picture of the national body that transcended traditional cleavages of ethnicity, class, region, and party. Beyond this, however, the two candidates differed somewhat in the specifics of their rhetoric and argumentation. Haya was more intellectual and verbose; Sánchez Cerro's speeches were shorter and simpler. Haya's assessment of the state of Peruvian social and economic realities was more complex, informed by socialist, anti-imperialist, and *indigenista* thought. Sánchez Cerro's reading of reality was more conservative and patriarchal, focusing less on the importance of restructuring social relations than on morally cleansing the national body. And importantly, the candidates constructed their targets—the anti-popular elite—differently. For Sánchez Cerro, the architect and executor of Leguía's ouster, the enemy was clear: the economic and political associates of the former dictator, who had benefitted under his reign at the expense of the

Peruvian people. Although he had systematically purged these Leguiístas (as supporters of Leguía were known) from governmental posts in 1930, during his time as head of the military junta, Sánchez Cerro painted their resurgence as a very real threat—a threat that only he, the vanquisher of Leguía, was capable of averting. Haya de la Torre, for his part, focused on the old political and economic elite of the Aristocratic Republic—which he generically called *civilistas*—as the real popular threat.[42] These were the connected, wealthy, liberal politicians who had sold the nation to foreign bankers while colluding to exclude the masses from political participation. Haya depicted a possible resurgence of this old socio-political order as the real threat. Naturally, he painted Sánchez Cerro as being in bed with the *civilistas*, whereas Sánchez Cerro accused Haya of being a Leguiísta. There could, of course, be only one legitimate representative of the popular national body.

As Pedro Ugarteche—Sánchez Cerro's personal secretary and advisor—would later reflect, the campaigns of 1931 "had neither precedent nor equal in all the republican life of Peru" (1969, 2:xli). When the election was finally held on October 11, 1931, Haya de la Torre and Sánchez Cerro dominated the polls—receiving, between the two of them, a combined 86 percent of the national vote (Tuesta Soldevilla 2001, 607). Other candidates who failed to break with the routines and habits of traditional political practice did not stand a chance. Of the two major candidates, Sánchez Cerro came out on top—and by a notable margin.[43] The final tally was 152,149 votes for Sánchez Cerro, 106,088 votes for Haya de la Torre (ibid.). Election day itself was remarkably tranquil (see figure 1.2). And despite APRA's cries of fraud, the election is now widely recognized by historians as having been the least corrupt in Peruvian history up to that point.[44]

It is not the aim of this book, however, to explain why Sánchez Cerro bested Haya de la Torre at the polls. To do so, it would be necessary to attend to much more than just the candidates' mobilizing practices. What is important is that, regardless of who ultimately won, the creative, problem-solving

---

42. As noted above, the term "Civilista" technically referred to adherents of the Partido Civil, a dominant force in the Aristocratic Republic. Haya used the term more broadly to refer to the traditional political and social elites of that era. I use the lower case to indicate generic use of the term, upper case to indicate adherents of the Partido Civil.

43. He would not enjoy the fruits of his victory for long. Sánchez Cerro was assasinated by a follower of Haya de la Torre just eighteen months after taking office.

44. While APRA did raise allegations of fraud—at the time of the election and for years afterward—the current consensus among historians is that these allegations were unfounded. The most cogent refutation of APRA's claims, as well as the best existing explanation of the electoral outcome, can be found in Stein 1980 (188–202).

FIGURE 1.2. Orderly crowds gather in Lima to vote on election day, photographed here awaiting their turn at the polling place on the Calle de Copacabana (top), anticipating the opening of the polling place on Avenida Francisco Pizarro (middle), and gathered around the booth and urn installed at the Plaza de las Nazarenas (bottom).
Source: *Variedades*, October 14, 1931, 35.

actions of APRA and UR revolutionized political practice in Peru. As sociologist Manuel Castillo Ochoa put it, "The '31 elections would mark a new way of 'doing politics' in Peru" (1990, 57). This was a moment of profound innovation. Only under these unstable circumstances, when confronted with novel challenges and possibilities, did Sánchez Cerro and Haya de la Torre develop a distinctly Latin American style of populist mobilization. In so doing, they introduced a radically new set of political practices into the Peruvian political repertoire.

Dictators, Democrats, and Populists, 1932–Present

The 1931 election was a critical turning point in Peruvian history that transformed the landscape of political possibility. Once demonstrated, the strategic value of populist mobilization was impossible to ignore. It produced clear results, indicating that it was appropriate to the changing socio-political context and that it resonated with broad swaths of the Peruvian public. And the candidates who did *not* embrace the new practices being developed by their competitors were thoroughly trounced at the polls. That this would be a game changer for later generations of Peruvian politicians was clear; but it did not mean that the mode of practice would be thenceforth endemic. Indeed, going forward, most political actors would continue to rely on nonpopulist practices most of the time. Still, after 1931, populist mobilization was "thinkable"—it had entered into the toolkit of available practical options. Ordinary people had been familiarized with the tactics and rhetoric; and some even came to expect it of their leaders. Under the right circumstances, populist mobilization could be used by leftists or rightists, authoritarians or democrats, in support of a range of agendas. Significantly, all political actors—regardless of how they felt about the practice—had to be prepared for it to be used against them.

The events of 1931 initiated what would become a persistent pattern of oscillations between episodes of populist mobilization and reactive antipopulist periods of elite political consolidation that arguably persists to this day (Collier and Collier 1991). One might be tempted to think that this cyclical pattern in the trajectory of political practice would map onto the country's broader alternations between democratic and authoritarian rule; but this would not be entirely correct. It is true, and not surprising, that populist mobilization has been more likely in periods of democratic opening (like the one ushered in by the 1931 electoral reforms). And it is also true that those conservative politicians who remained opposed to the mode of practice had to rely increasingly on military means for securing power—leading nonpopulist practices to be more strongly associated with authoritarian periods (Masterson 1991; Villanueva Valencia 1975). However, not all democratic political actors embraced populist mobilization; and perhaps more interestingly, some military authoritarians, under particular circumstances, did.

In the wake of 1931—fueled by what would become a longstanding feud with the now clandestine APRA party—the Peruvian military strongly opposed anything that smacked of populist mobilization, and could be counted on to step in to support more traditional elites if they became embattled. But even such a strong antipopulist reaction *itself* demonstrates that populist mobilization had become a knowable threat—a possible type of practice that political actors would have to contend with. Perhaps surprisingly, some military leaders came over time to embrace the practical modality themselves (if cautiously). Military dictator Manuel Odría was the first to break the mold in this way, when he used populist strategies in the 1940s to court the support of shantytown dwellers (Collier 1976). Then, two decades later, when the politically leftist General Juan Velasco came to power through a coup d'état—in what sociologist Ellen Kay Trimburger (1978) has called a "revolution from above"—he attempted a massive populist mobilization of workers and urban squatters to consolidate his power and secure support for his reformist programs. Velasco was not using populist mobilization to win at the polls, but rather to drum up support for policies that were controversial among elites, in an effort to delegitimate—and hopefully stave off—any possible coup attempts.[45] On Velasco's death in office, the "Second Phase" of the military government ceased relying on populist mobilization and courted elite support, eventually moving toward a cautious democratic opening in the early 1980s. Politics again turned populist in 1985, under the democratically elected president Alan García (himself an Aprista—the first to successfully win the presidency); and then even more dramatically so in the early 1990s under Alberto Fujimori, who used populist mobilization, first, to win an election, and then to maintain support while enacting neoliberal "shock therapy" and overthrowing his own government in an *autogolpe* (self-coup) aimed at achieving total political control.[46] Finally, after another period of nonpopulist politics, center-right candidate Lourdes Flores lost the first round of the 2006 election to two candidates who made populist mobilization a centerpiece of their political strategies: center-left candidate Alan García targeted

---

45. On Velasco, see McClintock and Lowenthal 1983 and Stepan 1978.
46. On Fujimori, see Cameron 1994, Conaghan 2005, and Kenny 2004.

the working and middle classes, while Ollanta Humala—a leftist in the image of Hugo Chávez—targeted peasants and the urban poor.[47]

In the years after 1931, then, the practice of populist mobilization proved to be both useful and extremely versatile, cropping up repeatedly and in a variety of situations. Not only was it (predictably) in the arsenals of democratic reformers, but it was even translated into a tool that could be used in nondemocratic settings. Some used it in democratic contexts as a way to secure support at the polls. Others used it while authoritarian heads of state, in attempts to secure popular legitimacy and support when facing opposition on other fronts. The majority of successful democratic candidates, and even some military dictators, would at least toy with the mode of practice at one time or another (Stein 1999; Stepan 1978). Even if it was far from ubiquitous or chronic, it was always a possibility—or a threat—that had to be taken into account. Populist mobilization was thus firmly established in the Peruvian political repertoire; and it had been born out of the radically innovative activities of Haya de la Torre's APRA party and Sánchez Cerro's Unión Revolucionaria party in 1931. The remainder of this book will explain why and how this happened.

---

47. Stein 1999 provides a useful summary of Peru's populist episodes.

2

The Social Context of Action
Economy, Infrastructure, and Social Organization

This book advances an argument that is largely political, micro- and meso-analytic, and eventful. In its efforts to explain why political actors invented a new mode of practice at a particular point in time, why that practical modality took on the characteristics that it did, and why it "stuck" in a way that would change the political repertoire in the long run, it foregrounds the lived experiences and perceptions of individual political actors, as they organized themselves into collectivities to act—in cooperation and competition with one another—in a dynamically changing political field, within the relatively short timeframe of an unfolding eventful situation. Ultimately, the book claims that, had these political, micro- and meso-level, and short-term eventful dynamics not played out as they did, it is unlikely that there would have been any political innovation at all in Peru in 1931, let alone that a Latin American style of populist mobilization would have entered into the political repertoire at this time.

Still, it is important to emphasize that these processes did not play out in an ahistorical social vacuum. Rather, they were critically conditioned—albeit not wholly determined—by broader, macro-historical, social-structural changes that had been taking place in the decades preceding this moment of political change. Before the turn of the twentieth century, a number of factors kept anything like populist mobilization effectively off the table. But by 1931, significant social changes had rendered this mode of practice newly possible—even if it remained far from inevitable. Thus, before turning to more political, micro- and meso-analytic, and eventful processes, it is necessary first to attend to the broader changes in the social context of action that the political actors of 1931 found themselves facing.

This chapter explores how the social-structural changes that took place in

Peru in the first part of the twentieth century mattered for the rise of populist mobilization in 1931. In so doing, it strikes a balance between recognizing the very real significance of these changes for the processes that produced the outcome, on the one hand, and understanding that these changes did not themselves directly produce populist mobilization in any sort of automatic way, on the other. In an effort to walk this tightrope, the chapter proceeds in three parts. The first sketches out the broad social transformations that Peru underwent in the early years of the twentieth century—and especially in the decade just prior to the 1931 election. The second part makes the case that, by the standards of the structuralist strand of the populism literature, conditions in Peru were decidedly *un*ripe for populist mobilization in 1931, casting the Peruvian case as something of an anomaly vis-à-vis this literature. Finally, drawing on the theoretical approach outlined in the introductory chapter, the third part provides an alternative way of thinking about how social change mattered for the outcome at hand that resolves the apparent paradox of the Peruvian anomaly. In short, the argument is that rapid changes in social-structural conditions (even if these changes remained small in absolute terms) spurred creative action by contingently empowered political outsiders who were attuned to the new opportunities that they afforded.

The Changing Landscape of Social Life, 1900–1930

In the late nineteenth and early twentieth centuries, Peru experienced quite dramatic economic, social, and political transformations. Between when Peru achieved independence from Spain in 1824 and the presidential election of 1931, the country went from being an underdeveloped, traditionalist society dominated by regional *caudillos* fielding private armies, to a liberalizing, industrializing, and modernizing society in transition. As discussed in chapter 1, politics shifted from military to civilian control, the state bureaucracy expanded, liberal politicians achieved dominance over conservatives, and new social and political movements emerged to challenge the status quo. At the same time, foreign investment rose and products were increasingly produced for international markets; communicative and transportation infrastructures expanded and cities modernized; rural populations migrated to cities; and basic formal schooling became more widespread as embryonic working and middle classes began to form. These transitions produced significant changes in how social relationships were structured, in ways that would have profound political consequences. A brief discussion of the changing landscape of social life in Peru should make this clear.

In the early republican period, the Peruvian economy revolved around mining and *hacienda*-based agriculture, much as it had during the colonial era. During this time, up through the turn of the twentieth century, most of the indigenous population was rural and concentrated in the Andean highlands. Mining operations supported commercial activities in highland towns and small cities. But the majority of the highland indigenous population was concentrated in and around large landed estates, or *haciendas*, which existed primarily to sustain the household of the landowner. Those who resided outside the *haciendas* lived in what were called "Indian municipalities," which in effect served to supply *haciendas* with surplus labor. For the average Peruvian, it was a life of poverty. As Peter Klarén (2000, 136) has put it, "Peru at the beginning of the republican era was a mosaic of regional agrarian societies resembling a feudal order." Independent civic organizing was strongly discouraged. Instead, whether on *haciendas* or in Indian municipalities, political loyalties and grievances were channeled through traditional clientelistic relationships with the *hacienda* owners or local community leaders (Aljovín de Losada 2005; Forment 2003; Mallon 1983). The clientelistic structures of the *haciendas* and municipalities provided the main channels for the redress of grievances (or, in cases of rebellion, its target). In urban areas, relationships were similar between notable patrons and their workers. Such relationships bound up loyalties, circumscribed options for political action, and undermined possibilities for political choice. This inwardly focused economic structure combined with rough terrain and formidable distances, which impeded travel and communication, to produce profoundly localized social worlds.

Peru experienced some gradual economic development throughout the nineteenth century. Most significantly, the guano boom of the 1850s represented republican Peru's first major moment of economic dynamism. But for the same reason that this boom fueled the expansion of the Peruvian state—because the government sold the rights to harvest the guano to foreign (largely British) interests—it did not lead to sustainable economic growth. As the nineteenth century progressed, however, liberal elites attempted to transform the economy from an inwardly focused, quasi-feudal, agrarian one into an externally oriented capitalist one. Peru saw more emphasis on the export of primary products and, eventually, the development of small industry (see figure 2.1). The pace of development quickened in the early twentieth century—and especially in the 1920s—when foreign investment, rising prices for oil and copper, and a cotton boom fueled unprecedented economic growth (Klarén 2000, 242–44, 263–65).

In concert with their attempts at economic transformation, Peru's politically ascendant liberal elites spearheaded projects to expand transportation and communication infrastructures (Karno 1970; Pike 1967). These efforts

FIGURE 2.1. Textile factory in the La Victoria neighborhood of Lima (c. 1924).
Source: Compañía Anónima La Victoria 1924, 21.

reached their height under the Leguía regime of the 1920s (Capuñay 1952; Giesecke 2010, 18–21; Karno 1970; Pike 1967, 217–49). While he had regularly repressed political opposition throughout his eleven-year rule, Leguía was also a modernizer (Pike 1967). During his tenure, there were massive expansions in the road and railway networks, in telegraphic communications, in the national mail service, and even in steamship and air travel (Giesecke 2010, 48–53).

Most notably, Leguía expanded Peru's transportation systems. The pace of railroad construction reached its height in the 1920s. Peru's first railroad, which connected Lima with the port of Callao, had been completed in 1851 (Bromley and Barbagelata 1945, 80); and in this year, Peru had 24,478 km. of finished track. By the end of 1929, this figure would rise to 4,522,323 km. (República del Perú 1939, 186). Of this number, nearly 23 percent (1,033,722 km.) had been laid by Leguía since 1920 (República del Perú 1939, 185).[1] The number of annual

---

1. It is important to remember that Peru's infrastructural expansion was uneven. While rail service began in 1851, the great Incan capital of Cuzco was not connected to Lima by rail until 1908 (Jacobsen 2005, 281). Also, Peru's level of rail connectivity at the time of the 1931 election was still comparatively low. In 1932, for example, Peru had 0.4 km. of track for every 100 square kilometers of national territory and 6.9 km. for every 10,000 inhabitants. By way of comparison, Argentina in 1933 had 1.4 km. of track for every 100 square kilometers and 32.8 km. for every 10,000 inhabitants; the U.S. (in 1934) had 4.5 km. of track for every 100 square kilometers and 37.7 km. for every 10,000 inhabitants; the U.K. (in 1934) had 13.6 km. of track for every 100 square kilometers and 7.0 km. for every 10,000 inhabitants (República del Perú 1939:48*–49*).

passages on conventional rail lines (i.e., not including electric tramlines, which will be discussed below) grew accordingly, from 2,943,465 in 1908 to 5,784,710 in 1919; they then held steady in the six million range through 1929 (at which point the number was 6,031,372) (República del Perú 1939, 186). At the same time, in 1920, Leguía reinstituted a system of obligatory labor on road projects called the Conscripción Vial (Highways Conscription Act), which had been abolished in the late colonial era (Klarén 2000, 250).[2] As a result, in 1928 alone, the total length of the Peruvian highway system increased from 12,614 km. to 18,069 km. (República del Perú 1939, 175). The Conscripción Vial "transformed the unconnected roads built over old Inca and colonial paths into a proper highway system that became the material base essential for mass migration" (de Soto 1989, 8). Even airline service was blossoming in these critical years. It started in 1928, with the founding of the first national carrier; and the number of passengers transported by airline jumped from 145 in 1928 to 5,768 in 1930, with the emergence of the first two private airlines (República del Perú 1939, 179).

Beyond these core transportation systems, other modalities of communication likewise expanded under Leguía. Although telegraphic service had been introduced to Peru in 1855 (Bromley and Barbagelata 1945, 83), the years between 1922 and 1930 saw the laying of an additional 4,072 km. of telegraphic wire (an increase of roughly 31 percent); and this expansion corresponded with a 97 percent increase in the number of telegrams transmitted over the same period (República del Perú 1939, 169–70).[3] Between 1916 and 1931, there was a 53 percent increase in the annual number of pieces of domestic mail sent and received (from 21,263,313 to 32,421,142) (República del Perú 1939, 165). And the advent of airmail meant the more efficient transportation of correspondence. While only 2,315 kg. of airmail was carried in 1928, this number jumped to 10,438 kg. in 1931 (República del Perú 1939, 182). Overall, infrastructural development clearly took off in the decade prior to the 1931 election.

Such infrastructural development facilitated unprecedented levels of internal migration within Peru, which was encouraged by the changes in agricultural and industrial production, coupled with economic hardship in the highlands. Some rural migrants moved off of *haciendas* or out of small villages to work on large, more industrial-style, residential plantations. Indeed,

---

2. As it was possible to buy out of one's service obligations, this act most negatively impacted the country's poor indigenous population.

3. In contrast, only 654 km. of new wire were laid in the subsequent nine-year period, between 1931 and 1939; and the number of telegrams transmitted in 1939 (1,932,323) represented an increase of only 19 percent over the 1930 number (República del Perú 1939, 169–70). (The figures on telegrams transmitted are for the 1923–1930 period, as no data are available for 1922. The total number of telegrams transmitted jumped from 826,777 in 1923 to 1,625,508 in 1930.)

THE SOCIAL CONTEXT OF ACTION 63

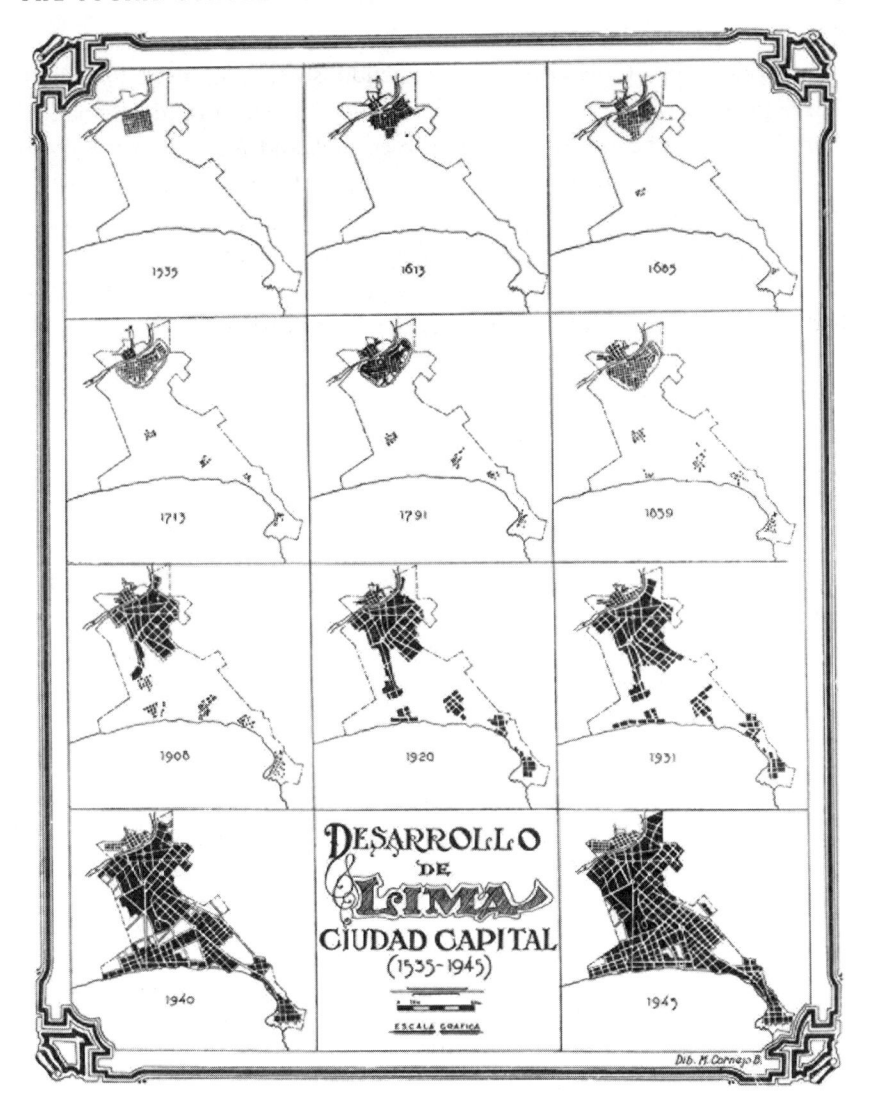

FIGURE 2.2. Growth of Lima, 1535–1945.
Source: Bromley and Barbagelata 1945, 4.

the managers of new sugar plantations along the northern coast actively encouraged and facilitated migration from highland communities to fill their labor needs (Klarén 1973). But the more preponderant migration pattern was from the agricultural areas of the highlands to cities, as new urban jobs—in industries like textiles, but also in shipping and construction—attracted large numbers of rural migrants (Bourricaud 1970, 15–16; Klarén 2000, 251).

The result was a rapid process of urbanization. While provincial capitals like Arequipa and Cuzco grew in the early twentieth century, Lima and the nearby port city of Callao expanded tremendously (see figure 2.2 for Lima). The population of the broader province in which Lima is situated (also named "Lima") grew by nearly 30 percent between 1908 and 1920 (from 172,927 to 223,807 residents) and then by another 67 percent between 1920 and 1930 (when it reached 373,875 people) (Departamento de Lima 1931, 45). By 1931, Lima and Callao had experienced over a decade of rapid urban growth. According to the urban census of that year, the city of Lima had 275,908 residents, while Callao had grown to 70,141 (ibid.).[4] This expansion was clearly fueled by migration from the provinces. As measured by the same urban census, more than 37 percent (140,044) of the residents of the province of Lima had been born in provinces other than Lima or Callao (Departamento de Lima 1931, 187).

Rural-to-urban migration was further fueled by the increasing availability in cities of modern amenities. At the same time as they were making great strides in developing national transportation and communication infrastructures, liberal politicians—and especially Leguía—undertook to modernize Peru's cities. Public works projects provided reliable electricity for the first time in history, while also improving sanitary conditions and easing urban transportation.[5] While Lima's electrification may have been the most impressive of these improvements to the city's newly arrived migrants, it was the elaboration of urban transportation systems that had the most profound impact on social relations and public life. While Lima had just eighty busses operating in 1931 (Basadre 1999, 12:3120), a system of electrified tramlines (*tranvías*) had recently come to provide much improved transportation within the city center. Soon, the various local lines were linked up with new commuter lines that connected central Lima with the port of Callao, but also with the newly developing coastal districts of Magdalena del Mar, Miraflores, Barranco, and Chorrillos (see figure 2.3). Busses were thus less important in the Lima metropolitan area than the new electric trams. Passenger data demonstrates the significance of these trams for urban life. While Lima's first electrified line was inaugurated in 1904, the city did not begin to record tram passenger data until 1908, when 22,575,083 individual passages were sold over the course of the year. By 1930, that number had increased to 29,239,045 (República del Perú

---

4. It is difficult to assess the reliability of official government statistics for nineteenth- and early twentieth-century Peru, but such figures are the only ones available. The 1931 census of Lima and Callao—cited here and relied on elsewhere—was commissioned by a government committee charged with measuring the impact of the 1929 Depression on the metropolitan area. For a critique of this census, see Derpich, Huiza, and Israel 1985.

5. For an illustrated catalog of Leguía's public works in Lima, see Fundación Augusto B. Leguía ([1935] 2007). See also Godbersen (2012, 149–237).

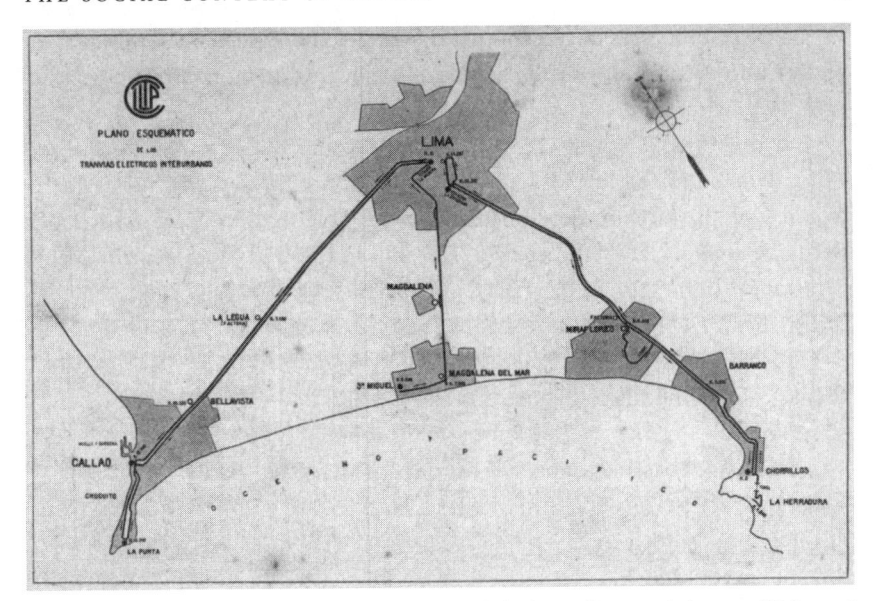

FIGURE 2.3. Map of the system of electric tramlines that linked central Lima with the port of Callao and the outlying districts of Magdalena del Mar, Miraflores, Barranco, and Chorrillos (c. 1925).
Source: Laos 1928, 110.

1939, 186).[6] Among other things, these trams made it easier for the residents of an ever-expanding periphery of outlying communities to journey to the city's historic center to participate in political events.

Peru's economic and infrastructural development resulted in a gradual but fundamental transformation in how civic life was organized. This change had two dimensions: the disruption of traditional social relationships and the development of new forms of social organization. The increasing waves of internal migration contributed to a loosening of traditional controls on social and political behavior. As indigenous peasants migrated down from the highlands, they left the spheres of influence of their former patrons and entered into new productive relationships that did not capture their social or political loyalties in the same way (Klarén 1973). Such social mobilization meant that individuals whose political loyalties had been locked into clientelistic social relationships were now, at least potentially, available for new political loyalties and actions.

6. For more information on the development of the tramlines, see Bromley and Barbagelata 1945, 96–97. See also "The Tramways of Lima, Peru" (http://www.tramz.com/pe/li/li30.html, accessed July 12, 2016), a website by Allen Morrison that presents a detailed history and bibliographies of Lima rail transportation. (This website also provides a more detailed map of the tramlines: http://www.tramz.com/pe/li/lim.html, accessed July 12, 2016.)

While these processes began toward the end of the nineteenth century, they really set in around 1925, at the height of the Leguía dictatorship (Bourricaud 1970, 16).

But this breakdown in traditional relationships did not mean the emergence of an atomized, mass society, as some variants of modernization theory would have it. Instead, new forms of social organization replaced the old. Peruvian civil society had begun to develop in the mid- and late nineteenth century, with the growth of mutual aid societies, political clubs, and elite social fraternities.[7] Between 1856 and 1885, 403 new civic and economic groups were formed; of these, 115 formed between 1876 and 1879 alone (Forment 2003, 285–86). These numbers include mutual aid and development societies, Masonic lodges and religious associations, ethnic and patriotic societies, scientific and professional associations, educational associations, banks and credit associations, charity groups, fire brigades, and leisure clubs (ibid., 290). Most of these nineteenth-century civic associations were reserved for elites. But as the populations of urban centers exploded in the early twentieth century, civic groups of various types proliferated, creating a culture of local organizing and an increasingly dense network of clubs and associations, even among the poor and working class.

New productive relations in both rural and urban areas prompted the beginnings of the formation of a working class, as well as the associational activities that go with it. In rural areas, the increasing industrialization of agriculture brought workers together onto residential plantations, where they both worked and lived in close proximity (Klarén 1973). In cities, artisanal guilds began forming in the late nineteenth century, preparing the foundations for the urban labor movements of the early twentieth century (García-Bryce 2004). The rural plantations and new urban industries alike became targets for increased labor organizing in the 1910s and 1920s (Blanchard 1982; Drinot 2011; Giesecke 2010; Klarén 1973; Sanborn 1995).

Lima in particular saw a fluorescence of labor organizing and civic associationalism in the 1920s, with increasing participation by poor and working class residents.[8] A quite comprehensive city guide, produced by the "Touring Club Peruano," provides detailed information on many of the civic associations that were active in Lima in the mid-1920s.[9] It discusses seventeen elite

---

7. Forment 2003 provides the most comprehensive picture available of civic life in Peru in the nineteenth century.

8. Stein 1986 and 1987 provide a good picture of everyday life among the Lima working class in the first part of the twentieth century.

9. This valuable source provides what appears to be a comprehensive catalogue of all major civic associations active in Lima in the mid-1920s (Laos 1928, 185–379).

THE SOCIAL CONTEXT OF ACTION   67

social clubs, seventeen cultural societies, twelve professional and four scientific societies, eleven religious and four patriotic societies, sixteen women's societies, nine university student societies, twenty-seven shooting clubs, and various sporting clubs—including eighty-one soccer clubs.[10] Perhaps most significantly, the guide also catalogues no fewer than seventy-seven workers' societies and forty-eight regional societies catering to provincial migrants to the capital (Laos 1928, 270–90). The workers' societies included longstanding artisanal guilds, as well as more recently formed labor unions, associations, and confederations. Of those workers' societies active when the data were collected, the longest standing—the Sociedad Fraternal de Artesanos—had been formed in 1860; twenty-four were formed between 1882 and 1911, at a regular but relatively low rate; eleven were formed in 1912 and 1913 alone, under the labor-friendly Billinghurst presidency; seven were formed between 1914 and 1918; and twenty-seven were formed between 1919 and 1924. As workers in the same factories often lived near one another, their societies sometimes identified themselves with particular neighborhoods, in addition to specific factories or industries. The regional societies were formed by provincial migrants to the capital and provided their members with trustworthy social networks, economic opportunities, and assistance in adapting to city life, while maintaining open channels of communication and social exchange with their communities of origin (Dobyns and Doughty 1976, 213–15). Of the forty-eight regional societies active when the data were collected, the oldest—the Sociedad Humanitaria "Hijos del Misti"—was formed in 1902. The rest were formed between 1911 and 1925. Eighteen were formed between 1911 and 1921; twenty-four were formed in 1922 and 1923 alone; and five more were formed in 1924 and 1925.

The emergence of new artisanal guilds, labor unions, migrant associations, veterans' leagues, patriotic fraternities, neighborhood clubs, community sporting teams, and other civic organizations marked a profound transformation in the structure of Peruvian social relations in cities; and in rural areas, the departure of increasing waves of migrants meant an equally important

10. Included among the elite social clubs are the esteemed Club de la Unión and Club Nacional, as well as the Club Lawn Tennis de la Exposición, the Club de Regatas de Lima, the Club Italiano, and the Cercle Francais. (*El Libro de Oro* [1927], a social register of the Lima elite, provides the names of the leadership of thirteen of the most prestigious of Lima's social clubs, as well as various charitable groups, in 1927.) The cultural societies include the national temperance society, the Asociación Humanitaria del Perú, the Rotary Club, the YMCA, and the Boy Scouts. The data on these civic associations appear mostly to have been gathered in 1925. For an interesting study of the development of soccer among the popular sectors of Lima in the early twentieth century, see Deustua, Stein, and Stokes 1984, 1986, and 1987.

transformation of the structure of agrarian social relations. The new forms of social organization replaced traditional social structures and provided a new organizational infrastructure for social—and ultimately political—life.

The transformations described above were partially enabled by, and themselves reinforced, shifts in the class structure of Peruvian society. Indigenous peasants who stayed behind on highland *haciendas* or in small villages remained mired in poverty. But those who moved away found themselves in a social world defined by a gradually emerging working class (as indicated by the blossoming of organized labor) and even an embryonic middle class. The consolidation of a modern bureaucratic state under Leguía played a critical role in the latter development, as the number of government employees rose from 5,329 to 14,778 between 1920 and 1931 (Giesecke 2010, 18). The growth of this sector in the provinces of Lima and Callao—where the number of public servants increased more than sixfold in the same span of time (from 975 to 6,285 [Departamento de Lima 1931, 206])—was even more stunning. Accompanied by related growth in lower-level professional occupations (in Lima: a doubling of the police, legal, accounting, medical, and artistic sectors, and a tripling of the transportation sector [Departamento de Lima 1931, 206]), this bureaucratic expansion heralded the first awakening of an urban middle class (even if it would remain quite small for years to come [Parker 1998]). Especially for urban Peruvians, social and economic prospects seemed to be improving.

But increasing dependence on exports and international finance left Peru particularly vulnerable to the crash of 1929. As foreign investment and the demand for exports dried up, the mining, sugar, cotton, textile, and construction industries were hit particularly hard (Giesecke 2010, 57–87; Klarén 2000, 262–71). While poverty in the highlands remained endemic as always, urban unemployment skyrocketed, despite the government's best efforts to combat it.[11] Indeed, by 1931, in Lima and Callao, around 25 percent of men between the ages of fourteen and sixty-nine were out of work (Departamento de Lima 1931, 250). In construction, the unemployment rate was nearly 70 percent (ibid., 257). The combined result of rapid development followed by depression was that new urban workers and a small but growing middle class experienced economic hardship precisely when they had first begun to enjoy a taste of modest prosperity, increased access to imported consumer goods, better educational opportunities, and improved employment prospects for themselves and their children (Blanchard 1982; Parker 1998; Stein 1986). It was against this backdrop that contingently empowered political outsiders developed a distinctively Latin American style of populist mobilization.

---

11. See Departamento de Lima 1935 and Decreto-Ley 7103 (ADLP).

Where Structuralist Explanations Fall Short

Peruvian society underwent dramatic changes in the first part of the twentieth century, in ways that are clearly relevant to the practice of politics. I have so far provided a description of these changes, but not yet a systematic consideration of their significance. What is the best way to understand how the changing landscape of Peruvian social life contributed to the historical emergence of populist mobilization in 1931? Before answering this question, it is necessary first to identify some common explanatory pitfalls. Thus, while the final section of this chapter will present my positive argument, the present section makes the case that what is perhaps a more common way of approaching the historical changes described above—according to traditional structuralist theories—is inadequate.

Arguably, the most promising body of scholarship to which we might turn for insight into the political significance of social context in the Peruvian case is the literature on Latin American populism.[12] Over the past half a century, scholars from various disciplines have attempted to make sense of this peculiar style of Latin American politics (even if they have largely neglected the case under consideration here). I have summarized elsewhere the various tendencies within this still-evolving interdisciplinary field (Jansen 2011); but for present purposes, I suggest that it is the first generation of this scholarship—which attempted to explain the pre-1955 era of "classic" cases by attending to the sorts of social-structural conditions discussed above—that is most relevant.[13]

The first generation of populism scholarship, which was propelled by currents in modernization theory and structuralist Marxism, was elaborated in

---

12. While "populism" has been identified in a variety of world-historical contexts, most of the scholarly literature produced over the past few decades has focused on Latin America, and it is with this regionally circumscribed literature that I engage here. Recent world events have highlighted the pressing need for a serious engagement with questions of "comparative populisms" (see de la Torre 2015 and Mudde and Kaltwasser 2012), but such questions are beyond the scope of the present enterprise.

13. There have been three generations of scholarly thinking about populism, comprising five distinct approaches. The first generation, which foregrounded social structural transformations and included both modernization and Marxist theories, is discussed here. The second generation was both an ideational and agentic corrective to the first. But while this generation also focused on the pre-1955 cases, it did not attempt systematic historical explanation, but rather focused on critiquing the first generation and reinterpreting the phenomenon of populism as a whole. The third generation—which has attended largely to the "neo-populist" cases—has usefully focused on how the failures of democratic institutions to incorporate citizens have continued to render populist strategies useful to politicians, but has had little to say about the classic cases.

the 1960s and 1970s and attempted to understand the social bases of support for classic populists like Argentina's Juan Domingo Perón and Brazil's Getúlio Vargas.[14] On one level, it can be said that this generation took as its outcome of interest the emergence of populist political parties. But because it took for granted that populist parties were themselves the relatively natural byproduct of the existence of populist class coalitions within a society, it is more accurate to say that they took this particular social-structural formation as their primary explanandum. In attempting to explain populist class coalitions, this generation focused largely on economic factors. Though disagreeing on specific points—and on their broader understandings of the nature of historical change—scholars of this generation generally agreed that the emergence of populism was the political expression of a structural shift in class relations that occurred in the context of peripheral late development. For modernization theorists, who drew in part on mass society theories, the disruption of traditional social structures by economic development and urbanization produced atomization and anomie; and this left masses of disadvantaged but socially mobilized people susceptible to manipulation by charismatic leaders who emerged out of a stratum of downwardly mobile or status-discontented elites (Di Tella 1965, 1990, 17–34).[15] For Marxists, dependent development produced conflict between ruling class factions and encouraged the formation of a new working class in urbanizing cities; but the partial nature of this class formation (leaving only some segments of labor as self-consciously organized) created conditions ripe for Bonapartism. For both approaches, populist parties were the political reflections of the resulting coalitions between disorganized masses and elite factions. In the end, although underwriting very different interpretations of history, both the modernization and Marxist theorists produced remarkably similar accounts of the emergence of populism in Latin America. This can be boiled down to the importance of five social-structural factors: late peripheral or dependent development, urban industrialization, the disruption of traditional social controls via social mobilization, working class formation, and the destabilization of the social bases of elite domination.

Thus, a structuralist theoretical framework would suggest that we emphasize particular elements of the broad historical narrative presented in the first

14. For examples of the modernization vein of first-generation populism scholarship, see Di Tella (1965), Germani (1963, 1978), Hennessy (1969), Ionescu and Gellner (1969a), Skidmore (1979), and van Niekerk (1974). For examples of the Marxist vein, see Grompone (1998), Quijano (1968), Spalding (1977), and Waisman (1982, 1987).

15. Classic statements of modernization and mass society theory include Deutsch (1954, 1963), Kornhauser (1959), and Lipset (1960).

section of this chapter. Given its emphasis on late peripheral or dependent development, it would point us toward the importance of Peru's position in the structure of global capitalist relations in the nineteenth and early twentieth centuries. This would likely mean beginning with the guano boom of the 1850s, in which Peru acted as a rentier state selling access to its island deposits, and continuing through the growth of oil, copper, cotton, and sugar exports into the 1920s. At the same time, this framework's emphasis on urban industrialization would focus our attention on the growth of cities—especially metropolitan Lima—in the 1910s and 1920s, which was fueled by the growth of urban industries like textiles. Relatedly, it would highlight the importance of the waves of rural migration, in which indigenous peasants moved off of highland *haciendas* to cities and to more industrialized agricultural plantations, leaving the spheres of influence of their former patrons and their broader webs of clientelistic relations. It would suggest that we focus with particular interest on the rise of working class organizations in cities in the 1910s and 1920s, on the development of working-class-like relations on coastal sugar plantations, and on various attempts to organize mineworkers. Finally, it would suggest attending to the social conflicts that threatened to undermine the dominant positions of particular elite factions. Here, of critical importance would be the rise to political dominance of liberal elites over traditional conservatives, which had its roots in the guano boom and was crystalized under the Aristocratic Republic (1895–1919).

All of these elements are of course important. The problem—which becomes apparent with even minimal comparison to other Latin American countries—is that these factors alone fail to predict the rise of populist mobilization in Peru in 1931. The structuralist populism literature was developed largely with reference to the Argentine and Brazilian cases. But populist mobilization emerged in Peru significantly earlier than it did in either Argentina or Brazil, both of which had by that time experienced considerably more pronounced change across all five of these social-structural factors than had Peru in 1931.[16]

While most Latin American countries experienced dependent development in the first half of the twentieth century, some developed considerably earlier and faster than others (Mahoney 2010). Leading the pack were the countries of the southern cone—Chile, Uruguay, and Argentina—with Brazil following

---

16. According to the definition outlined in chapter 1, Argentina and Brazil both experienced their first episodes of populist mobilization in 1943. (For further elaboration of this claim, see Jansen 2011, 87–88.)

close behind. Peru, although it certainly experienced economic development in the 1920s, looked more like Ecuador, Colombia, and Venezuela at the time. We run into similar comparative problems when considering urban industrialization, social mobilization, working class formation, and the destabilization of elite social positions. Argentina and Brazil both experienced significant urban industrialization in the first half of the twentieth century—much more than did Peru (where small textile factories made up the main proto-industrialized setting). In Argentina and Brazil, urban industrialization resulted in high levels of social mobilization and produced substantial sectors of new urban workers (both rural migrants and foreign immigrants).[17] While Peru saw the embryonic beginnings of working class formation in the 1920s, labor movements were only beginning to take hold at that time—and only tentatively—in Lima, on coastal plantations, and in some mining areas. Finally, developmental processes also fomented significant elite conflict in Argentina and Brazil—amongst industrialists, traditional conservatives, the military, the church, and an emerging sector of middle class professionals—which precipitated the populist moments in these countries. In both, the first populist episodes involved elite leaders capitalizing on the usefulness of popular urban support to triumph over other elite competitors. In Peru, although there were indeed important elite conflicts in 1931, these did not map neatly onto the types of social categories that mattered in Argentina or Brazil. Moreover, the critical period of development-induced, inter-elite conflict in Peru took place much earlier, in the late guano period, when market-oriented liberal modernizers gained social and political dominance over conservatives—a relationship that crystalized under the Aristocratic Republic. Thus, although the structure of elite conflicts mattered in Peru, a theory premised on the political realities of Argentina and Brazil in the 1940s would not identify 1931 as the moment at which populist mobilization should have emerged in Peru.

A few more points of comparison, here with negative cases, make the shortcomings of the structuralist approach unmistakable. While Argentina and Brazil were more developed than Peru across all five of the conditions noted above at the times of their populist episodes, these two countries had more similar

17. This is evident in the organizational content of the populist mobilizations themselves, which in each case drew heavily on urban labor. Perón began populist mobilization even before securing the presidency, as head of the Ministry of Labor—which in previous years had been a considerably less influential appointment (Horowitz 1999, 29–32). Similarly, the Brazilian Labor Party, which was at the core of Vargas's mobilization of 1943–1945, was formed from within his own Labor Ministry by his own Labor Minister—who also happened to be in charge of Vargas's mobilization campaign (Conniff 1982, 79–80).

peers that did *not* experience populist mobilization. Chile and Uruguay in the 1940s looked much more like Argentina and Brazil than did Peru in 1931, yet they saw no populist mobilization. Further, the Latin American countries that were more comparable to Peru in 1931 did not experience populist mobilization until much later. Peru had undergone some dependent development, urban industrialization, social mobilization, working class formation, and elite conflict by 1931, but so had Bolivia, Colombia, Ecuador, and Venezuela. If Peru experienced populist mobilization at this time, why not these countries also? The fact that populist mobilization did not emerge among Argentina and Brazil's equals (Uruguay and Chile) in the 1940s, let alone in countries positioned similarly to Peru in the early 1930s, suggests that focusing on structural conditions alone cannot take us very far in explaining the rise of the practice.

All in all, starting from the most plausible social-structuralist theories of populism, conditions in Peru actually appear to have been distinctly *un*ripe for populist mobilization in 1931. Yet the practice did emerge here at this time. Thus, while structuralist populism theories seem for the most part adequate for explaining the Argentine and Brazilian cases, their explanatory power seems to be largely limited to these, and Peru appears anomalous.[18] Perhaps this is why first-generation populism scholars tended to pass over the Peruvian case so quickly. Still, using their theories to situate Peru in comparative perspective is helpful, because without doing so, it would be all too easy to read the historical narrative presented in the first part of this chapter and conclude that this account represented an adequate explanation of the rise of populist mobilization. Instead, it is now possible to see Peru's social transformations of the early twentieth century from a higher vantage point, from which we can recognize the importance of a new set of questions about how relatively small changes in social conditions might prompt creative political action. That is, the fact that social-structural conditions were not ripe for populist mobilization in Peru does not mean that they did not matter; it simply means that it is necessary to rethink *how* they mattered.

---

18. The structuralist populism theories likewise fall short in explaining the Ecuadorian, Venezuelan, Colombian, and Bolivian cases, for similar reasons. Abel and Palacios (1991, 612) state the problem quite succinctly for Colombia, identifying a range of divergences from the paradigmatic Argentine and Brazilian cases: "A populist alliance of organized labour, the urban middle class, industrialists and progressive military was not viable. Organized labour was not sufficiently large; the urban middle class was tied to the ruling class through employment; the industrialists were beneficiaries of liberal economic policy; and a progressive military had not evolved." Similar statements could be made for Ecuador, Venezuela, and Bolivia.

How Social Change Shaped the Context of Action
(But Did Not Determine the Political Outcome)

The previous section highlighted some of the limitations of a structuralist approach to explaining the rise of populist mobilization in Peru. This final section will make the case that the Peruvian anomaly can be explained if we read the significance of changing social conditions from the perspectives of actors on the ground. It argues that, overall, it was relatively rapid change in some of these conditions—even if they remained relatively "underdeveloped" by comparison with conditions in Argentina and Brazil years later—that spurred contingently empowered outsider politicians into creative action by affording them new opportunities to outflank their traditionalist opponents.

If we take seriously the pragmatist perspective outlined in the introductory chapter, it shapes how we think about the relationship between social-structural conditions and creative political action. According to this framework, such conditions may facilitate, encourage, discourage, or even prohibit certain types of action. Among other things, they can produce the bases for new grievances that may figure in political claims making; they can contribute to the disruption of once stable social or political realities, making available new groups of potential supporters; they can make it logistically possible to reach these new potential audiences; and they can lay the social groundwork for political organization and mobilization. But for social conditions to result in the elaboration of new practices, they must become subjectively relevant to political actors—they must be perceived, interpreted, and taken into consideration by these actors as they formulate their lines of political action. When actors deliberate about their political practices, they orient toward the realities of the social context *as they understand them*; and they make decisions about how to act based on how they interpretively judge the opportunities for and constraints on action that these represent. In doing this, their attention is selective—they notice some things and overlook others, as conditioned by their prior experience—and actors vary in this selectivity.[19] Given all of this, we must ask ourselves not only about the objective realities of the terrain of social-structural conditions, but also about how these realities appeared to specific actors on the ground.

The same conditions may afford different opportunities to different actors, depending on how these actors are situated in the political field (see chapter 3).

---

19. This opens up the possibility that social-structural conditions can be *mis*read. Actors may misconstrue elements of social reality, perceiving an opportunity, possibility, constraint, or threat where none exists; but such interpretive "mistakes" can influence their decisions about political action—and prompt creative responses—as much as can "correct" perception.

If our concern is not just with political action, but with *creative* political action—with actors acting in unusual ways that break with routine—then we are focusing not on all actors, but on a more limited set of them who might be disposed to act in unconventional ways. The question that must be asked is: What about the conditions, and about how some actors might interpret them, has the potential to provoke a small number of actors to think about strategy and practice differently, and thus to make new types of action possible? Established actors, for whom traditional practices have worked well in the past, have no need to seek out new possibilities in the social landscape. Marginalized actors, on the other hand, are more likely be actively on the lookout for new options, as traditional practices are in their cases less likely to yield positive results. They are also more likely to be able to recognize new options as they present themselves, given the previous experiences with nontraditional forms of politics that they are more likely to have had. While insiders may remain oblivious to the potential opportunities (or threats) presented by small changes in social conditions, outsiders are more likely to be attuned to these.

Further, if what really matters is the actors' perceptions of conditions, then conditions that are undergoing change—and especially rapid change—might be particularly compelling, because they call attention to themselves. That is, changing conditions can prompt an anticipation of future states of affairs, even if the present social context is not objectively as amenable to the line of action under consideration as "objective" observers might think. And so, in the search for how social conditions might spur creative political action, change in such conditions—and especially rapid change—may be more important than their actual level of development.

Understanding that relatively modest changes in social-structural conditions may prompt creative political action provides a better way of looking at the significance of such conditions, but it does not provide a new determinism. Social-structural changes must be noticed by actors, interpreted as meaningful, and understood as promising; and acting on this promise is inherently risky—risky beyond what many political actors would entertain as reasonable. The changing conditions discussed above *matter*, then, by providing new practical possibilities and having the potential to spark some actors to orient to these possibilities in new ways. That is, they comprise a broader social-structural context of political action that is critically important to the political outcome, but that does not determine it.

In the previous section, I suggested that the five conditions identified by structuralist populism theories—late peripheral or dependent development, urban industrialization, social mobilization, working class formation, and the destabilization of the social bases of elite domination—are important, but not in the ways that structuralist populism theories think that they are. How, then, should we understand the significance of these conditions? The above discussion prompts a rereading of these, and also of two other important conditions that the first-generation populism scholarship did not highlight: the emergence of new forms of social organization and infrastructural development.

All of the factors highlighted by the structuralist populism literature mattered; but they mattered by establishing the conditions of possibility for action and, through even small changes (especially when somewhat rapid), by prompting recognition and response. In terms of peripheral dependent development, urban industrialization, social mobilization, and working class formation, Peru did not achieve the levels that would be seen in Argentina or Brazil in the 1940s. But as discussed in the historical narrative above, all of these conditions underwent rapid change in the decade preceding the 1931 election. This produced new grievances and provided new potential supporters who were not locked into existing systems of political loyalties. As will be shown in the following chapters, the APRA and UR leadership were particularly attuned to changes in these conditions in ways that their contemporaries were not. But also important were rapid changes in two social conditions that were evident in the historical narrative above, though not emphasized by structuralist populism theories.

First, while structuralist populism theories emphasized the social dislocation involved in modernization processes, they tended to neglect the fact that old forms of social organization were superseded by new ones. Traditional social structures were replaced in the late nineteenth and early twentieth centuries by artisanal guilds, labor organizations, migrant associations, veterans' leagues, patriotic fraternities, neighborhood clubs, community sporting teams, and other forms of civic association. And, as discussed above, this civic-associational landscape really blossomed in Peru in the 1920s. This provided a new organizational infrastructure that had the potential to become a foundation for populist mobilizing projects. Most critically, labor associations and unions provided potential access to networks of urban workers; and regional societies, which likewise concentrated groups of poorer and socially marginalized urban residents, offered the tantalizing promise of established social channels by which political ideas and sympathies might be spread throughout the country. As will be described in subsequent chapters, the outsider Peruvian political actors recognized and capitalized on this fact. This is one more critical—if often overlooked—piece of the social context of action.[20]

---

20. While the populism literature has done a good job of attending to the importance of labor organizing in the early twentieth century (see, for example, Collier and Collier 1991; French

Second, and finally, while social scientists have highlighted the importance of national transportation and communication infrastructures for the operation of political power (Mann 1984; Soifer 2015; Soifer and vom Hau 2008), this condition has been remarkably absent from treatments of populism (although see Conniff 1999).[21] Populist mobilization requires a certain level of development in such infrastructures, which are necessary for the efficient and effective organization of national-level campaigns able to reach beyond the capital city and provincial centers. The emergence of rail and air transport, highway networks, telegraphic and radio communications, and national mail systems greatly facilitated national political organizing. This was not only logistically necessary, but symbolically necessary: a political project claiming to unite a national people must be able to make at least symbolic moves to reach and connect with that people. A baseline level of infrastructural development thus made it objectively possible to court new populations and to mobilize these groups in new ways. But even more important in this regard than the absolute degree of infrastructural development was the pacing of that development. It was the rapid expansion of infrastructural density and penetration in the 1920s that mattered most for encouraging outsider political actors to pursue populist mobilization. Each stepwise increase in infrastructural capacity would make available new groups of people who national-level politicians had long dismissed as politically irrelevant. And the outsider political actors recognized this fact.

Conclusion

One potential danger of the pragmatist approach advanced in this book is that, if misinterpreted or misapplied, it could lead to a neglect of the broader social context of action that this chapter has highlighted as critically important. That is, there could be a tendency to focus too narrowly on micro-level events, interactions, and processes, and to neglect structured social relationships that transcend specific situations or material conditions with deep historical roots. The role of this chapter has been to ensure that such socio-historical

---

1989; James 1988), the historiography on other types of associations has only recently begun to pick up steam. On how the development of civic associations can provide an organizational infrastructure for new forms of political practice, see Riley 2010.

21. Modernization theory is attentive to the ways in which the development of communicative infrastructures and technologies can integrate regions and lead to the production of a national culture (Deutsch 1954). But the modernization strand of the populism literature generally neglects this point and is wholly inattentive to the ways in which stepwise increases in infrastructural penetration can make new populations available for national political mobilization.

realities—insofar as they shaped the processes and outcomes of this case—are given their due, such that the eventful situation of the 1931 election cannot be mistakenly understood as detached from these. At the same time, it would be an equally significant mistake (and a more common one in the comparative study of politics) to attribute too much determinative power to these broader conditions and to overlook the critical importance of more localized eventful processes.[22] As argued in the introductory chapter, a macro-structuralist approach alone would not be able to account for the rise of populist mobilization in Peru.

This chapter has shown that social changes in Peru over the course of the early twentieth century led to the crystallization of social conditions in the 1920s that were conducive to populist mobilization in 1931. In the absence of these conditions, populist mobilization would either have been not objectively possible, or it would have been so far outside the sphere of potential usefulness that no politician would have begun to try it. But it has also shown that these conditions alone did not produce the outcome at issue. They made the outcome objectively possible, and they encouraged some contingently empowered political outsiders to think about political strategy in new ways— but they did not make the rise of populist mobilization in Peru in 1931 inevitable. While this social context of action provides a critical piece of the puzzle that serves as a foundation for the explanation to come, we should not make the mistake of assuming that it is *itself* the explanation. Among other things, an adequate explanation of the introduction of populist mobilization into the political repertoire requires a more detailed consideration of the *political* context of action, to which we now turn.

---

22. Both structuralist populism theories and sociological approaches to repertoire change have tended to prefer macro-historical explanations based on the changing nature of structural conditions.

3

The Political Context of Action
Collective Actor Formation in a Dynamic Political Field

Just as the social context of action changed in Peru in the years leading up to the 1931 election, so too did the political context of action. Established regimes were overthrown, the institutional rules of politics were rewritten, political and military allegiances and antagonisms were reconfigured, old collective political actors dissolved, and new ones formed. These dramatic political shifts were the products of relational dynamics that were at least partly autonomous from changing social-structural realities. And, critically for our purposes, they contributed to the political ascendance of two outsider politicians, who would have had little hope of viability on the national stage in earlier times, as well as the formation around these politicians of semi-organized collectivities of supporters—not yet political parties, but proto-parties—that were primed to pursue innovative lines of political action in 1931.

In 1918, where this chapter begins, the stability of the Peruvian elite's domination of national politics appeared secure. Throughout the era of the Aristocratic Republic, a small number of insiders held a lock on political power, even if they struggled amongst themselves; and those not fortunate enough to have connections in the backrooms of Lima's social and political clubs were, in effect, politically irrelevant. In this context, the likelihood that a leader of radical movements or a junior officer stationed in a southern province could become a viable contender for national office was miniscule. To be sure, Víctor Raúl Haya de la Torre and Luis M. Sánchez Cerro were highly ambitious, charismatic, and politically savvy; and one might not have been surprised to see them rise to prominent positions within their own circumscribed domains. But these social and political outsiders would have had no chance at the presidency during the Aristocratic Republic.

Remarkably, however, by May 1931, the impossible had begun to appear quite probable. Not only did Haya de la Torre and Sánchez Cerro find themselves poised in the wings of a political stage that would normally have been off limits to them, but they found themselves increasingly recognized as *more* viable than any of the traditional political forces. Each figure had personally developed a national reputation and enjoyed widespread public support. Just as important, each had built up a network of loyal allies and close advisors, such that he stood at the helm of a potentially efficacious political apparatus. These were not yet fully fledged parties, but they were by this point loosely organized groups capable of making collective assessments about the situation and coordinating political action.

Furthermore, these collective political actors had formed in ways that primed them for political innovation. First, the candidates themselves, as well as many within their leadership circles, were social and political outsiders, with weaker than normal ties to established political authorities. This outsider status meant that riskier, more unorthodox political action would be necessary to secure victory. It also meant that they were not beholden to established interests or personalistic obligations, but instead would be freer than other political actors to deviate from political routine. And it meant that, in the eyes of the public, the candidates were untarnished by traditional politics. Second, the decision-making environments within these collective political actors were particularly amenable to innovation. The groups that coalesced around the outsider candidates came from a variety of backgrounds and brought with them a range of experiences—in many cases unorthodox experiences from outside the routine politics of the era. At the same time, however, they also placed authority firmly in the hands of the leader—whether officially or by virtue of his charisma. The leadership circles had personalistic connections to, and in many cases an elevated sense of faith in, the candidates, and dissenters were purged from the ranks. This meant that even unconventional political decisions were less likely to be questioned or checked internally, and were more likely to be implemented. Indeed, they would be marked by a distinction of association with the figurehead. According to the theoretical approach laid out in the introduction, these elements were conditions of possibility for political innovation that could become realized once the actors began to act.

How did two political outsiders and their inner circles of loyalists—who would never in previous eras have made it onto the national political stage—form as collective actors and then come to find themselves in such unlikely positions of political viability by May 1931? And what about their rise led these collective actors to form in ways that would make them more likely than others to break with traditional political routines and develop creative new lines of political action?[1]

This chapter argues that the formation of these actors with these characteristics was not an automatic byproduct of changing social conditions, but rather the result of unfolding political events and interactions that were shaped by a dynamically changing field of political contention. In support of this argument, it traces shifts in political relationships (both cooperative and antagonistic) and the formation and dissolution of relationally oriented collective political actors across four significant periods of reconfiguration of the political field that occurred between 1918 and 1931. The first of these periods took place in the months on either side of the 1919 presidential election, in which Leguía's dramatic rise to power undermined the stability of the old Aristocratic Republic. The second was the long period from July 1919 until August 1930, when Leguía's actions in power—and the various reactions to these by other actors—dramatically reconfigured the political terrain. The third was the six-month period in which Sánchez Cerro served at the head of a provisional military government, from when he overthrew Leguía in August 1930 until his own removal from office in March 1931. The final period extended from March through May 1931, during which time a new military junta reconfigured the field once again and rewrote the rules of the political game. The ultimate state of the political field—and the resulting composition and characteristics of the collective political actors that were formed in this era of profound instability—set the stage for the first steps toward political innovation in May 1931.

First Reconfiguration of the Field: The Rise of Leguía

The first reconfiguration of the Peruvian political field centered around the 1919 election that broke the back of the Aristocratic Republic. As discussed in chapter 1, the oligarchical Aristocratic Republic (1895–1919) was a long period of elite-dominated political stability. But a series of events that unfolded in 1918, and in the early months of 1919, broke this stability. While these events played out against the backdrop of economic, infrastructural, and social conditions that had changed significantly over the course of the first two decades of

---

1. To be clear, this chapter's outcome of interest is not the rise of actors primed to develop *populist mobilization* in particular, but simply the rise of outsider actors primed to innovate. The explanation for why this innovation took on the particular characteristics that it did is the subject of the next chapter.

the twentieth century, they were driven by political and interpersonal conflicts that were not reducible to longer-term structural transformations. Ultimately, the events of 1918–1919 unleashed a powerfully disruptive force—in the person of Augusto B. Leguía—into the political milieu, setting the stage for later reconfigurations of the political field in ways that had important consequences for the emergence of populist mobilization in 1931. But before turning to Leguía, it is necessary to map the state of the political terrain leading into 1918.

On the whole, the Aristocratic Republic was characterized by unprecedented political stability. Given how often the military had held political control in Peruvian history up until this time, the twenty-four-year period of civilian rule that the Aristocratic Republic represented was unique. The last military presidency—that of General Andrés Cáceres—had been overthrown in 1895, and civilians had been in charge ever since.[2] Political control remained severely limited during this period. A small number of elites—mostly wealthy men of European heritage who hailed from a handful of families and were members of a few select social clubs—were organized into a system of oligarchical parties. Suffrage was restricted and power sharing was arranged through backroom deals. In this sense, the Aristocratic Republic truly was a period of stable oligarchical domination. But stability does not necessarily mean elite consensus or cooperation. The Aristocratic Republic was not built on a foundation of clearly aligned interests or deep elite social cohesion. Just below the surface—and occasionally at the surface—the Aristocratic Republic was wracked by infighting, factionalism, and internecine struggle. The surface-level stability of this period rested largely on a tenuous balance of power between political parties, and between factions within these parties, and so was never guaranteed.

The most consequential split was between the members and allies of the liberal Partido Civil (called Civilistas), on the one hand, and their traditionalist opponents, on the other. The power of the Civilistas was based on a coastal plutocracy of capitalist, export-oriented wealth. The traditionalist opponents of the Civilistas derived from the old *gamonal* landholding class based in the central and southern highlands, who were semi-feudalistic, pro-military, pro-Church, and were represented at times by various political parties. For most of the Aristocratic Republic period, the Civilistas dominated the traditionalists. Thus the stability of the Aristocratic Republic actually represented not a broad

---

2. Cáceres was ousted by Nicolás de Piérola, who moved quickly to professionalize the military and reshape it into a "small but efficient standing army headed by well-trained and politically subservient officers" (Masterson 1991, 26). This professionalization, guided by French advisors who instilled an ethos of political obedience, was a critical condition undergirding the overall stability of the Aristocratic Republic.

consensus or the alignment of interests across the whole of the Peruvian elite, but rather the domination of the traditionally conservative elements of the oligarchy by a more powerful liberal branch.

Even within the political parties, however, there was regular conflict. The once formidable parties of the late nineteenth and early twentieth centuries had been built around the personalities of their founding members. These founders had been there at the institutionalization of the first national-level parties and had pulled the elites through the rubble of the aftermath of the war with Chile. Personalistic allegiances to these figures was a cornerstone of party loyalty. This was especially the case for the Partido Civil, which had been formed by Manuel Pardo, but also for the more traditionalist parties. As the original founding leaders aged, struggles for succession by the younger generation fragmented the parties (see Karno 1970). Steve Stein (1980, 38) put it colorfully but accurately when he said that, by 1919, the traditional parties "resembled the imposing colonial houses still owned by many of their most prominent members; impressive façades that hid aging structures beset by internal decay."

The dominant Partido Civil was particularly plagued by dissension and schism, almost from the start. While all Civilistas were broadly liberal in comparison with their traditionalist counterparts, the mainline leaders tended to be wealthy capitalists (and somewhat more conservative), whereas the internal opposition within Civilismo grew out of a younger generation that was more oriented to the plight of the emerging middle class (and was somewhat more progressive). Thus, just below the surface, the Aristocratic Republic was already quite unstable by early 1919. And it was finally brought to a definitive end by Leguía's rise to power.

Augusto Bernardino Leguía came from a secure but relatively modest background—what might reasonably be considered middle class origins.[3] He was born in 1863 in the town of San José, in the northern coastal province of Lambayeque, far away from the wealthy families, elite schools, and exclusive social circles of the Peruvian capital. While his mother hailed from a modestly wealthy family, his father made his living managing a sugar plantation for an absentee Chilean owner.[4] This landlord provided Leguía with the first of many opportunities for social mobility when he brought the young man to live with him in Valparaíso, Chile, to be educated in an elite secondary school that had cultivated former Peruvian presidents. Leguía left the school fluent in

3. For older and more recent biographical treatments of Leguía, see Capuñay 1952 and Alzamora 2013.

4. On Leguía's family, see Capuñay 1952, 9–18.

English and with a command of basic accounting and commercial practices. After finding his early ventures in business disrupted by the War of the Pacific, Leguía developed a very successful career, first in import-export enterprises, then in insurance, and later in agriculture, banking, and other areas. In all of this, his business skills and command of the English language facilitated ties with financial interests in New York and London. Leguía cemented his social position amongst the Lima elite by marrying into an aristocratic Limeño family. Although he would always remain culturally distant from, and even antagonistic toward, the exclusivist, high-living Civilistas, Leguía's business successes, coastal agricultural involvements, and newfound family connections brought him into contact with powerful figures in the increasingly dominant Partido Civil.

Over the course of the first two decades of the twentieth century, Leguía's relationship to the party was tempestuous. He was initially understood as a centrist figure who could appeal to multiple party factions. This sentiment, plus his experience in business, led to Leguía's first governmental post, as Minister of Finance, which he held from 1903 to 1907 (first under President Manuel Candamo, and then under José Pardo). Leguía then became the party's pick for the presidency and served what would be his first term in office, from 1908 to 1912. Along the way, however, Leguía drew the opposition of the more conservative wing of the Partido Civil, as he ultimately came to represent an upstart faction of Young Turks advancing more middle-class oriented, moderately progressive programs, against the wishes of the wealthy traditional party elite (Basadre 1999, 11:2857–68). While Leguía remained a member of the Partido Civil through this presidency, many Civilistas felt that he had betrayed them with his refusal to capitulate to party dictates. Leguía's opponents actively opposed him from Congress; and they even cooperated with their longtime rivals in other parties to back an alternative presidential candidate in 1912, effectively blocking Leguía's ability to install a handpicked successor.[5] On August 10, 1913, after Leguía had stepped down from office, his successor—Guillermo Billinghurst—sent the ex-president into exile in England (Karno 1970, 172). But the same moves that drew the opposition of the older, more conservative Civilistas, had also helped Leguía to develop a base of loyal support that would serve him down the road.

The struggles within the Partido Civil did not dissipate with Leguía's exile. Indeed, by 1918, those within the party who remained loyal to Leguía (called Leguiístas) were machinating to oppose the mainline Civilistas in the next presidential election, which was to be held in May 1919. Although Leguía remained in exile, he declared his presidential candidacy in March 1918. In decid-

---

5. The Peruvian constitution did not allow for reelection.

ing to run against his former party, Leguía was clearly aligning himself with the upstart faction. At the same time, however, it is important to note that he was also aligning himself with members of the emerging middle class, as well as with urban students and workers, who had become increasingly vocal in their opposition to the dominance of traditional Civilismo—especially as costs of living increased over the course of the First World War. The more radical elements among the growing student-worker movement viewed Leguía as a promising alternative. Similarly, important military leaders were sympathetic to Leguía, both because they valued the pro-military policies that he had enacted during his first presidential term and because they were increasingly dissatisfied with the current Civilista presidency of José Pardo (Garrett 1973, 37–40).

Leguía returned to Peru in February 1919 to begin campaigning in earnest against the Partido Civil's chosen candidate, Ántero Aspíllaga. Promising economic and political opportunities for the middle class, better conditions for workers, university reform for students, and financial support for the military, he ran on a broad platform of progress through modernization. But while most historians agree that Leguía won a majority of votes in the election that May, it took a military coup to put him in power (Garrett 1973, 46). Returns from the cities came in quickly and had Leguía leading by a large margin—but this had been expected. The rural votes, which were coming in more slowly and were likely to be corrupt, were assumed to favor Aspíllaga. This posed a problem for Leguía and his supporters, as a contested vote would be decided by the Congress, which was still dominated by mainline Civilistas. But Leguía did not acquiesce. Both sides claimed victory early on and charged the other with electoral corruption. In the end, the military intervened on Leguía's behalf, installing him in the presidency on July 4, 1919. With the help of his military allies, Leguía had wrested power from the hands of the Civilistas, marking the end of an era.[6]

Leguía's rise, and ultimately the actions that he would undertake as president, were products of the contradictions and struggles that were playing out just below the surface of the Aristocratic Republic. To put it most concisely: over the course of two and a half decades, the political bases of elite control shifted, from a power sharing arrangement between liberal and conservative elite parties, to the domination of the political field by the liberal party, and ultimately to the domination of the field by a more middle-class oriented offshoot faction that emerged from within the liberal party—with the endorsement of the military, and with some measure of student, worker, and middle-class support. In this way, Leguía was no exogenous political force descending onto

6. On the events of this paragraph, see Garrett 1973, 30–53.

the scene from on high. And once in power, he would continue to reshape the political field in ways that were informed by the political conditions of his rise to power. Thus a nearly twenty-five-year-long era of elite political control produced, in a very short period of time, a new force that would—both directly and indirectly—reconfigure the political field in dramatic ways.

Second Reconfiguration of the Field: Leguía's *Oncenio*

A second dramatic reconfiguration of the political field followed Leguía's upending of the Aristocratic Republic and unfolded continuously over the course of his eleven years in power, from July 1919 through August 1930. Leguía came into office with the aid of the armed forces and ruled with the support of key military officers and political appointees. After securing the presidency, he nullified Congress and took on authoritarian powers. While presidential elections continued to be held every five years as usual (in 1924 and 1929), their outcomes were never seriously in question. But it was Leguía's policing apparatus, through which he maintained tight control over political activities in the country, that mattered most for the changes in the field that would unfold over the next eleven years. During this period—commonly referred to as the *Oncenio*—Leguía's method of rule contributed to profound changes at both the elite and the popular ends of the political spectrum. On the elite side, Leguía's attempts to safeguard his power from his old political adversaries resulted in a thorough disempowering and disruption of the traditional political parties, politicians, and social elites who had long held a lock on politics. On the popular side, Leguía's actions against students and workers provoked these groups into further political action, fed dynamics of alignment and schism within these groups, and ultimately contributed to the formation and rise of APRA as a viable political force that was purified of dissent and ready to follow Haya de la Torre in new strategic directions.

The *Oncenio* was a dynamic period of transformation in Peru on multiple fronts. While Leguía was distinctly *not* a liberalizer when it came to politics, he was keenly interested in economic liberalization and development, and more generally in advancing a project of national modernization.[7] To facilitate economic growth, he spearheaded many projects to expand the country's transportation and communication infrastructures. He inaugurated Peru's

---

7. As Pike (1967) has argued, the historical focus on Leguía's authoritarianism has tended to impede recognition of his fundamental contributions to modernization at a critical point in Peru's history.

central bank, courted foreign investment, and encouraged the development of domestic industries. Leguía instituted educational reforms that (at least on paper) provided free public education to all children over the age of six. And, as discussed in chapter 2, he also significantly expanded the bureaucratic apparatus of the state, resulting in a more than sixfold increase in the number of government employees residing in Lima and Callao between 1920 and 1931. As a result of urbanization, industrialization, and state growth during the *Oncenio*, the urban middle class grew significantly. Other social groups also grew: skilled and unskilled laborers, small merchants, street vendors, white-collar workers, and students. But the most important of Leguía's actions for the reconfiguration of the political field were the moves that he made against both elite and popular political actors, as well as certain segments of the armed forces, in his efforts to stay securely in power.

In 1918, the elite political parties—and especially the Partido Civil—dominated the field of institutionalized politics. But as already noted, the stability of this domination was undercut by conflicts just below the surface that threatened to rend the fabric of the Aristocratic Republic. It was through riding the waves of these conflicts that Leguía was able to win the 1919 election and overcome the Civilistas' attempt to prevent him from claiming the presidency. The Civilistas were surprised that Leguía had done as well at the polls as he had, and were stunned when the military intervened to install him in the presidency. But they had managed to reassert their authority after upsets before. And so their defeat in 1919 did not necessarily mean that they were out of the political game. If things looked bad for Peru's traditional political elites in 1919, however, what Leguía did once in power made them significantly worse.

Leguía began his second presidency with his guard up. He was himself a product of the conflicts of the Aristocratic Republic. The Partido Civil had made him, politically, first by providing him with a cabinet position, and ultimately by elevating him to the highest office in the land in 1908. At the same time, high-ranking members of this same party had been behind his political downfall and exile in 1913. Accordingly, he was acutely aware of the dangers posed by his Civilista opponents; and he was equally wary of those who appeared to be his allies. On assuming office in 1919, Leguía's first priority was to preserve his own position and to prevent a repeat of what he had endured during his first presidency. The greatest threat, in his view, was the continued existence of the Partido Civil; and next in line were the other traditional parties.

Leguía thus took immediate steps to undermine the old political actors and to destabilize their relations with one another. He significantly expanded the size and powers of the Guardia Civil, the national police force that would direct the political persecution, and placed his own brother in charge of the force. He then began to systematically dismantle what remained of the traditional parties—including the Partido Civil—repressing their most prominent leaders, disrupting their networks, and undermining their capacity to act collectively (Karno 1970, 227–33; Stein 1980, 41–48).

But the elites did not go quietly. Most notably, they attempted to regain power in 1924, when Leguía stood for reelection. Much of Leguía's remaining opposition coalesced at this time around one candidate, Rafael Belaúnde Diez-Canseco. Belaúnde was a prominent figure in the Partido Civil: the grandson of a former president, brother of the prominent intellectual Víctor Andrés Belaúnde, a dedicated follower of the earlier Civilista leader Nicolás de Piérola, and even a former supporter of Leguía during his first administration (Basadre 1999, 13:3177). But Leguía would allow no opposition. In a typical move, he had Belaúnde arrested on September 24, 1924, and imprisoned on the island of San Lorenzo, where he was housing other political prisoners (Basadre 1999, 13:3177).[8]

After 1924, the traditional parties had little hope of mounting any viable offensive and the former political elites largely stepped back from politics. While Leguía had attacked them politically, he did not undermine them economically, and so many hoped that they would be able to enjoy a stable social existence and perhaps reenter political life at a later date. But as the *Oncenio* wore on, many encountered increasing economic hardship, which culminated with the Depression of 1929. This economic hardship, coupled with the political difficulties that they already faced, led many traditional politicians to focus inward and remove themselves from politics for good.[9] Add to this the fact that most of the party leaders were aging and that the old channels for cultivating new leadership were no longer in place, and this spelled the effective end of the traditional parties.

By the end of his time in office, in August 1930, Leguía had nearly liquidated Peru's traditional political parties and had thoroughly disempowered the traditional political elites who had for decades held a secure lock on politics. This had profound consequences for the layout of the political field, in that it left a vacuum at the elite end of the spectrum that was occupied only by Leguía and his Leguiístas. By undermining the capacity of the traditional elites to participate effectively in politics, Leguía had set the stage for a political opportunity for outsider contenders on his ouster.

At the same time, Leguía's actions while in office provoked equally dramatic changes at the popular end of the political field. Radical movements had

---

8. Rafael Belaúnde was ultimately exiled to France.
9. For details on the fates of specific individuals, see Castillo Ochoa 1990, 57.

already been picking up steam in the later years of the Aristocratic Republic; but Leguía's choices about how to respond to them were critically important for shaping the particular configuration of collective popular actors that emerged over the period of his long rule. Most important for present purposes is that Leguía's actions played a central role in facilitating the rise to prominence of Haya de la Torre—an outsider politician who might otherwise have been largely irrelevant to national electoral politics—as a political force to be reckoned with, the undisputed leader of a network of dedicated supporters whose ranks would eventually be purged of internal dissent.

Coming out of the Aristocratic Republic, the two main streams of radical activity were among workers and students; and between 1918 and 1923, Haya de la Torre would maneuver himself into a position of leadership within both movements—starting with the student movement. Haya had been born in the north coast town of Trujillo, the son of downwardly mobile aristocratic parents. On matriculating at the University of Trujillo in 1913, he became involved with an avant-garde literary circle made up of largely middle-class students who bristled at the conservatism of Trujillo society. Known as the "Trujillo Bohemia," this group included the now venerated Peruvian poet César Vallejo—author most notably of *Trilce*—as well as many who would go on to play important roles in APRA.[10] The thinking of this group resonated with a broader wave of student activism in Peru, which was itself inspired by university reform movements in other Latin American countries. But Trujillo, located some 345 miles up the coast from Lima, remained isolated from national student politics. Hoping to play a larger role in the broader movement, Haya departed for Lima in 1917 (Klarén 1973, 91–92). In the capital city, he quickly maneuvered himself into a position of leadership within the Federación de Estudiantes del Perú (Federation of Peruvian Students, or FEP), which was pressing for the secularization of university education and a student voice in university governance.

Haya's profile among the FEP leadership translated into his playing of a prominent role in a historic general strike that rocked the city of Lima in early 1919. By the end of the Aristocratic Republic, strikes had become increasingly frequent in Peru. Although the government of José Pardo had introduced new protections for women and child laborers in 1918, workers were not placated and continued to press for better wages and working conditions. A textile strike that began in Lima in December 1918, just six months before Leguía would come to power, snowballed in January into a general strike for an eight-hour workday that brought the city to a standstill. Hoping that the involvement of

---

10. On the origins of the APRA leadership in the Trujillo Bohemia, see Klarén 1973.

university students in the action might generate middle and upper class support (Stein 1980, 130n2), labor leaders looked to Haya de la Torre (of whom they were aware through a newspaper article that he had published the previous August calling for the establishment of popular universities to connect students with workers).[11] Thus, the young Haya—just about to turn twenty-four years old—became the principal liaison between students and workers, as well as the strikers' chief representative and negotiator in their talks with the government (Stein 1980, 130). The strike ultimately succeeded. As Peter Klarén (2000, 237) observed, this was "a huge victory for the strikers and has long been interpreted as the founding moment, the coming of age of the Peruvian labor movement." As chief negotiator, Haya was the one who had the honor of presenting the terms of the victory to the strikers, solidifying his image as a workers' hero (Stein 1980, 131–32). This—along with his already powerful oratorical skills and open defiance of government troops in the street during the protest—earned him popularity among both workers and students (Stein 1980, 130–32). And the general strike forged enduring bonds between students and workers, while building bridges between an older generation of anarcho-syndicalist labor leadership and a younger generation of student leaders.

The period immediately following the 1919 strike—during which time students and workers forged strong ties at both the leadership and rank-and-file levels—was particularly formative for Haya de la Torre and what would become his APRA leadership. Leveraging his newfound popularity, Haya—as well as those who would eventually help him to lead APRA—remained actively involved in organizing both student and worker movements during this period. The day after the strike ended, Haya presided over the founding of a new labor federation for Peru's textile workers (the Federación de Trabajadores en Tejidos del Perú), which would go on to become "the most powerful force in the Peruvian labor movement" of the 1920s (Stein 1980, 134–35n16).[12] Later that same year, in October 1919, Haya was elected president of the FEP; and in March 1920, he traveled to Cuzco to preside over the organization's first national student congress. It was at this congress that Haya pushed to make his popular university idea a reality (Klaiber 1975, 697). The congress ratified Haya's proposal.[13] The first popular university was founded in central Lima in January 1921; and the second would be founded just two weeks later on the outskirts of Lima, in the working class neighborhood of Vitarte (Klaiber 1975, 700; Stein 1980, 254n23) (see figure 3.1). The student movement went on to

11. For Haya's call for popular universities, see *La Prensa*, August 20, 1918, 7.
12. See Federación de Trabajadores en Tejidos del Perú 1921.
13. See Sabroso's 1970 interview with Stein (PUCP/AASM, AI 98a, 15).

FIGURE 3.1. Haya de la Torre (left of center) poses with students and workers at the 1921 inauguration of the popular university in Vitarte.
Source: Yarlequé de Marquina 1963, 36.

found a string of popular universities in quick succession. The concept was simple: as illustrated in figure 3.2, student activists would take on the role of "professors" and instruct worker "students" in regular evening courses on a range of subjects. The universities served dual purposes. On the one hand, they brought students and workers together for educational and consciousness-raising purposes (Chanamé 2006; Klaiber 1975); on the other, they helped to forge strong ties between these groups and served as an organizational basis for political action. With the system of popular universities in place, Haya then set off in 1921 on a tour through other Latin American countries to meet with student activists throughout the region (Klarén 1973, 100–101).

Haya de la Torre's role in student-worker leadership reached its pinnacle in May 1923, when he led another series of protests—this time against the Leguía regime (Sánchez 1985, 101–17). Leguía had risen to power in the immediate wake of the general strike; and at first, workers and students had looked on him with a sense of cautious optimism—thinking that he might be more responsive to their claims making than had been the old guard. They thus supported his rebellion against the Partido Civil; and one of Leguía's first acts in office was to release students and workers who had been arrested in the course of the general strike—an act for which he was thanked with a popular rally held in his honor. The Peruvian state under Leguía even encouraged the development of the popular universities, at least at first (Stein 1980, 146n47). But

FIGURE 3.2. Depiction of instruction in a popular university.
Source: Yarlequé de Marquina 1963, cover.

as the new president failed to follow through on his promises once in office, students and workers grew increasingly dissatisfied with him. The final straw came when Leguía attempted to appeal to the Catholic Church by consecrating the city of Lima to the Sacred Heart of Jesus. This consecration was an attempt to counter charges of anticlericalism while improving relations with the Church, in the hopes of securing its support for his planned reelection bid in 1924 (Klarén 2000, 253–54). Leguía had assumed that the consecration would be uncontroversial. He was wrong. Students and workers were outraged and, under Haya's leadership, took to the streets—with Haya declaring that the consecration "constituted in both spiritual and political terms a reactionary act which threatened freedom of thought" (Stein 1980, 142).

The protest that followed was even more momentous than had been the general strike of four years earlier. It was the first real test of the student-worker unity that had been sparked in 1919 and forged through the popular universities (which provided a fundamental organizational base for this contentious political action). The movement was galvanized, and the student-worker bond cemented, when two demonstrators—one student and one worker—were killed on the streets by police. Leguía buckled under pressure from the movement, and the consecration was called off.

Although the protests achieved their immediate aim of blocking the consecration, however, they prompted Leguía to take actions that had profound consequences for the popular end of the political field. He began a campaign of repression that decimated the organizational infrastructure of the student-worker alliance. Prominent leaders of the movement were exiled, including Haya de la Torre—who was put on a ship to Panama in October 1923 and would not be allowed to return to Peru for eight years. The Leguía government proceeded to shut down the various branches of the popular universities in the months that followed, sometimes by force. The popular universities became increasingly clandestine, first giving up their meeting halls and moving to workplaces, then meeting outside of workplaces, and finally meeting in the homes of workers.[14] But even these semi-clandestine meetings were eventually shut down by Leguía, as he raided homes and jailed or deported popular university leaders in 1924 (Klaiber 1975, 710).

During his time in exile, Haya de la Torre traveled extensively throughout the Americas and Europe, where he continued his political education and organizing activities as best he could.[15] After beginning his wanderings in Panama and Cuba, he spent a period of time in Mexico, where he came to know the leaders presiding over that country's agrarian reform and its consolidation of a corporatist party-state (see Ibáñez Avalos 2006). In 1924, while still in Mexico, he officially founded his Alianza Popular Revolucionaria Americana (APRA)—which was conceived at the time as a transnational, multi-organization front (Balbi 1980, 65)—giving a name and identity to the network of student and labor leaders with whom he had already been working for years. Haya then travelled to Moscow (via Texas and New York) in 1924, where he was a "visiting spectator" at the fifth World Congress of the Comintern and participated in the World Congress of Communist Youth. After traveling through

---

14. Sabroso 1970 interview with Stein (PUCP/AASM, AI 96 and 97). See also Stein 1980, 118 and 146n47.

15. On Haya's activities in exile, see Cáceres Arce 2006 (94–143); Chang-Rodríguez 2007 (94–101); Salisbury 1983; and Sánchez 1985 (118–223).

Switzerland and Italy, he enrolled at the London School of Economics and then at Oxford, where he studied anthropology, constitutional law, English politics, and economics. In 1927, he led an Aprista delegation to Brussels to attend the International Congress Against Imperialism and Colonial Oppression. Haya then returned to the Americas, where he visited New York, Mexico, and Central America; and he spearheaded an anti-imperialist campaign in Costa Rica. Finally, when the U.S. prevented him from disembarking to change ships in Panama (at the U.S.-controlled Canal Zone), Haya was in effect shanghaied back to Europe (Salisbury 1983, 13–14). There, he spent his last years abroad elaborating what he by then thought of as his Aprista ideas and working for the German economist Alfons Goldschmidt in Berlin, just as the Nazi Party was beginning its rise to power (Chang-Rodríguez 2007, 100). Throughout this period, Haya was a prolific writer, penning ideological tracts and journalistic pieces, while also corresponding extensively with Peruvian radicals at home and in exile, in an effort to remain politically relevant to workers, students, and his potential allies in leadership (Stein 1980, 147–48).

Haya's vision for APRA was that it would be a pan-continental movement with national-level parties in various countries.[16] He took advantage of his time abroad—and of the diffusion of other Peruvian activists abroad through exile—to take the first steps toward this goal. The branch that Haya had founded in Mexico in 1924 was the first; but it would be followed quickly by others. In 1927, on a break from his studies in the U.K., Haya and other Peruvian exiles founded an APRA cell in Paris.[17] On his trip through the Americas in 1927, he organized cells in New York, Mexico City, Quetzaltenango (Guatemala), and Santa Ana (El Salvador). And other Apristas-in-exile did the same. By the late 1920s, active APRA cells could also be found in Cuba, Bolivia, Argentina, and Chile.[18] But the international cells were always in a precarious state and had to compete for members constantly with the Communist Party.[19]

---

16. In *El Antimperialismo y el APRA*, written in 1928, Haya argued that national-level struggles would lead to the political and economic unification of the Latin American republics against imperialism (Haya de la Torre [1928] 1984, 4:153). See also Klarén 1973 (xiiin2).

17. César Vallejo was living in Paris at the time and was among the founding members.

18. For Cuba, see Klarén 1973, 110. For Bolivia, see Heysen 1933. For Argentina and Chile, see "Relación detallada de los documentos del Partido Aprista incautados por la policía . . . ," AGN/PL, Legajo 3.9.5.1.15.1.14.1, Folder 5, Documentos del P.A.P. Cartas Confidenciales 1930–32–33–34–35 y 1937.

19. For example, in a letter from Manuel Zerpa to César Mendoza dated September 1929, Zerpa implores Mendoza to leave APRA for the Communist Party in part by arguing that APRA

Although a few small APRA cells did manage to take hold in the south of Peru—most notably in Cuzco—overall, the party's presence in the country was minimal during this time. The popular universities had been broken up, many of the most prominent leaders of the Sacred Heart protest era were in exile or in jail, and Leguía continued to be particularly wary of Haya—as he threatened to compete for the middle class support on which Leguía relied. Thus, while APRA was not officially constituted until 1924, the movement out of which it emerged was much more effectively organized on the ground in Peru between 1919 and 1923 than it was between 1924 and 1930.

But Leguía's preoccupation with the particular threat posed by APRA created some room for maneuver in this same period for Haya's close ally, José Carlos Mariátegui. Remembered as one of Latin America's greatest socialist thinkers—for his masterful adaptation of socialist thought to the Andean context through its blending with the ideas of *indigenismo*—Mariátegui is best known for his *Seven Interpretive Essays on Peruvian Reality* ([1928] 1995).[20] But he also played an important role in sustaining pro-student, pro-worker, and increasingly pro-indigenous thought (and relationships between thinkers) in Peru in Haya's absence. Mariátegui had been exiled by Leguía also, but earlier (for his writings in favor of the 1919 general strike), and had returned two months prior to the Sacred Heart protests of 1923.[21] On his return, he joined with Haya in the popular universities project and took on the role of instructor. When Haya was exiled, Mariátegui stepped into his shoes, taking over the editorship of Haya's radical publication, *Claridad*. Haya continued to correspond with Mariátegui from exile, and their thought remained quite aligned.[22] Indeed, Mariátegui was arguably Haya's closest ally in Peru at the time. In 1926, he founded and began editing the important periodical *Amauta*, which served as a venue for developing his emerging synthesis of socialist and *indigenista* thought.[23] Because Mariátegui was an avowed socialist—albeit one that was remarkably independent in his thought from Soviet dictates—Leguía viewed

---

as a movement is practically dead, as represented by the state of its international cells: "The important [Aprista] cells of Paris and La Paz have dissolved, that of Mexico is in crisis.... The only one of significance still alive is that of Buenos Aires" ("Al camarada César L. Mendoza," AGN/PL, Legajo 3.9.5.1.15.1.14.1, Folder 5, Documentos del P.A.P. Cartas Confidenciales 1930-32-33-34-35 y 1937).

20. For the writings of Mariátegui, see Mariátegui [1928] 1995 and 2005.

21. Leguía had given Mariátegui the option of either accepting a government-subsidized foreign education in Italy or going to prison. Mariátegui chose the former and departed in 1920.

22. On the relationship between Haya and Mariátegui, see Luis Alberto Sánchez's memoir (1969, 1:295–320).

23. On *Amauta*, see Tauro 1986.

him as less of a threat than Haya. And so it was with Mariátegui's home-grown *indigenista* socialism (as represented in *Amauta* and other intellectual and artistic activities) that many Peruvian radicals identified in the second half of Leguía's *Oncenio*. It was because the student-worker movement that crystalized in the Sacred Heart protest had an eclectic, popular front feel—it included university reformers, ordinary workers, anarcho-syndicalists, socialists, and indigenists, and it made efforts to appeal to the embryonic middle class—that overlapping radical networks came together and were able to support one another in various guises.

It was this fact that made the eventual schism between APRA and the socialists—and later the Communists—so consequential for the composition of political actors on the popular end of the political field. As both Haya de la Torre and Mariátegui developed distinct bodies of political thought and interpretations of the social and political situation in Peru, they began to diverge on key points, especially with regard to political leadership and strategy (Burga and Flores Galindo 1979, 185–96). By 1928, Mariátegui was finding himself increasingly dissatisfied with Haya, his ideas, and his plans. Haya—who saw the fundamental political question in Latin America as one of power—was increasingly urging the importance of uniting behind APRA as a party, under his leadership, and pursuing a popular front strategy oriented toward the overthrow of Leguía and ultimately victory in electoral politics. Mariátegui—who was more focused than Haya on the long-term importance of organization and consciousness-raising—was critical of Haya's personalism, his political impatience, his desire to make electoral politics a cornerstone of his strategy, and especially his willingness to forge cross-class coalitions in pursuit of electoral victories. In part out of this dissatisfaction with the direction in which Haya was taking APRA, Mariátegui established the Partido Socialista Peruano (Peruvian Socialist Party) in October 1928.

That Mariátegui was not wrong in his assessment that Haya de la Torre was unable to participate in a political movement in which he was not the sole and undisputed leader became apparent in early 1929. Haya indeed *did* intend to pursue immediate electoral—and, ultimately, insurrectionary—strategies, and to make himself the figurehead of such efforts. On multiple occasions, Haya had toyed with the idea of coordinating the overthrow of Leguía through mutiny and rebellion. When Leguía scheduled a second unconstitutional reelection bid for 1929, Haya acted—putting into motion what he referred to as his Plan de México. Although it was broadly understood that the election would be a sham, Haya made plans to run anyway (Klarén 1973, 117; and 2000, 260). He would inevitably lose; but this denial of victory—in the face of what he assumed would be a landslide of popular support—would unmask the Leguía regime for the farce that it was. He would then coordinate a mutiny within the navy, where he had ties, with a popular rebellion in Peru, and overthrow Leguía once and for all (Salisbury 1983, 6). But Mariátegui refused to back the plan. He thought that it was doomed to fail; but more important, he also disagreed with the strategy of electoral participation and insurrection—not to mention the personalism that both evidenced (Klarén 1973, 113; 2000, 261–62). Although Haya would later abort his plan, he took Mariátegui's opposition as a profound sleight. This moment marked the fundamental split between Haya (and his APRA party) and Mariátegui (and his Partido Socialista).

The fissure was only deepened with Mariátegui's untimely death in 1930, at the age of just thirty-five. Mariátegui's successor in party leadership, Eudocio Ravines, swung the Partido Socialista in a more doctrinaire direction, aligning it with the Communist International and renaming it the Partido Comunista Peruano. The distance between APRA and the socialists only intensified with this drift toward orthodox communism, creating a schism that would force radical Peruvians to choose sides in an internecine rivalry that would endure for decades. But as bad as this split was for the Peruvian left, it ultimately helped Haya to coalesce much of the student-worker movement behind his undisputed leadership under the auspices of APRA.

Critically, the Peruvian military remained in the background through most of these changes in the political field, although their evolving relationship to—and dissatisfaction with—Leguía would be of the utmost importance for what was to follow. There was considerably less consensus in the army behind Leguía in 1930 than there had been in 1919, when it had initially helped to place him in office. In an effort to secure and maintain personal influence over the armed forces, Leguía had instituted a new "law of promotions" (*Ley de Ascensos*) among the officer corps immediately on coming to power. Essentially a patronage system by which loyalists were rewarded with key positions, this law undermined the neutral professional ethos that had been cultivated among officers since Piérola's military reform of 1895 (Masterson 1991, 53–55; Villanueva Valencia 1962, 53).[24] At the same time, Leguía sought to undercut the relative power of the army by reducing its funding and refusing to renew its longstanding contract with French advisors, while bolstering the strength

---

24. It appears that the political neutrality advocated by the French officers who guided the professional reform of the army was not enough to reassure Leguía. As Masterson (1991, 32) notes, "Although the French advisers disdained political intrigue, their neutral posture appears to have aroused the suspicions of the autocrat, who demanded open manifestations of loyalty."

of the navy, air force, and Guardia Civil (which was accountable directly to him).[25] To make matters worse, many officers were dissatisfied with what they interpreted as antinational resolutions of border disputes with Colombia and Chile (Masterson 1991, 33). All of this alienated and demoralized many officers, while introducing new lines of schism into the armed forces. As a result of these dissatisfactions and divisions, Leguía faced multiple coup attempts over the years. And it was these conditions that would ultimately make it possible for a lowly junior officer stationed at a provincial garrison to lead a successful coup and rise to national prominence.

In sum, the field of Peruvian politics underwent dramatic change between 1919 and 1930, in ways that were quite consequential for the constitution of and relations among Peruvian political actors—and in ways that are particularly important for explaining the political innovation that would take place in 1931. The most important force stirring up these dynamics during this eleven-year period was Leguía himself, as he machinated to safeguard his own political power. Ultimately, Leguía's actions had consequences that disempowered some actors while providing others with new opportunities. On the one hand, his actions undermined the political actors of the traditional elite, just as Leguía had intended. Nothing remained of the traditional elite parties; and most of their former leaders were definitively out of politics—back on the *hacienda* or plantation, looking inward and trying to salvage what was left of their own economic standing. This in itself represented the beginnings of a political opportunity for non-elite actors from outside the political mainstream. On the other hand, Leguía's actions had important unintended consequences for the popular end of the political field. His persecution of the members of the broad student-worker movement—through prison, exile, and the shutting down of their institutions—disrupted the movement (the intended result); but it also (inadvertently) sowed the seeds for APRA to innovate later. It did this by galvanizing cadres, providing experiences in exile, and contributing to creating a split in the left (by creating a strategic problem situation for them) that influenced the strategy and "purified" the organizational decision-making envi-

---

25. While the proportion of federal spending devoted to the armed forces declined during the *Oncenio*, funding for the Guardia Civil increased threefold; and while Leguía allowed the army's relationship with its professionalizing French advisors to dissolve, he brought in a Spanish mission to train the Guardia Civil (Villanueva 1962, 57–58; Masterson 1991, 32). Further, Leguía provided officers of the Guardia Civil with the same privileges, salaries, and even uniforms as those given to army officers (Masterson 1991, 57). Leguía also contracted a U.S. mission to reorganize the Peruvian Navy and establish a naval staff college (Masterson 1991, 31); and he appointed his son to head the air force, funneled resources to that service branch, and established an aviation school in Lima (Villanueva Valencia 1962, 58).

ronments of these actors. Leguía's actions also aided in the development of the national reputation of Haya de la Torre and contributed to the popularity and rise of the outsider APRA party as a viable political force. In both cases, Leguía could have acted otherwise—he could have been more conciliatory toward his conservative opponents, and he could have maintained his initially positive relationship with workers and students—and so this second reconfiguration of the field was not inevitable. But ultimately, over the course of his eleven years in power, Leguía instead sowed the seeds of his own demise, encouraging and facilitating his own overthrow by the military. This day finally came in August 1930, when a junior army officer stationed in the southern city of Arequipa—named Luis M. Sánchez Cerro—staged a successful coup against what was by then Leguía's largely unpopular regime.

Third Reconfiguration of the Field: Sánchez Cerro's Provisional Government

Leguía's ejection from office in 1930 marked the end of the second period of political reconfiguration and the beginning of a third. This third dramatic restructuring of the political field was in many respects a reaction to the dynamics of the second, and in this way still bore the imprint of Leguía's previous actions. It unfolded over a much shorter period of time—from August 1930 through February 1931, when Sánchez Cerro headed up a transitional military government. During this period, traditional elite actors were further undermined; and, while persecuted, APRA maintained its strength and core character while picking up some well-placed allies of its own. At the same time, Sánchez Cerro was transformed from an unknown outsider into a viable political force with a national reputation, widespread support, and well-placed allies. This gave him both the prominence and popular base that he would carry into 1931, and the taste of popular support that would contribute to the shaping of his strategic decisions at that time.

How did a junior army officer stationed in a provincial garrison rise to a level of national prominence? Nothing about Sánchez Cerro's social origins or early institutional roles could have predicted that he would become a powerful figure in national politics by 1930. He was neither a general nor a member of an elite family. Rather, born in the northern town of Piura on August 12, 1889, Sánchez Cerro was the son of a notary of modest means. He attended public schools until 1910, when he enrolled in the national military academy at Chorrillos, located just outside of Lima (Masterson 1991, 43; Stein 1980, 85; Ugarteche 1969, 1:1–4). Sánchez Cerro was thus a beneficiary of the professionalization of the Peruvian armed forces that had begun in the wake of the

War of the Pacific and that continued through the 1920s.[26] Yet while military careers provided a unique route to social mobility in Peru, they rarely led to real political power, economic wealth, or social prestige.

But Sánchez Cerro was ambitious. Indeed, his ambition—along with the nationalist sentiment that he developed in the military—seemed periodically to get the better of him. As a young officer, just twenty-four years old, he was seriously wounded while participating in the 1914 coup against Guillermo Billinghurst, in which he led the assault on the Palacio de Gobierno (Basadre 1999, 12:3094; Ugarteche 1969, 1:11–14).[27] Later, he would spearhead two coup attempts against Leguía—in 1919 and again in 1922—prior to his successful toppling of the dictatorship in 1930.[28] The punishments that he endured for his roles in these earlier actions—including imprisonment, removal to remote military outposts, and a quasi-exile to Europe to pursue professional training—only strengthened Sánchez Cerro's resolve.[29] On his return from his first European exile, in early 1930, he is reported to have expressed his continued drive to unseat Leguía at the home of José Carlos Mariátegui, saying "I must be president; I must overthrow this rogue" (Ravines 1952, 168–69; see also Ugarteche 1969, 1:100). And when his hosts expressed their disbelief, he continued: "I'm not bluffing—I do what I say I'll do, even though you don't believe me; . . . I swear on my mother that you haven't heard the last of me" (Ravines 1952, 168–69). But this was not the first time that Sánchez Cerro had voiced presidential aspirations. Ten years earlier, in 1919, he is reputed to have remarked to an orderly at the Palacio de Gobierno (probably in jest), "When I am president, I'll take care of such things"; and that same year he alluded, this time in writing, to what he would do when he was in power (Stein 1980, 85–86).[30]

By 1930, Sánchez Cerro was a lieutenant colonel garrisoned in the southern town of Arequipa. Virtually unknown in the civilian world, he enjoyed

---

26. On the modernization and professionalization of the Peruvian military, see Masterson 1991 (23–37) and Villanueva Valencia 1962 and 1973.

27. Sánchez Cerro suffered the amputation of his right index finger due to a bullet wound that he sustained in the action (Ugarteche 1969, 1:13–14).

28. For a brief discussion of the 1922 coup attempt, followed by a collection of newspaper articles and correspondence pertaining to the event, see Ugarteche 1969, 1:28–61, 63–67.

29. On Sánchez Cerro's imprisonment in 1922–1923, see the above-cited documents on the 1922 coup. On his removal to a post in the jungle region of La Pampa and subsequent exile to fascist Italy (where he remained from 1925 through early 1929), see the summary and supporting documents collected in Ugarteche 1969, 1:68–73.

30. The latter example comes from an entry that Sánchez Cerro wrote in the yearbook of a fellow officer, Capitán Peralta, on September 27, 1919. This entry is reprinted in its entirety in Ugarteche (1969, 1:27).

modest fame only within the small military circles of people who had either supported or opposed his previous coup attempts. In earlier eras, a junior officer from a provincial garrison would not have had a hope of becoming the head of a national governing junta.[31] But Leguía's popularity was flagging by the late 1920s, and dissatisfaction was spreading rapidly within the military ranks. While senior officers in the Arequipa garrison thought that any coup ought to be led by a high-ranking officer, junior officers supported Sánchez Cerro's bid for the leadership of such an effort (Villanueva Valencia 1962, 63). Through his connections to the Lima garrison, Sánchez Cerro developed the impression that officers there would not oppose a coup were it to take place. In light of this intelligence, and taking advantage of the generational factionalism within the Arequipa garrison, he and his co-conspirators set to work developing plans for a September revolt. When the plot was uncovered early, as had happened to him twice before, Sánchez Cerro acted before he could be arrested for a third time.

The subsequent events unfolded quickly. With the support of his fellow junior officers, Sánchez Cerro rebelled on August 22, 1930, seizing control of the Arequipa garrison. He immediately released a political declaration, called the Manifesto of Arequipa, that outlined his reasons for the coup and vision for a national renewal of Peru. Leguía was used to such intrigues and appeared unconcerned as word of the southern revolt reached the capital city, even going so far as to attend a horse race at Lima's *hipódromo* "as if nothing had happened" (Villanueva Valencia 1962, 62–63). On the twenty-fourth, the newspaper, *La Prensa*, reported "public order," declaring on its front page that "everything marches toward normalcy as along railroad tracks." But as the generals of the Lima garrison defected to Sánchez Cerro's side, Leguía's attempts to reassert control appeared increasingly futile.[32] At the urging of the Lima generals, Leguía agreed to resign on the twenty-fifth of August and was taken into custody. He was placed aboard a ship that would provide him with temporary protection and eventually take him into exile.[33]

By August 27, the lines of authority in Lima were clear, and the stage was set for Sánchez Cerro to travel safely to the capital city to convene with the rebel

31. As Masterson (1991, 33) has observed: "That Leguía was toppled by a coup d'état initiated by an army officer is not surprising. What is more revealing is that his downfall was initiated by a mere lieutenant colonel."

32. Villanueva Valencia (1962, 63) recounts that, on convening for an emergency meeting on the evening of the twenty-second, the top officers of the Lima garrison agreed that they would support the coup, as Leguía's dictatorship had to end, even though they recoiled at the notion that a "simple lieutenant colonel" was leading the movement.

33. For a firsthand account of the events of the fall of Leguía, see Villanueva Valencia 1977.

generals. After his triumphal arrival by airplane, the parties met and formed a military junta composed of representatives of all branches of the armed forces. At the head of this junta was Sánchez Cerro, the presiding officer who would sit as provisional president of the Republic.[34] In a move that foreshadowed the hard line that he would take against the Leguiístas in the near future, Sánchez Cerro ordered Leguía not exiled, but sent to the notorious island prison of El Frontón, off the coast of the port of Callao, where the dictator of the *Oncenio* had himself sent his own political prisoners. In a matter of just five days, he had gone from a lowly lieutenant colonel to holder of the highest office in the land. In the end, Sánchez Cerro's surprising rise to prominence was the contingent result of his savvy ability to read Leguía's waning popularity, to understand the potential utility of schisms between junior and senior officers in the Arequipa garrison, to predict the acquiescence of the national police force, and to foresee the willingness of the military bureaucracy in Lima to support a change of leadership (Stein 1980, 86–87; Ugarteche 1969, 1:107–9).

Not only was Sánchez Cerro's coup d'état seen as legitimate; it was hugely popular among most sectors of the Peruvian population. The event "produced a veritable popular explosion" of support for the figure (Villanueva Valencia 1962, 65). Sánchez Cerro's grand arrival in Lima, in which he was "received as a hero" (Villanueva Valencia 1962, 65), sparked what Steve Stein (1980, 84) has noted was "the largest public demonstration in Peruvian history up to that time" (see figure 3.3).[35] There is no evidence that Sánchez Cerro anticipated, or in any way orchestrated, this popular showing—indeed, he would make no real effort to politicize his popular support until months later. His calculations had been based on the old-fashioned methods of military-political positioning.

Nevertheless, an outpouring of support from all corners of the country continued in the wake of the coup, with people eager to offer their congratulations and declare their loyalty to the new regime. Sánchez Cerro received a constant stream of visitors, offering their services and asking for favors, at the temporary residence and office that he had set up at a private home on Calle Arenales, near the center of Lima. Congratulatory telegraph messages poured in from around the country: from military leaders pledging their support, from local officials and notables renouncing Leguía and offering their loyalty, from civic organizations proclaiming their gratitude and offering symbolic gestures of adhesion, and from ordinary citizens. Newspapers from across the political

---

34. Decreto-Ley 6874 (ADLP).

35. For accounts of Sánchez Cerro's arrival, see *La Prensa*, August 27, 1930, Second Edition, 1, and *La Prensa*, August 28, 1930.

FIGURE 3.3. Supporters of Sánchez Cerro march through central Lima on August 27, 1930, in celebration of the Revolution of Arequipa.
Source: 1930 photograph, "Manifestación en Lima, a la llegada del Comandante Luis M. Sánchez Cerro de Arequipa," courtesy of the Archivo Fotográfico of the Biblioteca Nacional del Perú.

spectrum reprinted these telegrams, ran lists enumerating Sánchez Cerro's many daily visitors, and wrote stories praising the Revolution of Arequipa and denouncing Leguía (and supposed Leguiístas).[36] Throughout the country, patriotic Sánchezcerrista clubs were formed—and existing civic associations appended the figure's name to their own—in expressions of support for the coup and its architect. In just a matter of weeks, "ties were forged between large segments of the Lima populace and the revolutionary hero that would later form the basis of the political movement to elect Sánchez Cerro to the presidency in 1931" (Stein 1980, 84).

Political actors throughout the country scrambled to respond to the new political reality. Former Leguiísta politicians and bureaucrats either kept a low profile or attempted to downplay their ties to Leguía and demonstrate their loyalty to the new regime. Ex-members of the Partido Civil and other traditional parties, who had been persecuted by Leguía, were enthusiastic about the coup, which was popular also amongst a newer generation of conservatives who favored a quasi-fascistic national revival. Even leftist radicals expressed

36. See, e.g., *La Prensa*, August 29, 1931, 4; *La Prensa*, August 29, 1931, Second Edition, 1.

support. Hoping that the fall of Leguía would signal a moment of real change for Peru, APRA and the Partido Comunista issued statements in favor of Sánchez Cerro's coup; and various unions and workers' organizations either issued similar statements or sent representatives to visit the provisional president on Calle Arenales.

Thus, by the start of 1931, Sánchez Cerro had established a network of supportive relationships among certain political elites and enjoyed the support of a loosely integrated but widespread Sánchezcerrista movement—all with minimal coordination on his part. Virtually overnight, the junior officer had taken command of the national spotlight, in front of what seemed to be a profoundly sympathetic audience (see figure 3.4). But Sánchez Cerro's popularity must be viewed in the context of the intense opposition to Leguía that had developed by 1930 (Molinari Morales 2006, 18–19). It was not so much a product of the content of his vision (the text of the Manifesto of Arequipa was open enough to be read in any number of ways), but of the fact that he symbolized a definitive end to the *Oncenio*.

The junta declared that it intended a return to democracy in the near future, after having dealt with the problems brought on by the Leguía regime. For Sánchez Cerro, the primary objective was clear: to root out Leguiísmo, or loyalty to Leguía, and to dismantle its organizational underpinnings—just as Leguía had done to Civilismo. He thus initiated a campaign to cleanse the nation of Leguiístas by persecuting the former leader's allies and supporters (Basadre 1999, 13:3093–113). He convened a commission—called the Comité de Saneamiento y Consolidación Revolucionaria (Committee for Healing and Revolutionary Consolidation)—to punish former members of Leguía's government for corruption (Basadre 1999, 13:3196; Molinari Morales 2006, 17).[37] The commission held hearings, seized personal property, and exiled and jailed people who it identified as Leguiístas. At the same time, Sánchez Cerro moved quickly to purge senior military officers whose loyalty he questioned, especially within the navy and Guardia Civil (Masterson 1991, 43).

As for the former dictator himself, he was still being held at El Frontón, under terrible conditions, where he was becoming increasingly ill. The conditions at the island prison were bad enough that some dared, despite the immense risks involved in appearing sympathetic, to write requesting that he be allowed to receive better medical care. Despite calls by some for Leguía's release, or at least exile, he was left to waste away in the prison, and ultimately died in the

---

37. The Manifesto of the Junta Directiva of the Comité de Saneamiento y Consolidación Revolucionaria, including a list of members, can be found in Ugarteche (1969, 2:69–71).

FIGURE 3.4. Sánchez Cerro addresses a crowd from the balcony of the Palacio de Gobierno during his 1930 provisional government.
Source: 1930 photograph, "General Luis M. Sánchez Cerro, Presidente del Perú, 1930-31, 1931-33. Pronunciando un discurso en los balcones de Palacio de Gobierno," courtesy of the Archivo Fotográfico of the Biblioteca Nacional del Perú.

naval hospital at Callao in 1932. Sánchez Cerro essentially dispatched the ruler of the former regime without technically having him executed.

APRA was initially optimistic and experienced a brief revival in Peru with the overthrow of Leguía. Haya de la Torre and the APRA leadership had anticipated Leguía's downfall and had been poised to return to the country immediately upon the event (Klarén 1973, 120). Some Apristas even started trickling back while Leguía was still in power. For example, we know from correspondence dated as early as April 1930—four months before the coup—that APRA was at least beginning to coordinate a campaign in country.[38] They began encouraging their cadres to stay true to APRA and to reject the Socialists and Communists.[39] But they knew that the battle would be uphill. As Aprista leader Luis Eduardo Enríquez (1951, 72, 80) later recalled, in the final days of the Leguía dictatorship, after the failure of the Plan de México, "Aprismo did not exist in Peru," apart from a few small cells in the south; those who first took on the task of renewing Aprista organization in Peru in 1930 were "a tiny group (hardly enough to fill a park bench)." And not only did APRA lack organizational infrastructure in country, they had to revive the popular memory of a long-absent Haya de la Torre. As Peru's only English language newspaper noted one year later, at the height of the 1931 campaigns, "Not one in a hundred had ever heard of APRA . . . until it burst upon an astonished Peru as a fully-organized party in August 1930."[40]

When Sánchez Cerro acted against Leguía, APRA pressed the new junta to release political prisoners who had been jailed by Leguía—which it did. Along with released Aprista prisoners, the cornerstone of APRA's rebuilding effort was the return from exile of former students who had been involved previously with Haya (Stein 1980, 158). While Haya de la Torre remained in Berlin,

---

38. On April 26, 1930, four months before Sánchez Cerro's coup, Rómulo Meneses sent a letter from La Paz, Bolivia, to César L. Mendoza in Peru. Based on a synopsis provided in a police memo, we know that Meneses told Mendoza that he had been well received at the university; and we know that the letter evidenced that an Aprista campaign for Peru was in the works. Mendoza replied to Meneses that, although he was in danger of being detained by Leguía for having contributed to a workers strike, he was ready to work toward the reorganization of APRA in Peru. (The two letters were seized by police in 1933; the memo describing them remains, but the letters appear to be lost to history. See "Relación detallada de los documentos del Partido Aprista incautados por la policía . . . ," AGN/PL, Legajo 3.9.5.1.15.1.14.1, Folder 5, Documentos del P.A.P. Cartas Confidenciales 1930-32-33-34-35 y 1937.)

39. In a confidential letter from APRA's Comité Ejecutivo Internacional (from exile in Berlin) to the Cuzco cell, dated February 25, 1930 (AGN/PL Legajo 3.9.5.1.15.1.14.1, Folder 5), the executive committee encouraged the Cuzco cell to reject the Lima socialists.

40. *West Coast Leader*, August 25, 1931, 4.

through ongoing correspondence with cadres on the ground, "he oversaw the first steps in the construction of an Aprista political machine in Peru" (Stein 1980, 158).

One of Haya's most important leaders in Peru at the time was Luis Eduardo Enríquez. Having been living in exile in Germany, Enríquez returned to Peru prior to the fall of Leguía to aid in the nascent organizing efforts in the south. He was promptly arrested by Leguía, but granted amnesty and released by Sánchez Cerro after the coup. In a letter dated August 31, 1930, Haya explained to Enríquez that it would be necessary to win the support of the indigenous population and middle class—and he suggested in particular that Enríquez should court the support of labor leaders (many of whom were at the time allied with the Partido Comunista). As Haya put it:

> In order to capture power, Aprismo has to cloak itself in its nationalist mission. As our anti-imperialism is nationalism, we must also present our platform for the Indians and the middle classes under that aspect. The *compañeros* who go to Lima should try to convince the labor leaders; but if they don't agree to collaborate, it will be better to leave them to form a well-defined communist group, by which they will serve Aprismo by negation, since Aprismo will appeal to them later.[41]

In other correspondence, dated September 16, 1930, an Aprista living in Bolivia instructed another operating in Peru to coordinate with various others who were trying to reorganize APRA in the country, to take advantage of Sánchez Cerro's coup.[42] On September 20, the Peruvian branch of the APRA party (the Partido Aprista Peruano, or PAP) was officially founded, with Enríquez assuming leadership as secretary-general of the party's new executive committee (Enríquez 1951, 72; Haya de la Torre and Sánchez 1982, 1:26). The PAP began to set up grassroots party branches, and generally engaged in propaganda activities to revive popular memory of the once famous Haya. In correspondence from this period, Haya insists time and again on the need for political organization—indeed he makes it a precondition of his return.[43] The

---

41. Letter from Haya de la Torre to Luis Eduardo Enríquez, August 31, 1930 (excerpted in Enríquez 1951, 95).

42. This correspondence was another letter sent from Rómulo Meneses to César Mendoza. As above, the letter has been lost, but it is summarized in a police memo ("Relación detallada de los documentos del Partido Aprista incautados por la policía . . . ," AGN/PL, Legajo 3.9.5.1.15.1.14.1, Folder 5, Documentos del P.A.P. Cartas Confidenciales 1930–32–33–34–35 y 1937).

43. Klarén (1973, 113) likewise notes Haya's insistence on the need for organization in Peru, even prior to the fall of Leguía. He discusses this as among the reasons for Haya's split with Mariátegui.

correspondence gives the impression that at least some progress in political organization was made between September and early November 1930.[44]

But Sánchez Cerro moved quickly to stymie APRA's renewed organizing efforts, beginning yet another wave of repression. In November, the important Aprista leader Carlos Manuel Cox was arrested and another, Manuel Seoane, was deported to Chile (Basadre 1999, 12:3118). Also during this period, other key members of the first Aprista directorate—including Luis Alberto Sánchez, Luis Eduardo Enríquez, Magda Portal, and Alcides Sepulcín—were persecuted and the return of Haya de la Torre to Peru was officially impeded (Basadre 1999, 12:3118; Haya de la Torre and Sánchez 1982, 1:26).[45] APRA was thus once again prohibited from organizing in Peru, this time until Sánchez Cerro's removal from power. This repression of APRA coincided with equal repression of other leftist dissidents within the labor movement and Communist Party.[46] While Leguía had viewed the Socialists and Communists as less of a threat than APRA, Sánchez Cerro was more hostile toward them. During his brief tenure as head of the provisional junta, he persecuted Socialist and Communist unions and party members, repressing worker cells (Ramos Tremolada 1990, 97) and notably banning the Confederación General de Trabajadores del Perú—an important labor federation, founded by Mariátegui

---

44. Excerpts from this correspondence are reprinted in Enríquez 1951 (81–101). This correspondence, however, also evidences tension between Haya, who emphasized the need for immediate organization and called for an immediate campaign for the presidency (despite the fact that no elections had been called), and Enríquez, who took a more realistic perspective on possibilities for action and the remaining dangers of repression. On APRA's initial organizing efforts in Peru in September through November 1930, see Klarén (1973, 119–20) and Stein (1980, 158–59). Manuel Seoane's letters to Luis Alberto Sánchez provide some insight into both the initial steps that APRA was taking to organize immediately following the August coup and the repression that the APRA leadership was already beginning to face by late October (Sánchez 1982, 393–95).

45. See Luis Eduardo Enríquez's public letter to Sánchez Cerro, dated December 9, 1930, which details repression of APRA and asks the provisional leader to end this persecution (AGN/PL, Legajo 3.9.5.1.15.1.14.1, Folder 5, "Documentos del P.A.P. Cartas Confidenciales 1930–32–33–34–35 y 1937"). Haya de la Torre's trusted advisor, Luis Alberto Sánchez, described the tensions of this period in a letter to Haya dated December 21, 1930 (reprinted in Haya de la Torre and Sánchez 1982, 1:27–30). He opens the letter with the following summary of events: "You will have already been informed by the *compañeros* of the very real situation that began on the 23rd of this past month, as a result of which [Carlos Manuel] Cox has been imprisoned, [Manuel] Seoane has left [the country], others remain underground, and others—myself included—are persecuted" (ibid., 27). For more on the persecution of APRA in late 1930, see Enríquez et al. 1930, Heysen 1931, and Seoane 1931.

46. See Decreto-Ley 6926 (ADLP); see also Basadre 1999, 12:3093–144.

in 1929, that claimed more than 19,000 members.[47] Sánchez Cerro, then, effectively prevented the formation of political actors that might have opposed him from the popular side of the political field as well.

Thus, the transitional period of Sánchez Cerro's short provisional presidency was marked by uncertainty, and its consequences were critically important. Following his overthrow of Leguía, Sánchez Cerro was in power as head of Peru's provisional military government for just six months, but he enjoyed a great deal of popular support during this time. This represented a profound opportunity for him. But during this period, he acted in traditional—not innovative—ways. He took his popularity for granted, assumed that his position of power was stable, and attacked his opponents. He dealt further blows to the elite, and especially to supporters of Leguía. At the same time, he repressed actors of the left, especially APRA and the Communist Party. And, like a traditional *caudillo*, he assumed that he should be rewarded with the presidency for having overthrown the previous regime. In all of these ways, he essentially shot himself in the foot; he stirred up the political field in ways that distinctly disadvantaged himself. He squandered his own opportunity and, as will become clear in the next section, ended up creating one for APRA. Although the Aprista leader Manuel Seoane had noted just before Sánchez Cerro's removal from office (in a letter dated February 15, 1931) that Aprismo "is a state of conscience, not yet an organization" (Sánchez 1982, 395), this was about to change.

Fourth Reconfiguration of the Field: The Samanez Ocampo Junta

Sánchez Cerro's first taste of power would be short lived. Just a few months into his provisional military government, his intention to install himself in the presidency became known (Basadre 1999, 12:3123). The other members of the junta disapproved of his plans and, by March 1, 1931, forced his resignation and prompt exile (Basadre 1999, 12:3126–27). And so by March 1931, the old parties were gone, the Leguía dictatorship that had replaced them had been overthrown, and Sánchez Cerro—the military leader who had filled the gap—had been forced into exile by his own junta. This moment marked the start of yet a fourth major reconfiguration of the political field, which lasted through the new junta's declaration of elections and promulgation of electoral reforms on May 26 of the same year. This was the shortest of the four periods

---

47. Stein (1980, 78) indicates that these membership claims were largely unfounded, although it is difficult to estimate a more modest figure. Regardless of the size of the membership, however, the CGTP was a particularly central institution of the labor movement in 1930.

of reconfiguration discussed in this chapter, but its consequences were profound for what would come later.

By January 1931, Sánchez Cerro had fallen out of favor with the other members of the military junta. It was becoming increasingly clear that he was not content merely to shepherd the country through a transitional period, but that he intended to use the advantages of his present position to secure personal power. In his view (which was shared by many Peruvians at the time), the nation owed him as much, according to the well-worn *caudillo* tradition whereby he who overthrew the dictator should be rewarded with the mantle of the presidency. That Sánchez Cerro was thinking along these lines was no secret: in a cartoon published in the December 11, 1930, issue of the anti-Leguía newspaper *Libertad* (figure 3.5), he is depicted as fantasizing about trading in his military uniform for the presidential sash. But Sánchez Cerro failed to anticipate the extent to which significant elements within the armed forces—including the other members of his junta—would oppose his plan. As Sánchez Cerro's ambitions became increasingly apparent, the tide turned against him. Most critically, an attempt at auto-election would violate the key professional principle of civil-military autonomy that had become so ingrained within the reformed army. The members of the junta were products of the professionalization of the armed forces and saw themselves as guardians of the nation and its political processes. They fancied themselves democratic reformers, and wanted Peru to be at the forefront of democratization in the region. This had, in their view, been the very reason for the coup in the first place. At the same time, some senior officers were upset at the prospect of seeing a subordinate ascend to the presidency, others felt that they had not reaped the benefits of the Arequipa coup, while still others either remained loyal to Leguía or simply disliked Sánchez Cerro personally (Giesecke 2010, 94; Klarén 2000, 269; Masterson 1991, 44). The conflicts within the armed forces that Leguía had strategically fomented needed only a small spark to be rekindled, and a spate of no fewer than six military-led insurrections broke out across the country (Villanueva Valencia 1962, 66).[48] Under immense pressure, Sánchez Cerro stepped down abruptly, tendering his formal resignation on March 1 and leaving the

---

48. These insurrections were accompanied by labor and student militancy. Some labor organizations assumed a revolutionary strategy as Sánchez Cerro moved to consolidate his authority (see Giesecke 2010, 87–88; and "A la Clase Proletaria del Perú," AGN/PL, Legajo 3.9.5.1.15.1.14.1, Folder 5, Presos Políticos y Sociales, Asuntos Políticos, 1930–1945). Student activists likewise opposed Sánchez Cerro's auto-election bid and occupied the campus of a major Lima university ("Al Señor Teniente Coronel . . . ," AGN/PL, Legajo 3.9.5.1.15.1.16.50, Folder 10, Subprefectura de Lima, 1931).

THE POLITICAL CONTEXT OF ACTION 111

FIGURE 3.5. Sánchez Cerro paints a self-portrait in which his presidential aspirations are revealed. Source: *Libertad*, December 11, 1930, 1.

country for voluntary exile on March 7.[49] He had botched what could have been for him a major opportunity.

The days following Sánchez Cerro's departure saw Peru on the brink of civil war as a new junta—led very briefly by the president of the Supreme Court—worked to contain the insurrections now raging throughout the country. After a period of negotiation, a stable junta was constituted.[50] Its official leader was

49. Sánchez Cerro's resignation letter is reprinted in Ugarteche 1969, 2:91–92.
50. Decreto-Ley No. 7060 (ADLP). See Basadre 1999, 12:3138.

David Samanez Ocampo, but he was "little more than a figurehead" (Pike 1967, 252–53). Lieutenant Colonel Gustavo Jiménez—Minister of War and commander of the Lima garrison (Masterson 1991, 44)—was "clearly the moving force" behind the new junta (Stein 1980, 191). Though he had once been close friends with Sánchez Cerro (Stein 1980, 190), Jiménez was also a noted APRA sympathizer (Masterson 1991, 45; Pike 1967, 252–53) who strongly opposed the notion of a Sánchez Cerro presidency. Thus the new junta was at least somewhat disposed in APRA's favor. On May 26, 1931—in a move that would reestablish appropriately autonomous civil-military relations, in keeping with their professional training—the new junta declared that elections would be held, instituted electoral reforms, and lifted martial law to facilitate the electoral process.[51]

As the junta was relatively insulated from outside political pressures, the reforms of its new Estatuto Electoral (Electoral Statute) marked a quite dramatic departure from the electoral politics of the past. First, the reforms encouraged transparency and broad representation, while dramatically reducing the possibilities for corruption and voter coercion, by altering the political process. They guaranteed minority representation in Congress, introduced the secret ballot, and instituted departmental scrutiny of the ballots. This last act was particularly important, in that it took the electoral process out of the hands of the centralized voting authority, which had been run by a cadre of corrupt elite officials throughout the Aristocratic Republic. Second, the reforms made voting compulsory for those who were eligible. Third, they expanded suffrage by taking the historic step of removing property qualifications. This enlarged the voting-eligible segment of the national population, when compared to the most recent contested election (in 1919), by roughly 92 percent.[52] But some context is necessary to interpret this figure.

Suffrage remained quite limited, with only around 7 percent of the national population eligible to vote.[53] While APRA had been lobbying for universal

51. Elections were declared in Decreto-Ley 7160 (ADLP); the law setting forth the electoral reforms is contained in Decreto-Ley 7177 (ADLP). Both documents are dated May 26, 1931. For a useful summary and analysis of the electoral reforms, see Basadre 1980 (141–60). The election date was initially set for September 13, 1931, but this was later pushed back to October 11.

52. This figure is in tension with the one offered by Klarén (2000, 269), when he notes that "the size of the electorate rose 59 percent, from 203,882 in 1919 to 323,623 in 1931." This is because Klarén appears to have been comparing the number of registered voters in 1919 with the number who *actually voted* in 1931. The more appropriate comparison for present purposes is between registered voters in both years. The number of registered voters in 1931 was 392,363 (República del Perú 1933, 23). As voting was obligatory, I use the number of registered voters (here and below) as a proxy for the number eligible to vote.

53. This figure is only approximate, as no national-level population statistics are available for Peru in 1931. Indeed, no census was conducted in the country between 1876 and 1940. Us-

male and female suffrage over the age of eighteen (Klarén 1973, 122), the junta was unwilling to go so far. The Estatuto Electoral continued to exclude women and kept the voting age at twenty-one. These two rules alone immediately rendered more than three-quarters of the national population ineligible to cast a ballot.

Thus, when discussing a 92 percent expansion of the electorate, it is important to remember that all of this took place among adult men (roughly 23 percent of the total population).[54] If we focus only within this limited slice of the population, the expansion of suffrage looks somewhat different: while around 19 percent of adult men could vote in 1919, about 31 percent were allowed to do so in 1931.[55] The newly eligible were those adult men who would not have met the property qualifications in 1919 and who thus benefitted from their removal in 1931.

But although the lifting of property qualifications opened up the franchise to some of the country's poorer citizens, it did not prevent the continued exclusion of the majority of even the adult male population—an estimated 69 percent of which remained ineligible to vote in 1931. Who were these excluded adult males? In short: those who were identified as indigenous. This becomes clear on examining the relationship between voter exclusion and ethnic identification at the department level. The 1940 census identified around 41 percent of the national population as indigenous; but this rate varied significantly by department (from around 1.5 percent in Tumbes to over 92 percent in Puno).[56] By far the highest rates of indigeneity were found in the southern and central Andean highlands; and, as figure 3.6 illustrates, these rates correlated

---

ing methods detailed in appendix B, I have calculated a 1931 national population estimate of 5,434,617.

54. This figure is also approximate: the 1940 census found that 22.75 percent of the population was both male and age twenty or older (República del Perú 1941, 52–54). It should be noted that the percentage of males age twenty-one and older would be slightly lower.

55. These percentages are again based on estimates. I estimate the size of the country's male population age twenty and older in 1919 and 1931 to have been 1,047,601 and 1,249,559, respectively. (See appendix B for details on how the 1931 estimate was generated. The same method was used for 1919, assuming stability in the department-level age and gender distributions.)

56. República del Perú 1941, 65. Any historical statistics on indigenous ethnicity in Peru must be taken with a large grain of salt, given the fluidity of the mestizo (or mixed) ethnic category and the conflation by many contemporary state officials of "Indianness" with ethnic cultural practices, indigenous language use, lack of education, rurality, and lack of economic means (see de la Cadena 2000). It should also be noted that, in the 1940 census, only 13 percent of ethnic assignations were *self*-identifications, while 87 percent were made by the enumerators; and individuals who could not be clearly identified as white, black, Indian, or amarillo ("yellow," or Asian), were coded as mestizo (República del Perú 1941, 60–61).

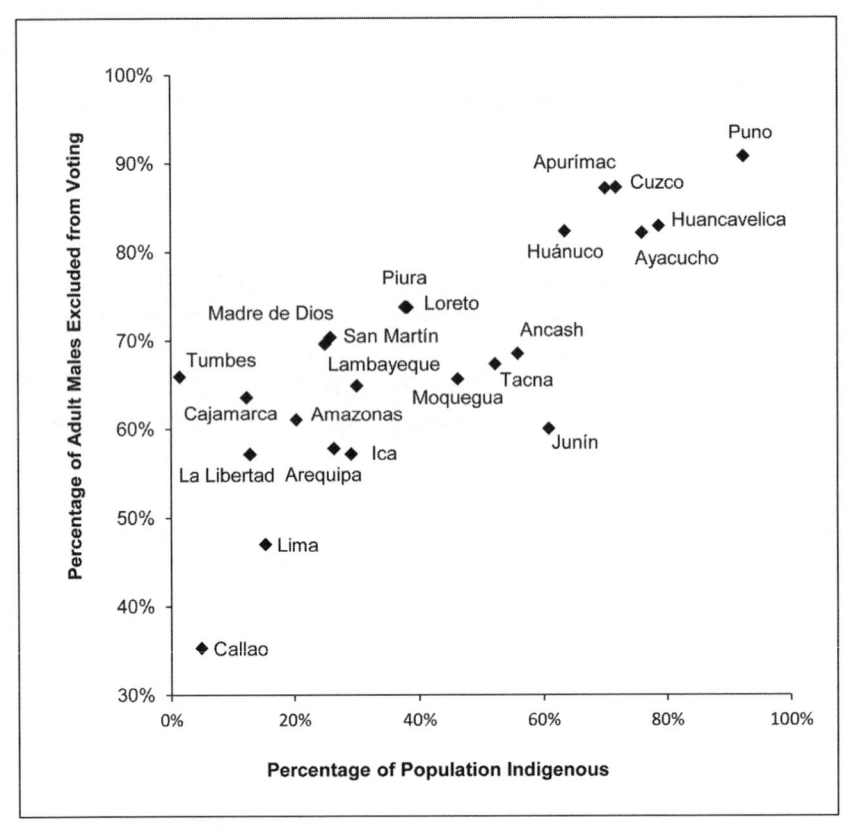

FIGURE 3.6. Indigenous electoral exclusion, 1931.
Source: See appendix B.

quite strongly with the rates of exclusion of adult men from the franchise. Only in Callao and Lima were fewer than 50 percent of adult men excluded from voting (around 35 percent and 47 percent, respectively).[57] In contrast—in an extreme example of what can only be called hyper-exclusion—there were six departments (Puno, Cuzco, Apurímac, Huancavelica, Huánuco, and Ayacucho; all geographically clustered in the southern and central Andes and together comprising around 34 percent of the national population) in which more than 80 percent of adult men were ineligible to vote. Not coincidentally,

---

57. In the *province* of Lima (the most urban of the seven provinces that composed the greater department of Lima), only 37.6 percent of the voting aged male population was excluded—comparable to Callao. (In 1931, the province of Lima had 65,903 eligible voters and a total population of 373,875, of which 105,601 were men over the age of twenty [Departamento de Lima 1931, 99; República del Perú 1933, 135].)

these six departments also had the highest proportions of indigenous population in the country.

The main mechanism of indigenous disenfranchisement was the Estatuto Electoral's literacy requirement. That this (Spanish language) literacy requirement should have such an effect on indigenous suffrage is unsurprising, given that 65 percent of those classified as *Indio* in the 1940 census were monolingual in either Quechua or Aymara (República del Perú 1944, 172). But the point can be underscored by comparing the percentages of adult males excluded from voting with those of people who remained illiterate, who lacked formal education, and who were monolingual in an indigenous language. As shown in table 3.1, the six cases of "hyper-exclusion" noted above also had the highest illiteracy rates in the country (all above 75 percent, and as high as 87 percent in Puno and Apurímac) and the highest percentages of their populations who by age fifteen had received no formal schooling (all above 72 percent, with Apurímac above 87 percent). And in five of these departments, more than 78 percent of the population were monolingual speakers of an indigenous language.

TABLE 3.1. Illiteracy and electoral exclusion, 1931

	Department	Adult Males Excluded from Voting (%)	Indigenous (%)	Illiteracy (%)	No Formal Schooling (%)	Monolingual in Indigenous Language (%)
Hyper-exclusion	Puno	90.7	92.4	87.0	85.8	83.4
	Cuzco	87.2	71.7	82.3	81.8	79.4
	Apurímac	87.1	70.0	87.2	87.4	86.2
	Huancavelica	82.9	78.7	84.7	83.2	78.8
	Huánuco	82.3	63.5	75.2	72.2	52.6
	Ayacucho	82.1	75.9	85.5	85.3	82.4
	Piura	73.7	37.8	63.1	58.3	0.0
	Loreto	73.7	38.2	54.4	50.8	13.5
	Madre de Dios	70.3	25.9	46.4	46.8	5.4
	San Martín	69.6	25.0	45.8	42.3	12.5
	Ancash	68.5	55.8	69.9	68.6	54.9
	Tacna	67.3	52.2	43.4	41.7	16.1
	Tumbes	65.9	1.5	43.7	34.3	0.0
	Moquegua	65.6	46.2	59.5	56.0	24.3

(continued)

TABLE 3.1. (continued)

Department	Adult Males Excluded from Voting (%)	Indigenous (%)	Illiteracy (%)	No Formal Schooling (%)	Monolingual in Indigenous Language (%)
Lambayeque	64.9	30.1	47.0	39.8	2.8
Cajamarca	63.6	12.3	68.4	64.0	1.1
Amazonas	61.0	20.4	57.8	55.9	5.3
Junín	60.0	60.9	62.4	59.6	31.7
Arequipa	57.8	26.4	41.8	38.5	17.2
Ica	57.1	29.2	30.5	23.6	1.8
La Libertad	57.1	12.9	54.6	50.0	0.2
Lima	47.0	15.3	20.1	15.4	2.4
Callao	35.3	5.0	11.5	6.6	0.0
NATION	68.6	41.2	57.5	54.3	28.4

Sources: See appendix B.

Leguía's educational reforms of 1920 had clearly failed to reach the highlands. In the urban, working class province of Callao, by contrast—where only about 5 percent of the population was identified as indigenous—the illiteracy rate was under 12 percent, the unschooled rate was below 7 percent, and there were no recorded monolingual indigenous language speakers. With the indigenous population largely excluded from participating, the 1931 election remained an overwhelmingly white and mestizo affair.

As figure 3.7 illustrates, the result would be an election in which certain departments were considerably more important than others. In the populous highland departments of Cuzco and Puno—which once formed the heart of the Incan Empire—candidates would find just 13,992 and 10,341 eligible voters (respectively).[58] Indeed, they would find around 3,000 *fewer* eligible voters in Puno (despite that department's seven-fold advantage in overall population size) than they would in the tiny province of Callao—which had the added appeal to politicians of being located conveniently adjacent to the capital

58. This amounts to just 12.8 percent of the voting aged male population in Cuzco and only 9.3 percent in Puno (see appendix B). The lowest number of eligible voters was to be found in the Amazonian lowland department of Madre de Dios, which had just 357 (República del Perú 1933, 216).

Department	Eligible Voters
Madre de Dios	357 (0.1%)
Tumbes	1,670 (0.4%)
Moquegua	2,671 (0.7%)
Tacna	3,029 (0.8%)
Amazonas	4,727 (1.2%)
San Martín	4,936 (1.3%)
Apurímac	6,588 (1.7%)
Huancavelica	7,708 (2.0%)
Loreto	7,720 (2.0%)
Huánuco	7,802 (2.0%)
Puno	10,341 (2.6%)
Ayacucho	10,782 (2.7%)
Callao	13,003 (3.3%)
Ica	13,053 (3.3%)
Cuzco	13,992 (3.6%)
Lambayeque	15,661 (4.0%)
Piura	19,801 (5.0%)
Arequipa	23,902 (6.1%)
Ancash	25,340 (6.5%)
Cajamarca	31,957 (8.1%)
La Libertad	32,838 (8.4%)
Junín	34,299 (8.7%)
Lima	100,186 (25.5%)

Number of Eligible Voters

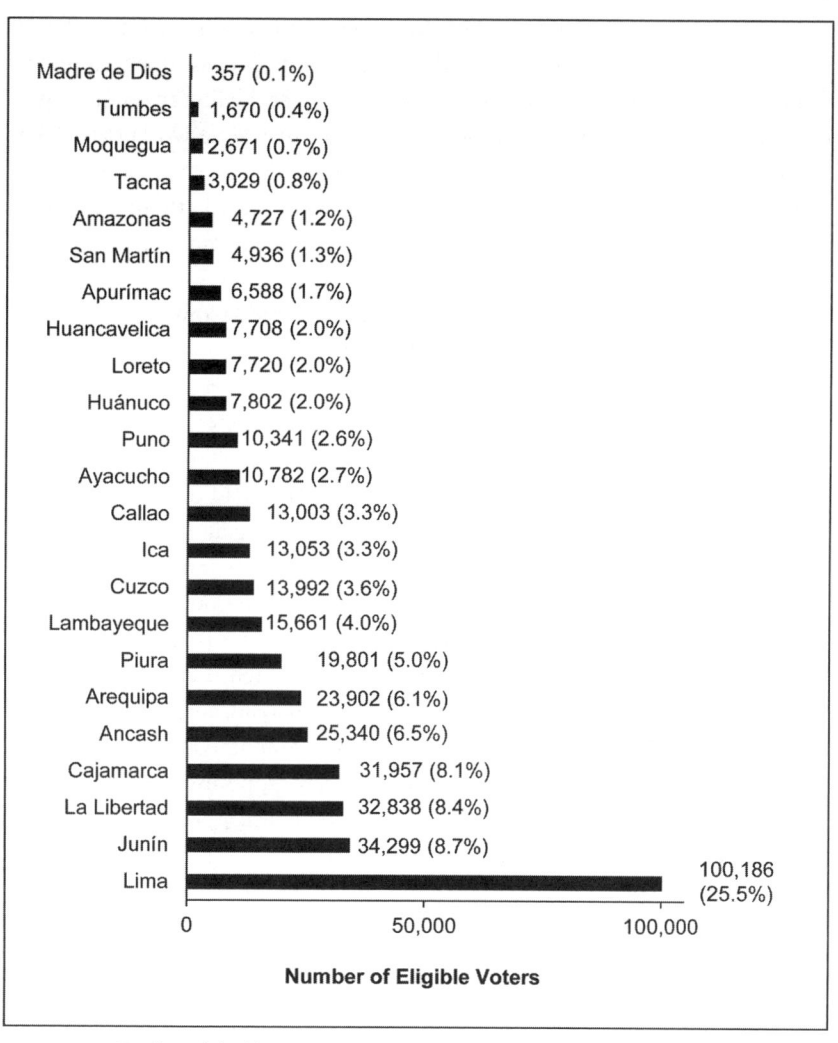

FIGURE 3.7. Number of eligible voters, 1931. (Note: the total number of eligible voters nationally was 392,363; percentages indicate the share of the national electorate represented by each department.) *Source*: República del Perú 1933, 230.

city.[59] Overall, more than half of the electorate was concentrated in just four departments; and a full quarter resided in the department of Lima alone.

In sum, the Estatuto Electoral reconfigured the Peruvian electorate in a very particular way. Its lifting of property restrictions and maintenance of a literacy requirement opened up the possibility (indeed, the obligation) of

---

59. In 1931, Callao had 13,003 eligible voters out of a population of 70,141; Puno had 10,341 eligible voters out of an estimated population of 494,856 (see appendix B).

political participation only for a specific slice of the adult male population. Who were these newly enfranchised? The individuals most likely to remain unpropertied yet achieve enough education to meet the literacy requirement were the laborers, artisans, and lower-level administrative workers of urban areas (especially Lima and Callao) who, although still working in low-earning occupations, had access to education.[60] And it was precisely these individuals that Haya de la Torre and Sánchez Cerro would target most aggressively in their campaigns.

The junta suspended active repression of the Partido Comunista, although it did not allow the party to participate in the election. In the end, in early July 1931, the junta even grudgingly allowed Sánchez Cerro to return from exile to undertake a legitimate campaign for the presidency (Masterson 1991, 45). When elections were announced in late May, both Haya de la Torre and Sánchez Cerro were in exile. On May 17, the junta had announced that it would *not* allow Sánchez Cerro to return to Peru to campaign, going so far as to prevent him from securing a reentry visa from the Peruvian consular service in Europe (Basadre 1999, 3178–79; Masterson 1991, 45; Pike 1967, 253).[61] The candidate—who it must be remembered was still quite popular among the general population—was only allowed to return when it became clear that the country risked civil war over the issue (Stein 1980, 191). Even then, the junta had already made sure to deny him governmental support in the upcoming election by removing all Sánchez Cerro appointees from office at both local and national levels and replacing them with appointees loyal to the Samanez Ocampo junta (Stein 1980, 191).

In just three months, Peru had gone from rule by a popular authoritarian leader to the declaration of elections by a military regime. This marked a historic shift in Peruvian politics and represented an important moment of political opportunity. But political opportunities are not necessarily opportunities for all. The restructuring of the political game that culminated in the electoral reforms of May 1931 advantaged some actors while disadvantaging others. It favored those who had the social recognition and capacity to court voters broadly, and it disadvantaged those with ties to old regimes or who had attempted opportunistic power grabs. Most distinctly, it was an opportunity

---

60. As Margarita Giesecke (2010, 28–29) notes, Leguía's education policies "played a decisive role in the incorporation of *mestizos* and the assimilation of Indians into industrialized areas.... In this way, [they] contributed to the creation of the voting masses in 1931."

61. The preliminary ban was largely the work of Lieutenant Colonel Gustavo Jiménez (Masterson 1991, 45).

for APRA. For Sánchez Cerro, it seemed to close the door on an opportunity squandered. For the Communists, it was an irrelevance. And for elites, it was not an opportunity but a threat.

Thus the fall of Sánchez Cerro, reconstitution of the junta, and promulgation of electoral reforms did much more than change the rules of the political game—these changes fundamentally altered the relations of collective political actors to one another. And this was itself in many ways a product of the competitive political dynamics of the previous periods. Sánchez Cerro misread his support within the junta, which led him to extreme—if still rather routinely conventional—actions that led to his ouster and disposed the junta to favor APRA over himself. He retained popular support, in a context in which this would be key, but came into the electoral cycle institutionally disadvantaged. APRA came into the same period enjoying a rare reprieve. The traditional elites remained disempowered, and seemed not to have much sway over the junta. And the Communists remained marginalized.

Conclusion

This chapter has shown how the rise to national prominence of two groups of nontraditional, outsider political actors by May 1931 was the result of dramatically changing field dynamics over the course of four distinct historical periods. By that time, the political terrain looked fundamentally different than it had in 1918. The country was being run by a democratizing military junta, which was quite autonomous from particularistic elite interests and had a firm grip on the reins of political power through its control of institutions. Unlike others in the past, this junta was at least sympathetic to claims to power that were based on popular support. On the elite side of the field, the former major players were not collectively organized. The infrastructure of their traditional parties had been dismantled, many were aging and struggling to stay afloat economically, and the few who remained invested in politics did not form a united front. There was effectively a vacuum where elite actors had formerly exercised thoroughgoing control. Furthermore, the dictator who had ruled the country for eleven years, Leguía, was in prison; and his former affiliates were disempowered and stigmatized. And the military leader who had planned and executed the overthrow of Leguía was himself no longer in power. At the opposite end of the political continuum, the Partido Comunista, for its part, remained an important actor, at least insofar as it anchored the far left, exercised influence among significant sectors of the working class, and conflicted publicly with APRA over strategy.

At the same time, Leguía's actions had unintentionally facilitated the rise of collective political actors that would never have had a chance to achieve prominence under the conditions of the Aristocratic Republic, and which had characteristics that would prime them for innovative political action. First, as political outsiders, the followers of Haya and Sánchez Cerro were already in a position that would make them more likely to innovate, as they were unconstrained by strong relationships with powerful social and political actors who would oppose radical departures from traditional political practice, and as they would likely have to undertake riskier actions if they wanted to continue to circumvent more established actors. Second, while neither Haya de la Torre nor Sánchez Cerro could boast an extensively organized and coordinated political party by May 1931, the core loyalties and networks on which these parties would ultimately be based were already in place. These loosely formed political collectivities drew in people with a diverse range of political experiences from outside the mainstream—in many cases from outside the country. Third, the leadership circles of Haya de la Torre and Sánchez Cerro had been purged of dissenters and half-hearted followers; those who remained were intensely loyal to their charismatic leader and more likely to be open to following through with unorthodox political strategies.

This was the context of political action that would be facing all of the political actors of the 1931 election—in addition to the social conditions described in chapter 2. But the rise to prominence of outsider politicians by no means predicts the political innovation that was seen over the course of the 1931 election. To fully explain that innovation—and especially to explain the content of that innovation—it is still necessary to examine how these actors responded to the situation that presented itself.

4

The Sources of Political Innovation
Habit, Experience, and Deliberation

By May 1931, Peruvian political actors were facing an unprecedented situation. A democratically oriented military junta had created a political opening that introduced a historically unique set of political rules and electoral realities; the political field had undergone dramatic transformations in a relatively short period of time; and profound changes in economic, infrastructural, and social conditions had produced novel challenges and opportunities for political action. But while it might be reasonable to expect that these socio-political realities would have encouraged some measure of political adaptation—and even of popular-oriented political experimentation—in the run-up to the 1931 election, the existence of these realities cannot explain which actors would take steps toward innovation (and which would not), let alone what their new political practices would look like. That is, even at this late stage in the game, the socio-political realities did not render the historical emergence of populist mobilization inevitable.

All Peruvian political actors, regardless of their characteristics, faced the same configuration of social and political conditions going into the election. But these actors understood and responded to the conditions differently in the first few months of campaigning. These early differences were highly consequential. By late July, the leadership circles around both Haya de la Torre and Sánchez Cerro were pursuing increasingly innovative lines of political action that were taking on the characteristics of populist mobilization. But other political actors—to both the left and the right of Haya and Sánchez Cerro—reacted differently. Most elite actors continued to machinate in ways consistent with the traditional practice of politics under the Aristocratic Republic. And on the opposite end of the political continuum, the Partido Comunista advocated an increasingly militant insurrectionary strategy. Neither the elites nor the Communists broke with their regular habits to innovate, even though they faced the same socio-political realities as the proto-parties that were forming around Haya and Sánchez Cerro. What explains this variation among the collective actors? And among those who did innovate, why did the practices that they developed come to look as they did and not otherwise?

I have already argued that the leadership networks gathering around Haya de la Torre and Sánchez Cerro were in positions that might prime them to innovate. But this does not explain why and how they did. Explaining this outcome requires a more detailed analysis of how these collective political actors experienced, understood, and responded to the social and political realities changing around them. Across all of the organized political actors in the field at the time, variation in their internal decision-making environments—and in the experience and worldviews of their leadership—led to differences in whether the objective political opportunity was read as a problem situation in a way that would create an impetus to break with previous habits; and these same considerations led to variation in the sorts of actions that these organizations began to practice.

Unlike the elites and Communists, the leadership around both Haya and Sánchez Cerro experienced the situation as problematic. As this chapter will show, although these leaders emerged out of political traditions with their own routine practices that had made sense under previous conditions, by 1931 their reliance on these practices had been frustrated. For both APRA and what would become UR, then, the circumstances leading up to the election precluded the effectiveness of the practices on which they had relied in the past. Each organized group recognized that the election presented a unique opportunity; but each was also savvy enough to understand that existing practices would be inadequate for capitalizing on this. It is precisely when confronted with such problem situations—when actors recognize that habit has failed—that creative practical action is spurred. But simply encountering a problem situation does not guarantee a solution. To innovate successfully, the individuals constituting these collective political actors had to have the creative skills and capacities to break with routine, as well as adequate exposure to alternative practices that they could draw on to construct something new. Both APRA and Sánchez Cerro's nascent Unión Revolucionaria party did this in 1931. Each found inspiration in a range of practices from other times and places; and each adjusted its understanding of the situation and reformulated its political strategies on the basis of these influences. In this way, each developed a similar practical response to the problem situation that it faced. That is, the parties of Haya de la Torre and Sánchez Cerro did not innovate simply because they were in outsider positions, or because they stood in opposition to elites. They innovated because the contingencies of their rise to prominence endowed them with certain experiences and decision-making capacities that formed their understandings and shaped their strategic choices in particular ways.

This chapter thus tells the story of how political opportunities—as a result of the state of the political field more broadly—got experienced as generative problem situations by some actors and not others; and how this combined with the experiences and stock knowledge of political actors to generate the beginnings of a break with routine and experimentation with cobbling together innovative packages of political practices. In this way, this moment in the process is a critical fulcrum in the overall explanation of the historical emergence of populist mobilization—it was the moment at which some political actors, and not others, translated conditions of possibility into specific modes of political practice.

As our ability to understand why some actors innovated at this moment is enhanced by making sense of why others did not, this chapter attends to the whole political field—to the non-innovators as well as the innovators. In doing this, it focuses specifically on the first half of the electoral campaigns, from the opening of restrictions on political activities in April 1931, until just before Haya de la Torre and Sánchez Cerro returned from their respective exiles in July 1931. This is because the divergence in how the political actors understood and responded to the political situation was established in this period, and it only became more pronounced in the second half of the electoral process (which is the subject of chapter 5). For ease of exposition, this chapter will treat each actor in turn, from least innovative in this early period to most innovative: first the traditional political elites, then the Communists, then the forces of Sánchez Cerro, and finally, Haya de la Torre's APRA party. In each section, particular attention will be paid to the social constitution and internal dynamics of the collectivity responsible for strategic decision making, to the political experiences and knowledge of the members of these collectivities, and to how these came together to shape particular understandings of the situation and initial responses to it.

Reluctant Elites

We can begin by looking at the political actors who did *not* explore new modes of political practice in 1931, starting on the right side of the political spectrum. It is true that many of Peru's traditional elites had been hit hard by the Depression, and that Leguía had repressed the most prominent leaders of the once-dominant Partido Civil. But just because the old parties were gone did not mean that the political field was vacant of elite actors or that the liberal oligarchy had disappeared. Various members of the social and political elite remained involved in politics in 1931, although their positioning in the field and degree of organizational cohesion had changed over the years. And while differing somewhat in their visions of the future, they all shared a desire to maintain political control at elite levels. Many were threatened by the political situation in the first half of 1931 and felt compelled to act. But they tended to do so in quite predictable, routine ways, drawing on past modes of responding to what they took to be historically similar situations. Given the extent to which conditions in Peru in 1931 favored populist mobilization, why did at least some elements of Peru's political elite not attempt to regain political control by developing this strategy? The answer varies, depending on the groups and personalities in question; but it amounts to some combination of a failure to see political conditions clearly and an opposition, on principle, to popular participation in politics. More specifically, these elites did not innovate in 1931 because their prior experiences led to poor readings of the situation, their visions of what was an acceptable social future precluded nontraditional thinking, and their lack of organizational cohesion led the initiatives that they did undertake to be fragmented. Ultimately, they failed to perceive a problem situation, in the pragmatist sense, and proceeded to act in traditionalist ways in the first few months of the electoral period.

As it became clear that Haya de la Torre and Sánchez Cerro might be threats, the elites continued to machinate. Some amongst the new generation of Peru's social elite advocated a more moderate approach that would have maintained the country's gradual trajectory of cautious modernization and liberalization—either in line with what Leguía had begun, or in some modified form—while preempting any dramatic shifts in political practice. Their primary concern at this time was the maintenance of tradition and ensuring social and political stability in what they saw as a moment of national crisis.

This tendency found expression in the actions of Rafael Belaúnde, a former Civilista who had been exiled by Leguía for opposing his reelection efforts in 1924. Belaúnde was the grandson of a former president (Pedro Diez Canseco) and had important historical ties to Piérola's Partido Demócrata. He was also a friend and old political ally of David Samanez Ocampo and a former prisoner on the island of San Lorenzo with Gustavo Jiménez—both of the current junta (Basadre 1999, 13:3177). According to historian Jorge Basadre, Rafael Belaúnde saw a clear problem with the political field in 1931: while there had been strong opposition to Leguía during his reign, "the old opposition to Leguía did not have a candidate of high enough stature on his own to put forward for the presidency in 1931, and so it was necessary to find a way to consecrate someone through a convention" (Basadre 1999, 13:3177).

Samanez Ocampo and Jiménez had asked Belaúnde to return to Peru to become an advisor to their new junta (Basadre 1999, 13:3177). Belaúnde did return at this time, but he had other plans. Declining the junta's offer, he instead moved to form a group of moderate professionals—doctors, lawyers, intellectuals—that would be called Concentración Nacional (National Unity, henceforth CN).[1] The aim of this group was simple: to present an alternative to unappealing outsider candidates who would be seen by the various elements of the fragmented elite as a satisfactory compromise. Instead of campaigning, however, this group tried—in thoroughly traditionalist fashion—to circumvent what was likely to be a contentious electoral process by making overtures to the junta to arrange a peaceful transfer of power through a negotiated pact that would have been generally acceptable to most elite factions (see Ugarteche 1969, 2:xxvii).

Concentración Nacional released its founding declaration on April 7, 1931.[2] The declaration began: "Surely the country will receive with patriotic satisfaction the initiative of the distinguished citizens who, foregoing all personal and partisan interests, advocate for a national coalition of forces capable of finding a happy solution to the delicate public problems now facing us" (Ugarteche 1969, 2:117). They wanted to "organize a representative assembly of the regions and active forces of the country to designate a candidate for the presidency of the Republic that it can recommend to the mass electorate in order to facilitate the electoral proceedings" (Ugarteche 1969, 2:119; see also Basadre 1999, 13:3177).

Their ideas came from experience and knowledge of Peruvian history; and based on this, they had reason to believe that their effort might succeed. The elite had put their differences aside to reach similar agreements in past moments of crisis—in 1895 and 1915—and it was the hope of the Concentración Nacional leadership that a similar arrangement would be possible in 1931.[3] The CN proposal was thus an attempt by some elites to cling to the old

---

1. On the Concentración Nacional, see Basadre (1999, 13:3177–78) and Ugarteche (1969, 2:xxxv–xxxvi). Acción Republicana represented a similar elite effort. For its January 1, 1931, manifesto, see Ugarteche 1969, 2:14–24.

2. This document is reprinted in Ugarteche 1969, 2:118–21.

3. Orazio Ciccarelli noted the elite's reliance on past political experience at this moment of change: "the moderate elements constituted narrow self-interested groups seemingly oblivious to the fundamental crisis which had gripped Peru. . . . The examples they most often wanted to emulate were the governments of 1895 and 1915" (Ciccarelli 1969, 105–6).

politics of backroom dealing, having failed to realize that "the gentlemanly and aristocratic times when such a solution might have been possible were long gone from Peruvian politics" (Klarén 1973, 135). That is, these more moderate elites failed to recognize the extent to which the political situation in 1931 was fundamentally different from past moments of crisis. In retrospect, this proposal appears naïve and incognizant of the changes that had taken place in the intervening years. It was only when outsider candidates began to rely on populist strategies—and especially when a populist victory began to appear inevitable—that these elites abandoned their hopes of a traditional political pact.[4]

At the same time as the CN initiative was unfolding, a small handful of former party notables initiated their own presidential bids and proceeded to campaign in the traditional style. The two most prominent of these—Arturo Osores and José María de la Jara y Ureta—ran all the way through to election day. Seeming not to grasp fully the new political reality, neither of these candidates mounted anything even approximating a populist campaign (Miró Quesada Laos 1947, 160–63). Indeed, Osores—an old veteran of the Partido Constitucional and former member of Leguía's cabinet—spent most of his time attempting to wrangle a coalition of traditional elites to his side, apparently deaf to popular cries for political change (Miró Quesada Laos 1947, 160).[5] Notably, la Jara—then the Peruvian ambassador to Brazil—did not even return to Peru to participate personally in the contest. In keeping with a traditional political practice, he instead relied on his elite colleagues to mount a letter-writing campaign on his behalf (Basadre 1999, 13:3199; McEvoy 1999, 119–68).[6] In the end, while successfully garnering some elite support, both candidates

---

4. In July 1931, once it became clear that their political strategy would not yield the desired results, CN attempted to assert its relevance by endorsing a candidate. It requested that representatives of Haya de la Torre and Sánchez Cerro meet with them, to compete for the endorsement. Both declined the request. "Sánchez Cerro answered by reminding it [CN] that the circumstances had so changed that his supporters and the people themselves wanted an open electoral struggle rather than subordinating their choice to the political judgment of the concentracion" (Ciccarelli 1969, 109). Haya de la Torre declined under similar pretext.

5. Osores was involved in the 1914 plot to overthrow Billinghurst, and also led a revolt against Leguía in 1924, for which he was imprisoned. As one historian noted, "his credentials, therefore, as an enemy of Leguía—an important requirement for a candidate in the 1931 election—were more than solid, but he had little else going for him" (Ciccarelli 1969, 111). For a profile on Osores, see *West Coast Leader*, August 4, 1931, 2.

6. In his memoir, Carlos Miró Quesada Laos (1947, 162–64) remarks that the candidacy of la Jara had been premised on the misguided notion that there was a broad political center that would support him as representative of the traditional elite. La Jara believed that it was unneces-

performed exceptionally poorly at the polls. Of 299,827 valid votes cast, la Jara won 21,950 (7.3 percent) and Osores secured just 19,640 (6.6 percent) (Tuesta Soldevilla 2001, 607). In failing to recognize how changing conditions had reconfigured the political terrain, both Osores and la Jara seem in hindsight to have been as naïve as Belaúnde in their assessments of the political situation. All told, the moderate elites simply failed to recognize that candidates who did not pursue populist mobilization would be unable to compete with Haya de la Torre and Sánchez Cerro in the 1931 election.

Other elites appear in some respects to have been more situationally aware. After the fall of Leguía, others yearned for a renewal of tradition and began to call for a dramatic reversal of the former dictator's modernizing policies and a return to political dominance by the liberal oligarchy. These elites apparently did recognize that the political reality had changed, as indicated by their failure to support either Concentración Nacional or the moderate elite candidates. But even amongst those who read the situation clearly, populist mobilization was distinctly unappealing. To these elites, the populist route to power remained abhorrent—such a courting of mass support would simply have gone too far toward undermining the social hierarchy that formed the basis of the traditional power structure. These more traditionalist elites eventually recognized how times had changed, though this did not temper their fundamental discomfort with populist mobilization.

But as the Haya de la Torre and Sánchez Cerro campaigns picked up steam, it became increasingly clear to savvy observers that electoral success would come only to a candidate who was willing to encourage—and who could successfully channel—popular participation (see figure 4.1). That is, while they wanted to control the political process, it was becoming clear that victory would go to those who encouraged popular participation.

Lacking the organizational capacity or control of political institutions necessary to disrupt the new political reality, this group had only three options: to abstain from the electoral process, to support one of the other elite candidates' unrealistic presidential bids, or to throw in behind one of the two outsider candidates. To be sure, some opted for one of the first two choices. But the rest ultimately decided that Sánchez Cerro was the lesser of two evils and gave him their grudging support (Castillo Ochoa 1990, 60; Ciccarelli 1973, 23). On what was referred to as the "black night of the oligarchy," a group of elites met at the prestigious Club Nacional to chart their collective political response to

---

sary to hold mass rallies and marches to court this silent majority, but that they ("our masses") would make themselves known on election day.

FIGURE 4.1. Representatives of Peru's traditional elite and governing military junta watch apprehensively as Sánchezcerristas (left) and Apristas (right) parade through Lima in August 1931.
Source: *Variedades*, August 26, 1931, 7.

the dynamics of the election (Adrianzén 1990). Realizing that they "were displaced and playing on a chess board that was not their own," and that they did not have a plan that could defeat the dual threats of APRA and socialism, the group decided to support Sánchez Cerro—even though they despised him (Yepes 1990, 78–79). In their estimation, Sánchez Cerro was more likely to safeguard their interests and could be more easily controlled than Haya de la Torre.[7] Sánchez Cerro's mode of popular mobilization seemed to have its roots in a more traditional, authoritarian paternalism than in a genuinely revolutionary project; and his nationalism was of a fundamentally reactionary type, promising to restore Peru to its pre-Leguía state and little more. Finally, social networks between Sánchez Cerro's key advisors and conservative elites ensured some semblance of political control. These conservatives thus decided to maintain *social* tradition by conceding to the violation of *political* tradition. Nevertheless, although their willingness to support Sánchez Cerro demonstrates that they understood the political reality better than either Osores or la Jara, this group of young elites disapproved of the populist mobilization that was being elaborated in the course of the election—and they certainly would never have developed it on their own.

Resistant Communists

On the opposite end of the political spectrum—on the ideological left—the leadership of the Partido Comunista Peruano (PCP) also did not innovate in 1931. In fact, they were strongly opposed to the populist mobilization being developed by the nontraditional candidates, albeit for very different reasons than the elites. Their objection was not that populist mobilization went *too far* toward toppling the old order, but rather that it did not go *far enough*. They were not disposed to take advantage of opportunities for political innovation due to their doctrinaire commitment to a different kind of politics.

Before the downfall of Leguía, Eudocio Ravines—who assumed leadership of Mariátegui's Partido Socialista (and changed the name to the PCP) in 1930—turned the party toward the Communist International. At its Sixth Party Congress in 1928, kicking off what is known as the Third Period, the Communist International had adopted the perspective that the world was ripe for proletarian revolution. Strategically, this meant establishing red trade unions and preparing for insurrectionary action. To reorient Mariátegui's party to the Communist International in good faith meant adopting the Comintern's Third Period strategy. In practice, this entailed putting forth the perspective that Peru, too, was ripe for workers' insurrection, organizing PCP-controlled unions, and engaging in strike activity. This interpretation of contemporary political events, and the subsequent strategy of Peru's labor left, were clearly articulated in the days immediately following Sánchez Cerro's Revolution

---

7. On prominent elites eventually throwing in behind Sánchez Cerro, see Castillo Ochoa 1990, 60.

of Arequipa by the Communist-dominated Confederación General de Trabajadores del Perú (General Confederation of Peruvian Workers, or CGTP). In a public announcement dated August 25, 1930, the CGTP explained that, "Our working class expects no decisive improvement to our situation from this staffing change [*cambio de hombres*]. The advantages we might obtain will be a consequence of the energy with which we assume the defense of our grievances."[8]

Considering the severely deleterious effects of the Depression on employment in Peru, as noted in chapter 2, it made sense to organize radical workers' actions. But in practice, following this approach ended up yielding diminishing returns in the last months of 1930. In September and October of that year, Communist-led unions organized a general strike against the Cerro de Pasco Copper Corporation. But the strike met with severe repression. Paired with the government's vow to repress the PCP, this "colossal failure" left the party "isolated and ineffective" (Klarén 2000, 271). In light of this defeat, the party could have regrouped and changed its political strategy. But in January 1931, the PCP passed a resolution that reaffirmed its Third Period position, stating that the country was facing an "objectively revolutionary situation," and that the foremost urgent task was to increase the profile of the PCP in the labor movement and engage in more insurrectionary actions.[9] Thus, on the domestic front, from the PCP's perspective, conditions seemed propitious again for strikes and worker insurrection leading up to the 1931 election.

The Partido Comunista remained an important actor in the political field as the electoral contest began to intensify. It anchored the far left and exercised influence among significant sectors of the working class. Indeed, it was APRA's greatest source of competition on the left. But the leadership of the party did not see the electoral opening as constituting a problem situation in the pragmatist sense. First, they were in a stronger position to pursue traditional labor organizing strategies than they had been under either Leguía's *Oncenio* or Sánchez Cerro's provisional government. The party was again legal and able to operate freely. Second, the Communist leaders did not interpret the present electoral moment as substantively different from any of the previous authoritarian, oligarchical, or otherwise "sham-democratic" elections in the country's history. They considered the elections to be a "farce" because they thought they

---

8. "A la Clase Proletaria del Perú," AGN/PL, Legajo 3.9.5.1.15.1.14.1, Folder 5, Presos Políticos y Sociales, Asuntos Políticos, 1930–1945.
9. "Resolución del Comité Ejecutivo," PUCP/CMAP, Folder 3.12/P.C.P, 1, see also 7.

could not produce substantive change.[10] That is, this aspect of the "political opportunity" did not present a problem situation that was distinct from the usual state of affairs. The Party did run protest candidates "to make our program known and understood to the masses,"[11] but they did not think elections could produce the kind of substantive political change that they wanted. Nor did they collaborate with other political organizations. The party stated variants of these views publicly, in polemics with APRA.[12] Thus the leadership of the PCP, at the time of the 1931 election, was dismissive of populist strategies.

Despite (or because of) many apparent similarities between the Aprista and Communist movements, the Communists directed their critiques most vociferously against APRA. Haya de la Torre had emerged from the ranks of the radical Peruvian left, and his movement competed directly with the Communists for organized labor and student support. In the wake of Mariátegui's death, the PCP clearly articulated its position on political strategy in intense polemics with APRA, in which it harshly condemned the party's mass mobilizing practices.

The party leadership had two fundamental problems with Haya's strategic choices—problems that echo the issues raised in the earlier schism between Haya and Mariátegui.[13] The first was that it encouraged premature political activity from Peru's poor masses. While APRA explicitly divorced labor organizing from political organizing, preferring to treat the two as separate activities, the Communist leadership believed that social, labor organization must precede political organization. Believing that their ongoing labor organizing activities had not yet reached a level of development appropriate for class-based political action, they argued that the most important political work remained at the level of production (in factories, on *haciendas*, and on plantations)—not on the national electoral stage.[14] Any movement built on such indiscriminate mass mobilization was, according to the Communist argument, intrinsically unstable and could be easily undermined by political elites who could use it to provide a veneer of popular legitimacy to traditional exploitative class relations. Second, and relatedly, the Communist leadership saw electoral mobilization as a dangerous deviation from their model of class conflict, given

    10. "Resolución del Comité Ejecutivo," PUCP/CMAP, Folder 3.12/P.C.P, 2.
    11. Letter from Eudocio Ravines to the Comité Regional de Junín, August 20, 1931 (PUCP/CMAP, Folder 7.1/P.C.P, 3); see also Giesecke (1992, 82).
    12. *La Noche*, April 28, 29, 30, May 2, 4, 8, and June 7, 1931.
    13. The analysis in this paragraph is based on the following documents: *La Noche*, April 28, 29, 30, May 2, 4, 8, and June 7, 1931.
    14. See "Resolución del Comité Ejecutivo," PUCP/CMAP, Folder 3.12/P.C.P.

that it required cooperation with the *petit bourgeois* middle classes.[15] These sorts of conflict-bridging class coalitions were seen by the Communists as inexcusable, especially given that they would not be led by a strong working class movement. For both of these reasons, they thought that Haya's populist mobilization was liable to produce an unstable cross-class movement that would be easily co-opted by political elites, providing a sheen of popular legitimacy to exploitative class relations.

The question was not one of whether APRA's political strategy was likely to bring success at the polls. Unlike some of Peru's traditional elites, the Communist leadership clearly understood that it would. They recognized that either Haya de la Torre or Sánchez Cerro would be victorious.[16] The issue was that the Communist leadership was opposed to populist mobilization on principle, as it threatened to undermine their long-term revolutionary objectives.

The Communist leadership, as might be expected from their earlier polemics with Haya, favored a worker-based insurrectionary approach to social and political change. This doctrinaire strategy aimed for proletarian revolution rather than political power through electoral victory. At the same time, their political ideas led them to be suspicious of "bourgeois democracy" and to worry about compromising their class antagonistic vision through electoral cooperation. The important work for the PCP, as its leadership saw it, was at the level of production, not in national electoral politics. And indeed, they believed that the latter could be quite dangerous. They were not "traditionalists" in the same sense as were the social and political elites, who enacted practices with long histories of routine use and success. But while the Communist's political practices were relatively new compared with the elites, they were not able to respond to opportunities on the ground as they presented themselves. Instead, they mostly applied the Third Period perspectives developed in Moscow to the Peruvian scene. This left them unwilling or unable to innovate based on national opportunities.

There is thus strong evidence suggesting that even *if* the Communists had been allowed to participate in the 1931 election, they would not have pursued populist mobilization. All indicators are that they would have maintained their long view and continued to pursue their disciplined, gradualist approach,

---

15. The party's general secretary states in correspondence to a provincial party cell that "APRA disciplines the bourgeois and petty-bourgeois reactionary forces as armed bands to pounce [*lanzar*] against the revolutionary proletariat" (Letter from Eudocio Ravines to the Comité Regional de Junín, August 20, 1931, PUCP/CMAP, Folder 7.1/P.C.P, 4).

16. They were less certain as to whether the junta, and the military in general, would allow an APRA victory; but this is a somewhat different matter.

focusing on labor organizing and shunning short-sighted mass mobilization in the service of an immediate and inherently compromised electoral victory.

This position was not inevitable. Mariátegui's death had created a window of opportunity for Ravines to bring the more ideologically and strategically eclectic Peruvian socialist movement into alignment with the dictates of the Communist International under the auspices of his newly formed Partido Comunista Peruano. While it is true that Mariátegui also opposed Haya's personalistic ambitions and electoral strategies, he was distinctly more autonomous from Soviet communism than was Ravines, and had been engaged in creative political thinking and action over the years. This is not to say that Mariátegui himself would have explored populist mobilization strategies given the electoral opening of 1931—he likely would not have. But he would have been more inclined than was Ravines to respond to the opportunity in creative ways; and another in his position might have remained aligned with Haya de la Torre and followed him down his path of populist mobilization. Under Ravines, however, the Communist response to 1931 was rigidly doctrinaire, and it decidedly did not include populist mobilization.

Overall, then, it is reasonable to envision a scenario in which this set of political actors—the elites of the right and the Socialists-Communists of the left—constituted the whole of the political field in 1931; and in this scenario, for the reasons outlined above, it is unlikely that any of them would have elaborated new lines of populist practice. On the left, the Communists would have continued organizing labor for insurrection. On the right, squabbling elites would have campaigned in the traditional fashion. And in the end, moderate elites would likely have been successful in brokering a deal with the junta.

Sánchez Cerro and his Unión Revolucionaria Party

Having discussed the collective political actors that did *not* break with routine in 1931, it is now possible to consider those that *did* begin to innovate in the early part of electoral campaigning—starting with the forces arrayed around the figure of Sánchez Cerro. As discussed in chapter 3, Sánchez Cerro responded to his first major political opportunity, on his overthrow of Leguía, with fairly traditionalist practices: he repressed the opposition and attempted to seize control through a sham election, in the style of a classic *caudillo* who had just ousted his predecessor.[17] Coming into May 1931, he and his advisors initially responded

---

17. In fact, even late into the electoral contest, UR propaganda soberly lamented the loss of the old *caudillo* order. As one editorial in the UR-partial *La Opinión* (October 3, 1931, 2) explained: "It is no longer possible to decide in intimate gatherings the future of the Republic.

in similarly traditionalist ways. Unlike Haya de la Torre, Sánchez Cerro was not already inclined for ideological reasons toward mobilizing the popular masses. But as he and his close advisors made their initial political moves under the new conditions, they realized that their traditional practices were not working—leading them to experience the situation as problematic. How they would respond to this problem situation varied across individuals. And regardless of their initial responses, they were not fully empowered to act, as Sánchez Cerro remained in exile and it was not clear that he would be allowed to return. But, especially as the period progressed into June and July, they started moves toward practices that looked like populist mobilization in anticipation of Sánchez Cerro's homecoming. This was made possible by the varied experiences of the leadership, their practical orientation to political ideals (that is, they were looking to achieve political power—or to prevent APRA from doing so—and this was more important than adhering to a particular vision of the Peruvian social order), and the centralization of their leadership (which enabled even audacious decisions to be followed by others in the group).

Sánchez Cerro's party was formed quite late in the game. The Comandante did not return from exile until July 2, 1931, did not officially announce his candidacy until the thirteenth of the same month, and finally founded his Unión Revolucionaria party on the thirtieth—less than three months before the election.[18] But loyalists were organizing on his behalf long before his party was officially constituted. Like with APRA, earlier political relationships formed the core around which the party would later build, even though a period of repression had impeded the continuity of their political organization.

Sánchez Cerro's inner circle of supporters—those who would form the nucleus of Unión Revolucionaria—did not for the most part have ties to him that predated his 1930 coup.[19] The social constitution of the Unión Revolucionaria's leadership corps was thus largely a product of the concrete political realities of the emerging situation. Some had first worked with Sánchez Cerro in his provisional government before it was disbanded, as members of the anti-Leguiísta

---

The cabinet politics of the men of 1910 cannot succeed in Peru. . . . The era of *caudillismo* was more pleasant and picturesque. The kind days of 1910, with its well-mannered intellectuals, its grandeoloquent orators, and its wise lawyers, have left us nice memories. But what are we to do? We are in the Peru of 1931."

18. Sánchez Cerro arrived by ship at the port of Callao on July 2 and disembarked on July 3 (see *El Comercio*, July 3, 1931; Basadre 1999, 13:3179; Miró Quesada Laos 1947, 151–52). For the announcement of his candidacy, see *El Comercio*, July 13, 1931, 3; on the founding of UR, see Molinari Morales 2006, 32.

19. An exception is Carlos Ugarte, who became one of Sánchez Cerro's close advisors in 1931, and who had visited Sánchez Cerro in prison after his failed coup in 1922 (Ugarteche 1969, 1:29).

Comité de Saneamiento y Consolidación Revolucionaria (Basadre 1999, 13:3196; Molinari Morales 2006, 17). But most of the group was more an ad hoc collection of professionals and politicians dedicated to Sánchez Cerro's election. The group eventually included lawyers, middle class professionals, and elites with ties to the old oligarchy. Sánchez Cerro's support amongst these well-situated allies solidified especially as the threatening realities of the political situation became clear (Cossío del Pomar 1977, 1:336). Indeed, many core UR leaders were involved more because they wanted to defeat APRA than because of their love for Sánchez Cerro, and some because they saw their participation as a way to keep the candidate from doing too much to upset the status quo. This particular group thus might not have come together under other circumstances. But Sánchez Cerro was more than happy to accept help from all quarters. And so the result was a party leadership that was considerably less cohesive than that of APRA, but that was nonetheless unified in its immediate practical goals by the pressures of the situation.[20]

But even if this group did not have ties to the candidate that preceded August 1930, some had historical ties to one another, providing a measure of cohesion to the leadership. Part of the group had its origins in a group of young university students who had held clandestine meetings during the Leguía dictatorship (Ugarteche 1969, 2:vii–xi). This group of elite, nationalist, "creole-fascist" students—which included, most notably, Pedro Ugarteche and Alfredo Herrera—stood opposed to the Hayistas that were so central to the formation of APRA. Steve Stein (1980, 119) quotes these politicians as seeing their university activism as "a kind of preparation for the larger national political arena." When the political conflict reduced to one between Haya de la Torre and Sánchez Cerro, the nationalists fell into line behind Sánchez Cerro.

Sánchez Cerro and his advisors entered into the new political situation with experience in routine strategies that had been better suited to prior conditions. Many founding members of the party came from elite families with ties to the old parties, and so embraced traditional methods of political practice premised on social control. Prior to Leguía's rise to power, such methods included the repression of labor organizing, declarations of martial law, the maintenance and enforcement of tight restrictions on suffrage,

---

20. The self-described independent, but powerful Sánchez Cerro supporter, Luis Antonio Eguiguren recounted an internal debate over party formation in the Casa de Arenales that illustrates the internal heterogeneity of the haphazardly organized party, and also the internal resistance to imposed homogeneity: "The Revolutionary Party is an alliance of diverse sectors of national opinion. Here we have Civilistas, liberals, democrats, social-nationalists, and independents like me. If the party attempts to reduce us to one single group, this would prove impossible for many of us" (Eguiguren 1933, 39).

the proscription of radical parties, the brokering of backroom political deals, electoral manipulation, and coups d'état. Although Sánchez Cerro had strong political ambitions, his actions made it clear that he did not see elections as necessary for realizing these. Instead, he embraced strategies that were more typical for his institutional position. In keeping with his martial and paternalist views, Sánchez Cerro's clear preference was for a military authoritarian solution to the problem of political succession. As one historian noted, "[Sánchez Cerro] lived most of his life as a conspirator specializing in clandestine meetings and the planning of coups" (Ciccarelli 1969, 25). He spearheaded two failed coup attempts prior to his successful 1930 coup.[21] And once in power as head of the provisional government, he did not attempt to mobilize his already enthusiastic supporters into a formidable political force, but rather to orchestrate a sham election. In the end, it is clear that Sánchez Cerro and his leadership circle preferred to ply the tried-and-true political tools of the traditional elite.

While Sánchez Cerro clearly aspired to political power, as evidenced by his coup attempts against Leguía and statements in the home of Mariátegui promising to become president (see chapter 3), he evidenced no predisposition to populist mobilization as a strategy for achieving it. If anything, he was ideologically *opposed* to the direct involvement of non-elites in politics. For example, he wrote the following in a letter to his brother:

> I've always maintained that this misunderstood system of strikes—typical of the rabble—is the worst of the ills recently introduced to this already degenerated and convulsed country. The stupid masses, who only give in when the stick is brought into play, are completely ignorant of who they should be listening to . . . ; in the best of cases, the result obtained [by a strike] doesn't remedy the ills that the strikers bring upon themselves. It truly irritates me, as if I were being personally attacked, every time such wretchedness is produced.[22]

He then goes on to tell his brother not to worry, because "it's easy to subdue these people—who are so boisterous and without firm conviction of their actions."

---

21. These attempts were in 1919 and 1922. For a brief discussion of the latter, along with a collection of primary documents pertaining to the event, see Ugarteche 1969, 1:28–61, 63–67. It is notable that Sánchez Cerro had also taken part in one *successful* coup many years before: as a young officer, he was seriously wounded while participating in the 1914 overthrow of Guillermo Billinghurst (Basadre 1999, 12:3094; Ugarteche 1969, 1:11–14).

22. Luis M. Sánchez Cerro to Antonio Sánchez Cerro, June 4, 1916 (reprinted in Ugarteche 1969, 1:17). See also Stein 1980, 86, 104–5.

Sánchez Cerro did have opinions about how he thought the masses should be "handled" politically. Essentially, he was a paternalist and an authoritarian, believing that they needed to be shepherded by a strong hand and rewarded, like children, with favors when appropriate (Stein 1980, 104–5). As he explained to a fellow officer in 1919, it is the job of a political leader to map out the right path and direct the "indolent and lazy rabble, with a piece of bread in one hand and a whip in the other" (Stein 1980, 86). Some historians have interpreted this paternalism as evidence of Sánchez Cerro's latent populist tendencies. But while such paternalist sentiment may resonate or be compatible with populist strategies, the two should not be confused as the same thing. Sánchez Cerro's earlier paternalism did not actually speak to the role of the masses as a basis for political support, so much as address how a political leader should manage their incapacity and unruliness. Sánchez Cerro's military experience and paternalist views point more toward an inclination to military authoritarianism than toward a tendency to pursue populist mobilization. His childhood schoolmates, after all, nicknamed him "The Dictator" (Ugarteche 1969, 1:3), not "The Savior."

This estimation of Sánchez Cerro as more inclined to military paternalism than populist mobilization is supported by the way that he came to power in 1930 and how he operated once seated as the head of the provisional junta. While mass support erupted in *response* to Sánchez Cerro's 1930 overthrow of Leguía, the coup itself was a military act not strategically premised on the mobilization of widespread popular support. It was based, rather, on a savvy assessment of the likely response of Leguía's national police force; of schisms between junior and senior officers in the Arequipa garrison; of disenchantment in Arequipa, among both the military and liberal intellectuals, with the Leguía regime; and of the likelihood of support for a coup among Lima's higher ranking officers (Stein 1980, 86–87; Ugarteche 1969, 1:108). The Manifesto of Arequipa that Sánchez Cerro proclaimed at the time of the coup was a combination of xenophobic nationalism, paternalist social reformism, and—most of all—anti-*Leguiísmo*.[23] Once in power, Sánchez Cerro shepherded the lower classes exactly as he had indicated that he would in 1919, with both a firm hand and the dispensation of favors. While implementing programs to create employment and distribute resources, Sánchez Cerro also vigorously repressed protests, strikes, unions, and the APRA and Communist parties. Finally, and possibly most important, when the time came to determine how he would perpetuate himself in power, Sánchez Cerro did not undertake the

---

23. Ugarteche's account of the authorship of the Manifesto can be found in 1969, 1:109–10. Villanueva Valencia (1962, 62) attributes its writing to José Luis Bustamante y Rivero.

mass mobilization of his already enthusiastic popular supporters; rather, he attempted to orchestrate a sham election from his seat as head of the junta.

But although these political routines had been effective in previous eras, they confronted their limits in 1931. Sánchez Cerro had personally experienced the shortcomings of a military route to power. As discussed previously, his two failed coup attempts had earned him, first, banishment to an obscure military outpost in the Amazon, and then later, full-blown exile. And even once successful in toppling Leguía, his backdoor route to the presidency had been effectively blocked by the junta. Later, after elections had been declared, Sánchez Cerro and the future Unión Revolucionaria leaders watched as the junta rebuffed Concentración Nacional's corrupt overtures. A problem situation had thus emerged for Sánchez Cerro and his collaborators by 1931. And it was only in light of their frustrated options that these leaders felt compelled to explore new political strategies.

Sánchez Cerro's pursuit of populist strategies in the 1931 election was thus not a result of his political ideology so much as a practical response to the contingent circumstances that he confronted. At first hostile to popular politics, Sánchez Cerro stumbled into a position of mass popularity and was enough of a political pragmatist to take advantage of the situation in which he found himself. His political genius was in realizing—in a way that should not be taken for granted for this era—that the tools for political success were already before him, in the form of popular support; and that neither the military establishment nor the traditional elite would be able to compete with this political resource. When the reconstituted junta declared elections, Sánchez Cerro pushed to be allowed to return to campaign. But while maintaining support at the popular level, he faced stiff opposition from the state when it came to organizing this support in a bid for the presidency.

These political experiences shaped Sánchez Cerro and his UR leadership's understandings of the opportunities afforded by conditions in 1931 Peru. Although lacking the more organic ties that APRA leaders had with organized students and workers, Sánchez Cerro received useful soundings of the political situation by virtue of his privileged political profile. Indeed, the declarations of support with which the leader was inundated when he overthrew Leguía painted a vivid picture of his adherents' grievances and desires.[24] With this understanding of political conditions already primed by his prior exposure to Mussolini from his time in exile in the 1920s, Sánchez Cerro started to see his political opportunities in a new light. Thus Sánchez Cerro and his advisors came to understand how they could take advantage of existing conditions.

24. See *El Comercio*, March 7, 1931, as well as Ugarteche 1969, 2:xxxix–xlii, lxvii, 100.

Confronted with what they saw as the necessary evil of a political campaign, Sánchez Cerro and his political advisors made the astute decision to capitalize on the popular support that he already enjoyed as the "Hero of Arequipa" who had ousted Leguía.

It was only when faced with limited options and a clear opportunity for capitalizing on the mass support for his overthrow of Leguía that Sánchez Cerro allowed his top advisors to construct a populist campaign around his already popular persona.[25] But while sharing largely similar assessments of the political situation, the UR leaders did not always agree about what their strategic response should be. For his part, having long ago set his sights on the presidency, Sánchez Cerro was both ambitious and opportunistic enough that the promise of victory trumped his otherwise conservative, antipopular political tastes. Sánchez Cerro and his Unión Revolucionaria leadership were influenced by the various political models (both domestic and foreign) to which they had been exposed.

Because the UR leadership was less cohesive than that of APRA, its political influences may appear to have been even less obviously consonant— ranging from nineteenth-century Peruvian party practices to Italian fascism. Sánchez Cerro himself was a military man without much experience in Peruvian politics; but many UR leaders had ties to traditional parties. And so earlier, paternalist, socially unthreatening ways of turning out supporters— through clientelist political clubs and election day mobilization around the ballot box—still resonated with some UR leaders as acceptable means of harnessing mass support.

For Sánchez Cerro himself, more influential was his firsthand education (in the wake of his coup) about the power of popular support to carry a leader past entrenched opposition. In a sense, Sánchez Cerro realized the power of populist mobilization after having already (but inadvertently) enjoyed some of the fruits of widespread popular support. In this respect, the power of the rally in his favor in August 1930, as well as all the telegrams of support he received, were critically important. And the enthusiastic reception that Sánchez

---

25. Sánchez Cerro is explicit about his motivations for capitalizing on popular support in a letter that he sent from Paris in April, in which he explains that: "above all, my decision to participate in the coming elections has been strengthened by the series of demonstrations of all forms and origin that I continue to receive" (cited in Molinari Morales 2006, 43; original citation from: "Carta de Luis M. Sánchez Cerro a un amigo." Biblioteca Nacional-Sala de Investigaciones; Archivo Sánchez Cerro). In this same letter, he requests that the recipient of the letter meet with his brother for the purpose of launching a political party: "With him [my brother] take the necessary steps to see the immediate formation of a party, with me as its leader and with principles based on the Manifesto of Arequipa" (ibid.).

FIGURE 4.2. Sánchez Cerro (center) is carried on the shoulders of his supporters upon his return from exile in July 1931.
Source: 1931 photograph, "Gral. Luis M. Sánchez Cerro, Presidente del Perú, 1930-31, 1931-33. A su llegada a Lima," courtesy of the Archivo Fotográfico of the Biblioteca Nacional del Perú.

Cerro received on his return to Peru in 1931 (figure 4.2) demonstrated that his support had not dissipated during his absence. Sánchez Cerro clearly must have been aware of his own popularity. This experience of having been the object of such adulation was profoundly formative for the leader. The overwhelming popular support for his coup against Leguía demonstrated to him the potential utility of populist mobilization as a route to political power.

Finally, Sánchez Cerro's prior exposure to Mussolini's Italy shaped his thinking about the Peruvian situation. As Pedro Ugarteche, one of Sánchez Cerro's closest advisors, later recalled: "times had changed, and leaders could no longer be elected by small coteries of distinguished personages, but only by powerful political organizations" (Ugarteche 1969, 2:xxxvi). Sánchez Cerro's experiences abroad made a powerful impression on the young officer—and the effects of this exposure ricocheted back into the Peruvian context in ways that Leguía could not have anticipated when he cast him into exile. In effect, Sánchez Cerro's experience of his own popularity and exposure to Mussolini's mobilizational successes quickly cured him of his previous aversion to seeing the masses in the streets (so long as those masses were supporting him). Thus, in his correspondence from exile, Sánchez Cerro praised Mussolini and wrote of the ur-

THE SOURCES OF POLITICAL INNOVATION 141

gency of forming a party in Peru—which should remain under his absolute control—to channel his preexisting support and serve as an apparatus for winning the election through mobilization (Molinari Morales 2006, 42–43). Like Haya de la Torre, Sánchez Cerro was a pragmatic political outsider who accurately discerned the potential utility of populist mobilization as a route to political power in 1931.

At the same time, less than comfortable with the candidate's newfound enthusiasm for seemingly extreme mobilizing practices, some of Sánchez Cerro's advisors tried to nudge him in more conservative directions. These UR leaders were more comfortable resurrecting and recombining ideas and practices from the recent Peruvian past, like basic nationalist principles, internally hierarchical political clubs, and elite-controlled street thuggery.

The result was a process of political innovation that involved ongoing practical negotiations between Sánchez Cerro and his top advisors. A middle ground coalesced around ideas and practices that were somewhat more authoritarian, paternalistic, and reactionary than those of APRA, but that nevertheless amounted to the contentious public mobilization of ordinary people motivated by populist rhetoric. Thus, while drawing on different building blocks than APRA, the Unión Revolucionaria party was moving in a similar strategic direction.

That Sánchez Cerro enjoyed a significant degree of continuous support, from his coup through the formation of Unión Revolucionaria, is well established. What remains unclear is the extent to which this support maintained an organizational basis in the form of grassroots political clubs, and thus whether the clubs that eventually linked up with UR after its formation had a substantial history of independent operation. Whether the clubs that declared their support for Sánchez Cerro in August and September 1930 remained active is difficult to establish. It is also not clear whether Sánchez Cerro encouraged or supported these clubs during his time in office. Conversely, while we know that the Samanez Ocampo junta antagonized Sánchez Cerro's supporters, we do not know whether this means that it actively shut down Sánchezcerrista clubs. Molinari Morales (2006, 17–18, 32) does claim that the Sánchezcerrista movement was sustained by a network of political clubs, both in Lima and in the interior, and that these played an important role in facilitating Sánchez Cerro's return from exile. And spotty evidence is available on the existence of specific clubs during this interim period.[26] Unfortunately, a more systematic study would be necessary to provide more detail than this on the origins, prevalence,

26. Drinot (2001, 337), for example, notes that the Centro Obrero Pro-Elección Sánchez Cerro No. 1 was in existence on February 7, 1931, shortly before Sánchez Cerro's removal from office.

and continuity of the Sánchezcerrista clubs. We know that Sánchez Cerro's removal from office and subsequent exile was protested by his supporters. We also know that pressure from Sánchez Cerro's supporters played an important role in lobbying the Samanez Ocampo junta and convincing them to allow the politician to return to campaign for the presidency (Stein 1980, 98–99). And we know that the formation of Sánchezcerrista clubs picked up considerably upon the Hero of Arequipa's return from exile. These Sánchezcerrista clubs were in many respects modeled on the traditional electoral clubs that played an important role in many elections of the late nineteenth century, before the consolidation of the Aristocratic Republic. In terms of their internal organization, practices, and procedures, they mimicked other associations—such as mutual aid societies, guilds, and unions—that had become an increasingly important part of urban life in Peru in the early twentieth century, and in which we can assume club members had at least some experience (Drinot 2001, 341). Most writers refer to this Sánchezcerrista support as a somewhat amorphous "movement," in contrast with what would eventually become the Sánchezcerrista *party* of Unión Revolucionaria.

But Sánchez Cerro might not have gone so far as to form his own political party, had it not been for the emergence of APRA as a viable political force. Indeed, in his search for a route to the presidency, Sánchez Cerro had first considered linking up with the more moderate Concentración Nacional initiative discussed above (Ugarteche 1969, 2:xxxv–xxxvi), before deciding to preserve his own, already privileged political profile by going his own way (Molinari Morales 2006, 41–42). At the same time, many of the elites who eventually formed UR's central leadership corps had likewise supported more traditionalist political options, at least initially. But APRA was quickly becoming a formidable political organization, even in its first months on the ground. And unlike the other adherents of the Concentración Nacional, Sánchez Cerro and his handful of elite supporters recognized APRA's growing power and understood that the moderate initiative was doomed to failure.[27] With the encouragement of his advisors, Sánchez Cerro came to see that it would be necessary to organize his own mass party if he wished to defeat APRA at the polls. Thus, the evolving competitive dynamic between APRA and the Sánchezcerristas played an important role in the crystallization of UR as a party. In this way, Sánchez Cerro's Unión Revolucionaria party was likewise a product of the context of action.

27. See Sánchez Cerro's July 30 letter to A. E. Pérez Araníbar (reprinted in Ugarteche 1969, 2:122–24).

Haya de la Torre and his APRA Party

The most innovative action in the early stages of campaigning came from Haya de la Torre and the leadership of his APRA party. Although Haya had founded APRA from exile in Mexico in 1924, and the party had appeared in Peru briefly at the fall of Leguía, it was only in late March 1931—after the ouster of Sánchez Cerro and in anticipation of the junta's move toward a democratic opening—that the party renewed its organizing efforts in Peru. APRA experienced at this time a respite from the repression to which it had been subjected since November of the previous year. The new junta released jailed Aprista leaders, allowed others to return from exile or to emerge from hiding, and relaxed restrictions on APRA organizing. The party leadership began even before the political opportunity of the electoral opening was made official to take advantage of this situation, as they understood it, to begin developing new political practices. Key to their ability to do this was the fact that exiled Apristas had collected new political experiences in other contexts and the fact that strategic decisions were being made in a setting in which the leadership had been selected to have a shared vision of politics consistent with that of their undisputed leader, Haya de la Torre. This led to the clear and shared perception of a problem situation and political opportunity. All together, this led the emerging APRA leadership to experiment with new practices that increasingly took on the characteristics of populist mobilization.

Haya de la Torre himself was a practical political strategist, open to whatever means were most likely to result in political success. His previous political experiences with students, workers, and socialist intellectuals had provided him with a small network of potential supporters, many of whom had also been exiled by Leguía or jailed by Sánchez Cerro's short-lived provisional government (Basadre 1999, 13:3118; Klarén 1973, 84–105). Haya had stayed in contact with these supporters from abroad through extensive correspondence.[28] The networks and ideas on which the party would build can be traced to Haya's involvement in progressive political movements in the years prior to his exile. Most of Haya's leadership circle had been working with him for years—many since the May 1923 protests against the consecration of Lima to the Sacred Heart of Jesus, some since the 1919 general strike for the eight hour work day, and a few since the earliest days of the Trujillo Bohemia movement.

---

28. See, for example, the letters excerpted in Enríquez 1951 (79–101); and "Haya de la Torre to La Célula del Apra del Cuzco," February 25, 1930 (AGN/PL, Legajo 3.9.5.1.15.1.14.1, Folder 5, "Documentos del P.A.P. Cartas Confidenciales 1930-32-33-34-35 y 1937").

Not only did the dynamics of the situation in 1931 contribute to the *occurrence* of APRA's formation as a collective political actor, but they also played a role in shaping the social constitution of its leadership corps. Haya de la Torre had emerged out of the protests of the late teens and early 1920s as a prominent figure among a broad group of student, anarcho-syndicalist, and socialist radicals. Although the 1931 APRA leadership was composed largely of intellectuals and workers who had been involved with Haya in these earlier struggles, situational dynamics already discussed had prompted two important moments of schism that shaped Haya's inner circle. The first was the split with Mariátegui. The second came in 1931, as Haya made preparations for a renewal of political activity in Peru. While the Apristas who had been charged with orchestrating a mobilizational push in the country were enthusiastic about the new atmosphere of political openness, there were disagreements both about whether to participate in the elections and about Haya's vision for leadership and political organization (see Enríquez 1951, 79–101). Such dissension led to a second wave of defections and purges. In the end, Haya allowed only his most trusted allies to become party leaders. In this way, the social constitution of APRA's leadership corps was critically shaped by the unfolding dynamics of the political situation.

After Sánchez Cerro's renewed wave of repression in late 1930, the APRA party was more or less starting from scratch when elections were called, although it would be able to build on networks and relationships—at both elite and rank-and-file levels—that significantly predated the fall of Leguía. After the junta took charge and sent Sánchez Cerro into exile (in March 1931), political controls were relaxed and Apristas were released from prison. APRA was allowed to operate openly in Peru after March 31, 1931, although there were no public party meetings in Lima until June 23 (Basadre 1999, 13:3181). Incorporating those who had supported the earlier struggles of the early 1920s into the party would be a major aim of APRA's organizing efforts. Preparations were made for Haya's return from Germany (Basadre 1999, 13:3181); and when the junta declared elections in late May, the party began campaigning in earnest and Haya began making arrangements to come home.

Organizing in the wake of Sánchez Cerro's exile began not at the grassroots level, but at the level of party leadership. Much of this leadership was drawn from the ranks of the university students who had taught in the popular universities of the early 1920s (Stein 1980, 136). In Lima, the national executive committee was reestablished—this time headed by longtime Haya confidant Carlos Manuel Cox—and the Partido Aprista Peruano (PAP) was officially registered with the government. APRA representatives—who for the most part had become involved with the party through the student and labor struggles of the early 1920s—were sent to begin organizing efforts in the provinces. On May 16, Manuel Seoane founded the official party newspaper, *La Tribuna* (Basadre 1999, 13:3181). This same month, APRA held its first regional congress in Trujillo—where Aprista networks were the most developed—bringing together representatives from adjacent departments to develop an electoral program (Klarén 1973, 122). As Peter Klarén has described, in Lima, "where the effects of the depression had radicalized much of the middle and working classes, it was not long before the newly organized PAP began to attract a large following" (1973, 122).[29]

APRA's early organizing efforts, in April and May 1931, focused more on middle class professionals than on workers. By late May, APRA had organized unions of engineers, doctors, and students in Lima; they were at that time also in the process of organizing lawyers and white collar workers.[30] In starting its organizing with middle class professionals, APRA was both securing what it knew would be a crucial base of support and establishing an infrastructure for the provision of important services to party members. In an article published on May 24, APRA stated explicitly that it was giving preference to these professional unions because the services that such workers would be able to provide to the party would be indispensable for the development of Aprismo.[31] This same article went on to elaborate on the usefulness of a study conducted by Aprista engineers and the importance of the social assistance being provided by Aprista doctors. It also explained that, "The manual workers of the party do not see this as a neglect of their interests; on the contrary, they understand that in this we achieve two important goals: party efficiency and the defense of our affiliates who count on the services of the Social Defense Committee."[32] The article goes on to say that the future organization of manual laborers will depend on the Aprista solidarity of the intellectual workers. Indeed, APRA's ability to offer professional services—such as education and healthcare assistance—to its members was central to its ability to develop popular support later on in the election cycle.

Haya de la Torre and his APRA leadership had cut their political teeth among leftist movements for whom grassroots organizing, disruptive protests and strikes, and even attempts at insurrection and mutiny had become regular practice. Haya de la Torre thus entered the 1931 presidential contest with a

---

29. On this political opening at the removal of Sánchez Cerro from office, and on early APRA organizing during this period, see Klarén 1973, 122–24.

30. *La Tribuna*, May 24, 1931, /.

31. *La Tribuna*, May 24, 1931, 7.

32. *La Tribuna*, May 24, 1931, 7.

good deal of experience in radical politics. Over the course of his career, he was directly or indirectly involved in mutinies, coup attempts, revolutionary uprisings, and the brokering of backstage deals with his political competition. In the repressive context of the 1920s, such strategies made good political sense for the radical left.

But although they resulted in minor successes in 1919 and 1923, these strategies did not produce enduring political change—and worse, they tended to provoke state repression. As discussed earlier, striking workers were frequently jailed and protesters were occasionally killed by government troops. The regime shuttered *Amauta* and drove the popular universities underground (Klaiber 1975; Klarén 1973, 114). And along with other student and worker leaders who were similarly expelled, Haya was compelled to leave the country. All the while, Leguía remained in power. And even once the dictator had fallen, leftists who remained in Peru were persecuted by Sánchez Cerro's provisional government (Basadre 1999, 12:3093–144). Thus, by 1931, a problem situation had emerged for Haya and his APRA leadership. Although returning to the political stage with a good deal of experience in radical politics, they recognized that the old strategies were not adequate to the present situation and that something new would be required.

Haya de la Torre was an ambitious political leader, an organizer, and a political pragmatist. He and his APRA leadership were exposed to a wide range of political models throughout the 1920s. Not insignificant among these were the models elaborated by the radical movements with whom they had been previously affiliated. As already discussed, these had not proved adequately effective on their own; but exposure to them nevertheless colored Aprista thinking (see Hirsch 1997 and Tejada 1985). Haya had also studied briefly for the priesthood; and while he ultimately decided that the "calling" he felt to politics overrode his calling to the Church, religious overtones continued to infuse his thought and rhetoric (see Stein 1980, 175–76, 265n39–40; Pike 1986).

During his exile, Haya drew on various strains of thought to elaborate a complex political philosophy that he would translate into a galvanizing populist rhetoric in 1931. His writings of this period carried heavy doses of anti-imperialist and anti-oligarchical thought and were clear about the importance of coordinating active political support from various social sectors, including students, urban laborers, coastal plantation workers, highland peasants, and middle class professionals (Alexander 1973; Pike 1986; see Haya de la Torre 1984).

In the same way, his strategic thinking about political organization and mobilization was shaped by his exposure to diverse movements during his years abroad. Haya had long been interested in the problem of political or-

THE SOURCES OF POLITICAL INNOVATION   147

ganization; and APRA's continued reliance on grassroots popular organizing drew heavily on his and his leadership's earlier experiences with Peruvian student and labor movements. Haya had been interested in organization from an early age. In a 1971 interview with Steve Stein (1980, 134), he described his childhood obsession with organizing:

> We had some very spacious rooms to play in, and we created a republic there. We had a President, we had cabinet ministers, deputies. We had politics. And there we practiced . . . at reproducing the life of the country with spools of thread. [. . .] I used to receive very nice toys: locomotives, trains. But I was not interested in these things. What interested me was to have an organized setup, like a country. . . . When I recall this, you can see how early I had a political imagination. It was quite noteworthy, because we imitated life, but we assured a life of order. Now I tell myself, how I've always had this thing about organizing.[33]

Haya's earlier experiences, both as a child and in radical movements, had thus already primed him to think about political organization in unconventional ways. And in correspondence between Haya and Enríquez from this period, Haya insists time and again on the need for political organization—indeed he makes it a precondition of his return from exile.

But APRA's emphasis on organization was further invigorated by Haya's exposure to corporatist, Marxist-Leninist, and fascist organizational models.[34] While in exile in Europe, Haya was "deeply impressed by the methodical operation and rigid stratification of European fascist and communist parties" (Stein 1982, 125). In many ways, he modeled the organizational structure of his APRA party on these European examples. Applying insights from these models to APRA as a whole, Haya and his leaders organized their party according to a complex vertical and hierarchical structure intended to facilitate disciplined mobilization, expressing an organicist conception of society and politics, with functionally differentiated units reflecting the structure of Peruvian society.[35]

The hierarchical character of the earlier student-worker movement was formalized in the renewed APRA of the 1931 campaign. In a pamphlet entitled *Vertical Organization of the Peruvian Aprista Party* [*Organización Vertical del*

---

33. As Stein notes, this childhood game is also discussed in Cossío del Pomar (1977, 1:33) and Haya de la Torre (1957, 6).

34. See, for example, "Haya de la Torre to La Célula del Apra del Cuzco," February 25, 1930, AGN/PL, Legajo 3.9.5.1.15.1.14.1, Folder 5, "Documentos del P.A.P. Cartas Confidenciales 1930–32–33–34–35 y 1937."

35. *La Tribuna*, May 24 and August 8, 1931.

Partido Aprista Peruano], released early on in the campaign, Haya de la Torre explained that "the very size of the Peruvian Aprista party and the enormous potential for action of its masses demand an increasing technification of its functions; that its structure be vertical in order to make the greatest use of the energies of its followers, channeling their activity into a series of specialized tasks" (quoted in Stein 1980, 154). At least on paper, all APRA organizations were assigned functional roles within the party and sought to represent all "organs" of Peruvian society in a holistic way. As an article in *La Tribuna* explained: "Our committees are organized in the form of functional democracy; that is to say, taking into account the specialization of groups to establish a strict division of labor, with the three classes that form our Great Unified Front being represented: peasants, workers, and the middle classes."[36] These three broad categories were broken down into no fewer than thirty-three separate categories of social position.[37] In this respect, APRA shows the influence of the same organicist conceptions of society and politics that played a role in Italian fascism.[38]

Further, although he rejected many elements of fascist thought, Haya's exposure to fascist movements led him to understand charismatic, nationalistic, election-oriented mass mobilization as a promising route to political power (Sánchez 1985, 220–23).[39] Indeed, he emulated fascist mobilization strategies to such an extent that his opponents accused him of importing dangerous foreign ideas. Interestingly, the comparisons to fascist leaders did not seem to bother Haya. On receiving an article written by Alberto Hidalgo, "in which Hidalgo praised Mussolini and Hitler as super-heroes, and affirmed that in Latin America Haya de la Torre more than any other was the man destined for greatness," he responded enthusiastically, saying: "Until today, only my conscience has said to me, 'greatness calls you.' But now . . . you have spoken to me in the name of destiny" (Pike 1967, 261). When asked about Haya's political loyalties, a former Leguía minister replied: "Haya has never been anything else but 'hayista' " (Klarén 1973, 109). At the same time, Haya "was impressed with the towering figure of Leon Trotsky not only as an intellectual but as a man of action, as well as with the fervor with which Russian youths had embraced communism, almost as a religious faith with strong mystical and moral strains" (Klarén 2000, 260). Through all of these influences, Haya discovered

36. *La Tribuna*, May 24, 1931, 7.
37. See *APRA*, August 8, 1931, 8–9.
38. On organicist conceptions of society and politics, see Stepan 1978.
39. See letter from Haya to Luis Eduardo Enríquez, dated August 31, 1930, excerpted in Enríquez 1951, 95.

FIGURE 4.3. Haya de la Torre depicted addressing the masses on the cover of an APRA party publication. Source: Partido Aprista Peruano 1933, cover.

new ways to channel his personal charisma to build a strongly affective relationship with his supporters (see figure 4.3).

Such strategic insights were consonant with—although not an automatic result of—the political ideology and populist rhetoric that he had been developing in his political writings. All together, then, Haya de la Torre and his APRA leadership started down a path of populist mobilization—of organizing and mobilizing previously excluded social groups into public contentious action, and motivating this action with anti-elite, nationalist, pro-popular rhetoric—in 1931 by stitching together a set of ideas and practices from diverse sources that, enacted in concert, represented something new for the Peruvian context. For Haya de la Torre, populist mobilization resonated with the quasi-revolutionary social and political ideology that he had developed over the course of more than a decade of radical political activity.

Haya's ideological perspective—coupled with his past experiences leading student and worker movements—also meant that he was particularly attuned to the conduciveness of current social and political conditions to populist mobilization, in a way that other politicians of his time were not. His assessment of political conditions and strategic options was conditioned by years of experience with popular movements and an ideological disposition to pro-popular politics. Even from exile, Haya de la Torre maintained close ties in Trujillo among the organized working class and middle classes. He was closely involved with the labor movement through Mariátegui, the anarcho-syndicalist Arturo Sabroso, and others; and he maintained ties with student organizations. Haya also maintained close ties with elements of the Lima professional middle class. Based on his personal history of radical political activity, he recognized the favorability of the conditions quite clearly and pursued a line of political action that was in keeping with his ideological commitments. This exposure provided Haya and his advisors with new tools for understanding the possibilities offered by domestic conditions in 1931. Haya had already demonstrated that he was a political opportunist, open to whichever strategies appeared most likely to result in success; but to evaluate his strategic options in 1931, he would first have to formulate an accurate and subtle reading of APRA's immediate political situation.[40] His time organizing students and workers in the early 1920s, and his ongoing correspondence from exile with observers who remained in country, gave him a leg up over other politicians of the day by attuning him to changing conditions in urban centers and along the northern coast—and by alerting him to the conduciveness of these conditions to novel mobilization practices. Likewise, Haya's experiences in exile provided him with new lenses for evaluating domestic political realities. His studies of economics and exposure to anti-imperialist thought informed his understanding of depression-era Peru (Salisbury 1983; Stein 1980, 149). And many influences prompted him to cultivate a deep sensitivity to the historical plight and political potential of social groups that had been previously marginalized. Perhaps most important, Haya's exposure to early German fascism encouraged him to recognize that moments of electoral openness in contexts of profound social and political dislocation provided tremendous opportunities for outsider politicians. Thus,

---

40. See, for example, Haya's attempt to do this in his January 31, 1931, letter to Luis Alberto Sánchez (reprinted in Haya de la Torre and Sánchez 1982, 1:30–34).

Haya's comprehension of domestic conditions—and of the possibilities that these afforded—was not automatic, but rather shaped through a decade-long period of political learning.

The fact that Sánchez Cerro and his supporters still posed a significant threat also played a role in prompting APRA to begin organizing when it did. Sánchez Cerro's overthrow of Leguía had been hugely popular; and many Peruvians still believed that he deserved to be granted the presidency as a reward for his actions (Stein 1980, 94). This popularity was ominous for Haya's followers. A Sánchez Cerro presidency would likely have meant more exile, or even prison, for many Apristas. Thus, even though APRA leaders began organizing in Peru about three months before the official formation of Sánchez Cerro's political party, it must be understood that they were doing so with a stark awareness of the threat posed by the figure's sustained popularity. The electoral opening, and the competition that it entailed, thus provided both the opportunity and the impetus for the formation of APRA as an organized political force in Peru in 1931.

Conclusion

By July 1931, the leadership of both Haya de la Torre's APRA party and of what would become Sánchez Cerro's Unión Revolucionaria party had confronted the limitations of their own routine political practices, recognized the situations in which they found themselves as problematic in various respects, drawn on diverse sources of political experience, and begun to cobble together new sets of political practices in creative ways. While this process played out differently for the two groups of political actors, the result was that both converged on developing practices that—while certainly not identical in every respect—generally took on the characteristics of what this book calls populist mobilization. At the same time, other political actors—with different stocks of experience, relationships to established political actors, decision-making environments, and strategic priorities—continued to act in fairly routine ways. The elite political actors pursued backroom deals and traditional campaigns reminiscent of politics under the Aristocratic Republic, either oblivious to the changing nature of political reality or unwilling to develop new practices in the face of it. The leadership of the Partido Comunista—who had split with Haya precisely over issues of strategy—eschewed election-oriented popular politics and continued to practice labor activism in line with the dictates of the Communist International.

But this was just the first phase of campaigning—a process that would become even more intense between August and October of the same year.

As the campaigns progressed, the outsider parties and their candidates circumvented the established political actors of both the left and the right, and escalated the popular drama of the election to such a point that the moderate elites' backroom deal quickly became impossible. As the non-innovators became increasingly irrelevant, the competition between the innovators intensified. This dynamic, which shaped the last months of the campaign in critical ways, is the subject of the next chapter.

5

Practicing Populist Mobilization
Experimentation, Imitation, and Excitation

In the previous chapter, we saw that some organized political actors experienced the social and political circumstances of early 1931 as constituting a problem situation, broke with their existing political routines, and began to explore new political practices—while others did not. But neither Haya de la Torre nor Sánchez Cerro had yet fully elaborated sustained projects of populist mobilization by this point. Political innovation is a process that unfolds over time, as new practices have to be tested on the ground, in specific situations in which others are also acting. It was only in the second half of their campaigns, between July and October 1931, that the nontraditional candidates' populist mobilization projects really crystalized and took on a comprehensible coherence.

By the time that Haya de la Torre and Sánchez Cerro returned from exile, it was apparent to most observers that their movements had become the dominant forces of the electoral moment. But they still had to contend with one another. No longer simply attempting to circumvent the reluctant elites of the right and upstage the resistant Communists of the left, these candidates now had to successfully out-mobilize one another. As they competed with one another, their practices continued to evolve and they adjusted their lines of action according to their own understandings of what was and was not working. The parties learned from and were constantly trying to upstage one another, via iterative interactional dynamics of trial and error over time, as they calibrated and solidified their populist practice over the course of the campaigns to the political climax of election day (see table 5.1).

This chapter follows the development of populist practices over the course of the second part of the electoral campaigns. It shows how the dynamic of competition that emerged between the two candidates and their parties, and

TABLE 5.1. Timeline of electoral competition, 1931

Haya de la Torre (HdlT) & APRA	1931	Sánchez Cerro (SC) & UR
	March	
• Apristas released from prison by new junta.		
• APRA reconstitutes its executive committee, officially registers as party in Lima.		
	April	
		21 SC supports CN initiative, in effort to maintain political relevance from exile.
	May	
1 Apristas organize May Day rally in Lima.		
• APRA's first regional congress held in Trujillo.		
16 APRA party newspaper, *La Tribuna*, founded.		16 SC expresses outrage over junta's decision to allow HdlT's return, while preventing his own.
• Aprista organizations begin to form throughout the country.		• SC leaves Paris for Panama, against junta's wishes.
	June	
		12 SC appeals to the Peruvian public from Panama, demands junta allow his return.
20 APRA convenes regional congress in Lima.		• Sánchezcerrista organizations begin to form throughout the country.
	July	
		2 SC arrives in port of Callao, disembarks the following day after confrontation between police and unruly crowd.
12 HdlT arrives in northern port of Talara.		13 SC announces his candidacy.
26 APRA rally held to welcome HdlT in Trujillo.		
29 APRA holds Lima rally.		30 UR party officially formed.
	August	
		1-19 SC and UR party leaders tour the south.
15 HdlT speaks at large Lima rally, accepts APRA's nomination to be the party's presidential candidate.		• Sánchezcerrista organizations affiliate with UR.
20 APRA convenes national congress in Lima.		22 SC speaks at large Lima rally, in commemoration of his Revolution of Arequipa, releases his *Programa de Gobierno*.
23 HdlT outlines APRA program at large Lima rally.		

TABLE 5.1. (*continued*)

Haya de la Torre (HdlT) & APRA	1931	Sánchez Cerro (SC) & UR
	September	
10 APRA national congress concludes in Lima.		
20 APRA releases its Programa Mínimo.		
	October	
		4 UR holds large Lima rally.
		7 UR holds large Arequipa rally.
8 HdlT speaks at large Lima rally.		
11 ELECTION DAY		11 ELECTION DAY

their assessments of their own strategic successes—that is, their experiential learning from themselves and from one another—led to a ratcheting up of the practices that they had been enacting since the start of campaigning. Focusing in particular on the parties' grassroots organizing efforts, their practices at mass rallies, and their political rhetoric, the chapter shows how populist mobilization crystalized over this period and presents a sketch of what this looked like in its final form.

Grassroots Incorporative Organizing

In the months leading up to the 1931 election, both Haya de la Torre and Sánchez Cerro departed from traditional Peruvian political practice by facilitating the development of extensive systems of grassroots political organization. Both relied on small, party-affiliated, popular organizations to attract new adherents and incorporate them into party activities. These organizations targeted populations that had traditionally been marginal to the political process: artisans, workers, low-level professionals, rural-to-urban migrants, students, women, and residents of poor and working class neighborhoods. As discussed in chapter 2, Peruvian civil society was becoming increasingly organized in the early twentieth century; and the grassroots incorporative organizing efforts of the candidates' parties took advantage of this fact. In some cases, the parties were able to co-opt or politicize preexisting associational structures; but even when their popular organizations did not map directly onto preexisting organizations, they did map onto existing social networks, patterns of routinized interaction, identities, social solidarities, and personal loyalties. While often altering or extending existing social networks, grassroots incorporative organizing created conduits to channel and coordinate political activity, and to bring new adherents into party life and loyalty.

The organizations contributed to mobilization in a number of respects, not least by providing an infrastructural basis for the enactment of the political rallies that will be discussed below. They also served as conduits for information and machines for the production and dissemination of party propaganda. But perhaps most important, participation in the day-to-day organizational life of party clubs was important for solidifying political loyalties and relationships among supporters. In both cases, networks of localized political clubs engaged ordinary Peruvians in party practices, politicizing them in ways that made their new participation in electoral politics coincide with party loyalties.

This was not the first time that popular political clubs had played an important role in Peruvian politics. But it was the first time that Peruvian presidential candidates had recognized the potential political utility of grassroots organization as a means to incorporate adherents and to channel support from sectors of society that had not yet been systematically integrated into politics. The organizations did not represent clientelistic hierarchies, as they had in the past, but distinct "popular" social groups that were mobilized *as* popular groups—that is, by virtue of, or because of, their popular nature. This, both symbolically and substantively, was quite different from the role that political clubs played in the nineteenth century.

To coordinate and incorporate grassroots support, both Haya de la Torre and Sánchez Cerro oversaw the rapid organization of their own political parties. As discussed in chapter 4, each candidate went into his campaign aided by a small but tightly knit inner circle of dedicated supporters who formed an elite corps at the top of a hierarchical party structure. In both cases, these groups played an important role in coordinating grassroots incorporation through dense networks of party-affiliated popular organizations.[1] By election day, the candidates had built two of the most extensive political parties that Peru had seen up to that point.

But while similar in many respects, the grassroots incorporative organizing projects of the two parties were characterized by different organizational structures and dynamics. Both parties were organized vertically; and a defining feature of each was the extensive network of popular organizations at the

---

1. Both candidates also drew on informal ties with sympathetic organizations and more diffuse networks of supporters (including unions, student groups, etc.). I limit the present analysis to organizations that were either directly affiliated with or that explicitly endorsed the populist candidates.

base of the party structure. But the parties varied in how the popular organizations were incorporated into the larger party structures. Haya de la Torre and the APRA leadership designed and created—from the top down—a web of small- and medium-sized organizations that reached down into popular sectors of society and were tightly integrated into APRA's hierarchical structure. Sánchez Cerro and his UR leadership, by contrast, took a less proactive approach. Still enjoying a good deal of popular support as a result of his anti-Leguía coup, Sánchez Cerro used his Unión Revolucionaria party to coordinate and channel the activities and support of popular organizations that were, for the most part, formed independently by his supporters and only loosely integrated into the party hierarchy. While integrating and coordinating their popular organizations in different ways, however, both parties shared in common a reliance on incorporative organizing to attract adherents, inculcate party loyalties, and organize political action.

Incorporating the large following that had supported Haya was a major aim of APRA's organizing efforts. At the core of APRA's incorporative organizing project was its use of the same types of organizations that it had been using to integrate middle class professionals (see chapter 4) to incorporate working class members at the grassroots level. In particular, these targeted urban workers and the burgeoning population of rural migrants in the capital (Stein 1980, 159–60). APRA's comprehensive organizational scheme was structured according to a preconceived vision of Peruvian society and instituted from above. That is, it did not simply cobble together preexisting organizations and clubs, but laid a systematic organizational blueprint on top of Peruvian social reality, which it would then attempt to realize. This blueprint stipulated a need for three main types of organizations: political, economic, and social.

The political organizations formed the backbone of APRA's party structure. APRA was organized into a series of nested political committees. The top administrative unit was the National Executive Committee (Comité Ejecutivo Nacional), which was headquartered in Lima and with which Haya—the undisputed head of the party—worked closely. There was then to be an Aprista committee for each administrative unit of the country, from the national to the most local. Making up the wide base of the pyramid were various neighborhood and district level subcommittees and other types of organizations—those popular organizations that performed the task of incorporative organizing under discussion here. Most of these were organized by neighborhood, such as the "Comité Aprista de Barranco" or the "Comité Aprista Vitarte" or the "Subcomité 2 de Mayo." Some were organized by region of origin (for rural migrants to the city), such as the "Comité Aprista Cerro de Pasco" or the

"Comité Ancashino." Some of these political organizations also had corresponding women's associations, such as the "Sección Feminina" of the "Comité Distrital de Rímac." These grassroots organizations reported to district committees above them, which reported to provincial committees, which reported to departmental committees—mirroring the nested administrative levels of the Peruvian state.[2] Peru at the time had twenty-three departments (roughly the equivalent of U.S. states). The APRA organizational scheme sorted these departments into eight national regions, each of which had its own Aprista committee. The popular organizations were thus integrated into the hierarchical structure of the APRA party through middle-tier organizations that were in turn linked to the party's Executive Committee. These were the *political* organizations under APRA's party structure.[3]

But also organized underneath the district level political committees were a large set of economic organizations. These were popular Aprista associations organized by employment sector. The working and middle classes were broken down into thirty-three categories, including teachers, engineers, mail and telegraph workers, textile workers, street vendors, and even barbers. The official organizational unit was the *sindicato* (union), although sectors that had not yet officially constituted *sindicatos* were often organized into less formal *agrupaciones* (associations), *células* (cells), or *federaciones* (federations).[4]

Finally, also reporting to the district level political committees were the Aprista social organizations. This set of organizations was oriented toward the provision of social services and education to workers and their families.[5] In 1931, there were three subareas of social organization: legal, medical, and cultural. In the first two, the Aprista *sindicatos* of lawyers and doctors provided free services to party members.[6] This is in keeping with the APRA strategy, outlined in chapter 4, of organizing the professions first so that they might provide services to entice worker supporters. APRA's cultural mission

---

2. In Peru, the largest administrative unit is the department. These departments are subdivided into provinces, which are in turn subdivided into districts.

3. The complexity of APRA's hierarchical organization is quite striking, especially in the context of 1930s' Peru. A complete organizational chart can be found in the August 8, 1931, edition of *La Tribuna* (8–9).

4. For example, workers at various trades (including bricklayers, carpenters, and painters) in the civil construction sector formed the "Agrupación Aprista de Construcciones Civiles" in mid-June, 1931 (*La Tribuna*, June 17, 1931). When this association had grown and become sufficiently organized, it was reconstituted as the "*Sindicato* Aprista de Construcciones Civiles."

5. Once they were formed, the Aprista *comedores populares* (popular kitchens) would fall under this heading. To my knowledge, there has been no study of these Aprista kitchens. On Sánchez Cerro's *comedores populares*, see Drinot 2005.

6. *La Tribuna*, September 11, 1931.

was to be implemented through popular educational organizations: the popular universities (in urban areas) and rural schools. Perhaps the most important of the Aprista popular organizations were the Universidades Populares González Prada (UPGP). As noted above, Haya had founded the original popular universities in 1921, and these had provided the institutional underpinning for the student-worker coalition of the early 1920s. While these were shut down by Leguía in 1924, Haya resurrected the organizational form for the 1931 campaign. The UPGPs, which Haya called "lay temples," had originally been organized "along lines similar to the neighborhood church that brought people together socially, culturally, and spiritually" (Stein 1982, 129). The general idea was that by lifting workers out of ignorance, to a "higher" cultural level, they would be less susceptible to exploitation and more able to take control of their own emancipation. As declared in the hymn of the UPGP: "The more ignorant the worker the more impossible for him to conquer his own liberty; for this reason, brave *compañeros*, we swear to defend our Popular Culture with our lives."[7] In 1931, the UPGPs continued to function in this way. Like before, they were centered on particular workplaces and brought students together with workers; and they held regular classes and public events, with substantial membership and attendance.[8] This time, however, they played an explicitly political role.[9] Like the other types of Aprista popular organizations, the popular universities served to attract new adherents, inculcate party loyalties, and organize political action. Similarly, the rural schools were formed for the purposes of educating (and, in so doing, mobilizing and gaining the political loyalties of) rural peasants. According to an article printed in *La Tribuna*, the first rural schools began functioning in April 1931 and involved agricultural engineers giving free instruction in agronomic practices.[10] Another *La Tribuna* article explains that APRA's women's organizations dedicated themselves to founding the rural schools and played an important role

---

7. See Sabroso's 1970 interview with Stein (PUCP/AASM, AI 98a, 15–16).

8. The exact number of popular universities functioning at the time of the 1931 campaign is difficult to estimate. A joint announcement for fifteen UPGPs posted in *La Tribuna* about one month after the election (November 8, 1931) lists thirty-two courses currently being taught at those locations, ranging from History of Civilization to Botany to Industrial Drawing to Constitutional and Political Law. A preliminary examination of announcements published in *La Tribuna* during the campaign yields at least twenty-one separate popular universities in the various neighborhoods of Lima. Sabroso, in his interview with Stein (PUCP/AI, 96 and 97), remembered that the popular universities were active in all seventy-six sectors of Lima, and in other locations throughout the country.

9. Stein 1980, 179. See also Sabroso Interview, PUCP/AASM, AI 96 and 97, question 40.

10. *La Tribuna*, September 11, 1931.

in their operation, through "anti-illiteracy" programs, the teaching of practical agriculture and drawing, and the provision of free medical assistance.[11]

In all of these popular organizations, the ongoing dynamics of organizational life were closely directed by the central party. The organizations met in a few centralized locations—referred to as *casas del pueblo* (people's houses)—that were set up by the party. APRA's first Casa del Pueblo was established by the Executive Committee in central Lima, at 1065 Belén Street, just off the Plaza San Martín, before Haya's return from exile. Large enough to accommodate the simultaneous meetings of multiple groups, this served both as the party headquarters and the principal meeting place in Lima for APRA's many political committees and other popular organizations. A handful of other Casas del Pueblo were established throughout the city—in places like Callao, Matavilla, and Lucanas—to provide meeting places for cells and organizations located further away from the city center. The Casas del Pueblo often housed popular universities and workers' libraries, and were the sites for social events as well as political meetings. Only rarely did Aprista organizations meet in private residences or commercial establishments (as the Sánchezcerrista clubs did).

The central party insisted that popular organizations maintain party discipline, in terms of the public and private conduct of their members and ideological positions espoused. "Every Aprista organization, from the National Executive Committee to the smallest local cell, had a disciplinary commission that was charged with maintaining central control" (Stein 1982, 126). The secretaries of discipline of each popular organization would monitor that organization, and then report periodically to superior bodies, in meetings of the disciplinary commissions that would be convened at the Casas del Pueblo. "Party discipline" is a concept that does not appear to have been in the Sánchezcerrista lexicon, but for APRA—which was virtually a "civilian political army" (Stein 1980, 160–61)—it was central. According to Masterson (1991, 46), APRA was the most disciplined political force in Peru at the time, its strict internal organization mirroring that of the armed forces. Even membership cards were closely scrutinized by the center; they were to be awarded only "after party chiefs were satisfied that prospective members would follow party discipline and ideological pronouncements" (Pike 1967, 244).

A structure of regular meetings up the organizational hierarchy ensured central control of the popular organizations. The most obvious manifestation

---

11. I have chosen not to translate "anti-illiteracy" into "literacy," because the double negative is important. The program is not framed as cultivating literacy, but rather identifies *i*lliteracy as a disease on the national body that must be eradicated. *La Tribuna*, May 24, 1931, 7.

of this dynamic was the holding of departmental congresses, to which all committees, *sindicatos, agrupaciones,* and cells within a given district sent elected delegates. These only took place in a handful of departments; but that they happened at all in such a short period of time is telling.[12] The various committee posts also met regularly. Cell and committee secretaries were accountable to superiors and integrated into the party's structure through regular meetings.[13] The secretaries of propaganda for the various organizations in the department of Lima met regularly at the main Casa del Pueblo.[14] The secretaries of discipline did the same, although they met at various locations, including the Casas del Pueblo at Lucanas 179 and of the subcommittee of Guadalupe.

Meetings, events, and activities at the popular organizations also tended to be dictated and facilitated by the central party. Meeting activities usually involved, as the main event, a speech by a worker or middle-class speaker who had been sent by the Executive Committee (Stein 1980, 159–60). The central party cultivated an active stable of speakers, many drawn from the party leadership (who all contributed in this respect), but also from the rank-and-file. It kept these speakers in rotation and made sure that local organizations had a steady supply of propaganda and events from the center. Some of these events were quite large. When the new district committee of San Miguel was inaugurated, for example, the party coordinated an event at the Plaza de Independencia in Magdalena del Mar with the committees of nearby Magdalena Vieja, Magdalena Nueva, and Miramar. The key Aprista leaders Manuel Seoane and Luis Alberto Sánchez spoke, along with others, attracting (by APRA estimates) around 800 attendees.[15] Locally situated events of about this size—coordinated with, if not planned by, the central party—were quite common throughout the campaign.

While all of these functionally differentiated organizational units were planned from above as part of a comprehensive system, however, the actual process of organizing unfolded gradually (Stein 1980, 129). APRA's grassroots

---

12. The first, for the department of La Libertad, was held in Trujillo on May 23, 1931 (*La Tribuna*, May 31, 1931). Perhaps the most important, the Lima congress, took place on June 20, 1931 (*La Tribuna*, June 8, 1931).

13. For example, on August 17 the secretary-general of the Lima Departmental Committee invited the secretaries general of the committees, subcommittees, *sindicatos, agrupaciones,* and cells from Lima and the nearby areas to meet at the main Casa del Pueblo to present their testimony to a newly arrived Haya de la Torre (*La Tribuna*, August 17, 1931).

14. *La Tribuna*, August 19, September 16, 1931.

15. *La Tribuna*, September 12 and 14, 1931.

organizing efforts became more extensive as they began to bear fruit and the central party attempted to call new organizations into being from the center.[16]

This discussion of APRA's organizational dynamics has thus far focused mainly on the department of Lima. It is difficult to know for certain the extent and importance of Aprista grassroots incorporation efforts in the provinces. Outside of Lima, APRA organizing was certainly the most extensive in the northern department of La Libertad. Indeed, Aprista organizing in Trujillo and the surrounding area may have even surpassed that in Lima for a time.[17] Elsewhere, APRA was probably not as well organized as it was in Lima or La Libertad; but Aprista cells, subcommittees, and cultural organizations certainly existed in most regions. They communicated and coordinated with the central party in Lima, not least in facilitating various Aprista campaigns to the provinces; and they effectively organized mass demonstrations from time to time.[18] In some regions of strong APRA support, the presence of party organizations cannot be doubted. In some peripheral areas where Aprista support remained low through election day, any existing APRA cells were likely of only symbolic importance. But even such symbolic importance should not be trivialized. Back in Lima, where both candidates courted the votes of recent migrants from the provinces, the symbolic value of the presence of Aprista cells in far-flung provinces was likely to have been quite important.

Sánchez Cerro's party, Unión Revolucionaria, was not formed until July 30, 1931, on the candidate's return from exile; but its formation was a product of the events that unfolded between August 1930 and June 1931. The party was formed explicitly for the purposes of supporting Sánchez Cerro's candidacy—"to serve as an organizational base" for the 1931 presidential campaign (Stein 1980, 120–21)—and so "was organized with incredible speed" (Miró Quesada Laos 1947, 156). Not out to revolutionize organizational practices, Sánchez

---

16. The party newspapers are full of examples of this dynamic. On May 30, 1931, for example, *La Tribuna* ran an announcement for all Apristas of Cerro de Pasco living in Lima to meet at the central APRA headquarters for the purpose of constituting an Aprista committee. On June 17, the Comité Aprista Ancashino announced in *La Tribuna* a meeting to organize the district committees within Ancash department.

17. Klarén (1973) documents extensively APRA's organizing both in Trujillo and in the towns and villages of La Libertad. By May 1931, the APRA leadership in La Libertad had already set up a grassroots political coalition that would last for decades, composed of disaffected intellectuals, small farmers, merchants, artisans, white collar workers, and sugar plantation workers (Klarén 1973, 123). Indeed, the first APRA departmental congress was held not in Lima but in Trujillo, and addressed key problems of industrialization along the north coast (Klarén 1973, 124).

18. APRA claimed, as of the early date of May 24, 1931, to have nineteen functioning departmental committees (out of twenty-three total departments), as well as provincial and district committees in these areas (*La Tribuna*, May 24, 1931, 7).

Cerro modeled the top of his party on past parties. But beyond the core leadership of its Comité Central Directivo, the party lacked the sort of complex internal party architecture that APRA had. Stein (1980, 122), in fact, suggests that Unión Revolucionaria remained quite disorganized throughout the campaign. It was a vertical organization with a "loose, ad hoc structure held together by a charismatic leader" (Stein 1980, 132). As the *West Coast Leader* reported, Sánchez Cerro was:

> acting under the advice of a powerful committee which includes many of the leaders of the bar, commerce, banking, mining and agriculture. It is formed from a new political group known as "Unión Revolucionaria" representing all the conservative elements of the country. The Central Committee meets twice a week and adopts resolutions which are then passed on to the different Departmental and Provincial committees. Not a speech is delivered, not a declaration of policy made, without its approval.[19]

In large part, the party was formed to coordinate the amorphous set of already existing clubs that had emerged to support Sánchez Cerro's return and candidacy.

Constituting the base of UR's loose vertical structure, and doing the practical work of incorporative organizing, were the Sánchezcerrista electoral clubs. These clubs were an incredibly diverse set of organizations that represented not an idealized differentiation of society into functional social organs (as was the case with APRA), but rather a social reality of associations and identifications closer to the experience of everyday life. The best sources of data on the Lima clubs are the political announcements that they regularly posted in sympathetic newspapers.[20] Any given issue of *El Comercio* in August 1931, for example, would typically publish between ten and fifty announcements of club meetings, activities, and recent declarations. An analysis of such announcements discovers a strikingly diverse set of popular organizations, all united around their advocacy of Sánchez Cerro's candidacy. Many clubs, such as the "Club Sánchez Cerro No. 1 Huancavelica" and the "Club Departamental Piurano," were formed around communities of recent migrants to the city from specific departments or provinces. Many others were neighborhood-based organizations, like the "Club Sánchez Cerro No. 10 La Victoria" and the "Club

---

19. *West Coast Leader*, September 1, 1931, 17.

20. My analysis draws most heavily on the announcements sent to Peru's longest running daily, *El Comercio*. While the paper was officially independent, its support for Sánchez Cerro's candidacy was no secret. The newspaper published no similar announcements for Aprista committees or cells. The ongoing opposition between *El Comercio* and APRA only intensified over time—in 1935, the editor of the newspaper and his wife were gunned down by an Aprista.

Sánchez Cerro No. 1 Surquillo Miraflores." Some were broad based clubs for workers, like the "Club Político Artesanos y Obreros—Candidatura Pro Sánchez Cerro," while others formed around specific workplaces, like the "Club Señoras de la Parada del Mercado Central de Lima Sánchez Cerro No. 1." Additionally, there was a notable number of women's and youth clubs.[21] Finally, some clubs, such as the "Club Defensor de la Patria Luis M. Sánchez Cerro No. 1" and the "Club Libertad No. 1 Pro-Elección Sánchez Cerro," invoked no distinctions in their names but only expressed support for Sánchez Cerro's candidacy.[22] Stein (1980, 125–26) estimates that the Lima metropolitan region supported upwards of 155 such clubs, of about 100–150 members each, at the height of the campaign, for a total of approximately 20,000 members. If these numbers are accurate, it means that about two-thirds of the Lima residents who ultimately voted for Sánchez Cerro participated in Sánchezcerrista clubs.[23]

Unión Revolucionaria's incorporative organizing efforts followed a different logic than did APRA's. Whereas APRA's organizational impetus originated in the National Executive Committee, which exerted control downward over the cells and subcommittees, much of UR's organizational dynamics came from below, as Sánchezcerrista electoral clubs reached upward to connect with the central party. For the most part, Unión Revolucionaria did not directly create the Sánchezcerrista clubs that performed the incorporative role that in the case of APRA was carried out by party cells, unions, and committees. Each Sánchezcerrista club had its own unique origins, and, unfortunately, the local histories of these clubs are difficult to determine. Many seem to have formed out of—or on the basis of social networks consolidated through—preexisting civic associations. For example, those clubs oriented to migrants from specific departments or provinces appear to represent the politicization of the preexisting migrant associations that proliferated in Lima in the 1920s.[24]

Not only were the Sánchezcerrista clubs largely independent from the central party in terms of their origins, but they maintained a significant degree

21. Some of these were organized around auxiliary categories (such as neighborhood, as in the case of the "Club Juventud Pro Candidatura Sánchez Cerro Chirimoyo No. 1"), while others (like the "Club Femenil Sostenedora de la Libertad") remained generic.

22. The above statements about the social composition of clubs are based on inference from the club names. It is possible—indeed likely—that what appear to be generic clubs or regional clubs were also limited to specific neighborhoods, or that seemingly generic workers clubs were actually specific to certain factories.

23. Sánchez Cerro received 29,131 votes in Lima (Stein 1980, 250n63).

24. For numbers on the proliferation of migrant associations in the 1920s, see chapter 2.

of autonomy in their operation—much more so than their Aprista counterparts. Accounts of Sánchezcerrismo emphasize the social, cultural, and organizational distance between the popular clubs and the central party. Whereas the central party was composed mainly of elites, the electoral clubs had a distinctly "popular" character (Castillo Ochoa 1990, 64). As Sánchezcerrista Máximo Ortiz told Steve Stein in an interview, "Those of us who were the most enthusiastic formed our own political clubs without help from anyone. In the central campaign headquarters, we did not have a dominant position. People of another social class dominated. These were two distinct organizations" (Stein 1980, 123). Stein (1980, 123–25) claims that the clubs "overtly maintained a high degree of autonomy, manifesting a certain mistrust toward the central headquarters." Molinari Morales (2006) concurs, arguing that the operation of the popular clubs had a dynamic that was quite distinct from that of the central party. This contrast could be seen quite clearly at mass demonstrations, or in the contrast between the social makeup of the clubs compared with the central campaign headquarters (Stein 1980, 121, 125).

At the same time, Unión Revolucionaria increasingly attempted to exert authority over the clubs, as it tried to centralize and to provide leadership for what was in reality a quite diverse movement. As petitions to recognize pro-Sánchez Cerro political clubs accumulated at the UR party headquarters, more active efforts were made to fund, develop, and coordinate such clubs as grassroots party affiliates. Many clubs did receive some measure of funding from the central party—indeed, this was one of a handful of ways in which the party encouraged the incorporative organizing of the clubs—but this support was not systematic.[25] Another mode of connection between the party and the clubs was through the activities of what were called *capituleros*. In exchange for the promise of government employment after the election, *capituleros* acted as intermediaries between the central party and the clubs, ensuring the continued flow of propaganda between the central headquarters and the local organizations, as well as providing alcohol for club meetings and demonstrations (Stein 1980, 126–27 and 126n66).[26]

---

25. Luis Antonio Eguiguren, a close ally of Sánchez Cerro who was running for a seat in the Constituent Congress, had a much better organized campaign headquarters than did UR (Stein 1980, 121). A former mayor of Lima, Eguiguren bore much of the burden of distributing UR propaganda in Lima and helped to cover the overhead for over sixty Sánchezcerrista clubs out of his own pocket (Stein 1980, 121). (He also "paid for over 18,000 photographs to be affixed to the voter registration cards of Sánchez Cerro supporters in Lima" [Stein 1980, 121].)

26. *Capituleros* had been a traditional fixture in Peruvian politics, when the electorate was small enough that vote-buying was feasible and when electoral clubs were organs for the exchange of patronage for political action. They were essentially agents of the party charged with

But while the central party controlled the planning of major events and the development of propaganda, the clubs managed to maintain control of local decision making. Club members were responsible for their own neighborhoods. They did word-of-mouth canvassing, registered voters, stoked turnout for demonstrations, distributed handbills, put up election posters, and got out the vote on election day, while women made posters and badges (Stein 1980, 126).[27] Unlike APRA, Unión Revolucionaria did not try to enforce a rigid party discipline over its popular organizations. Clubs commonly met in the private residences of their presidents or other prominent community members, rather than in shared locations arranged by the central party (as was the case with APRA's Casas del Pueblo). UR seems to have had very little control over the selection of club officers or the programming of club activities (with the exception of the major UR events). Indeed, communication and exchange between the central party and the clubs was quite spotty. It seems that individual clubs coordinated much more with each other than they did with the center. Often, clubs arranged local meetings with other clubs in the nearby area, either to deal with pressing problems or to celebrate UR events.[28]

The relationship between the central party and the clubs can be seen more clearly by taking a closer look at a specific example. The Club Sánchez Cerro de Magdalena del Mar No. 1 was the local club for the Magdalena del Mar neighborhood, located to the south of central Lima. The club was formed on July 6, 1931, and was active with meetings at least weekly through the election. It is the only Sánchezcerrista club whose minutes books from the 1931

---

the task of coercing political support (using both gifts and threats). It is unclear how widespread the employment of *capituleros* was, however; and at any rate, they acted more as free agents than as agents of the party. For evidence of UR's use of *capituleros* in 1931, see "URGENTE, Al Sr. Jefe de la Brigada de Asuntos Sociales . . . ," AGN/PL, Legajo 3.9.5.1.15.1.16.50, Folder 10, Subprefectura de Lima, 1931.

27. One function that seems *not* to have been at the core of the missions of these clubs is fundraising for the party. If anything, UR clubs appear to have been a *drain* on party resources. The minutes of the Club Magdalena del Mar (AGN/PL, Legajo 3.9.5.1.15.1.14.2), for example, recount multiple instances of the leadership imploring members to comply with dues requirements.

28. For example, the presidents and secretaries of the various Sánchezcerrista clubs of the district of Rímac met together at Jirón Libertad #280 on August 21, 1931, at 6 p.m., to deal with "urgent matters," most likely having to do with the mass political rally set for the following day (*El Comercio*, August 21, 1931, 8). In another example, the Club Social Lince y Lobatón Sánchez Cerro No. 1, apparently on its own initiative, organized a gala event in honor of Sánchez Cerro for August 22, 1931, to which it invited the directorates of all Sánchezcerrista clubs (*El Comercio*, August 22 [morning edition], 1931, 15).

election have been preserved.[29] In these records, it is clear both that the club took the initiative in its relationship with the central party, and that the club maintained closer ties with neighboring clubs than with the party headquarters. The first meeting of the club was held at the private residence of a local notable. At this meeting, the members formed a directorate and a propaganda commission and elected officers to each. The members also chose a delegation of six members to visit Sánchez Cerro's Casa Política, "in order to inform the *Jefe* [Sánchez Cerro] of the foundation of the club that will be supporting his candidacy in the district of Magdalena del Mar." At the second meeting, the members agreed to send a circular to the various institutions of the Partido Nacionalista to establish relations with them (although after a brief debate agreed not to append "Club Nacionalista" to their name). At the third meeting, the members endorsed the candidacies of two prominent Partido Nacionalista candidates for the Constitutent Congress—Luis A. Flores and Luis Antonio Eguiguren—and agreed to send a delegation to inform these candidates of their support. At this same meeting, the announcement was made that the club had requested that Sánchez Cerro himself pay a visit to the club; Sánchez Cerro had turned down the request, but had agreed to send his brother—the doctor Pablo E. Sánchez Cerro—in his stead. Also at this third meeting, a secretary of the neighboring Miramar club was in attendance to give a speech; on hearing of the pending visit of Sánchez Cerro's brother, he asked if his club could send a delegation to greet him also. Sánchez Cerro's brother did visit the club for its fourth meeting. He gave a speech; and as a delegation from the Miramar club was in attendance, the president of the Miramar delegation also gave a speech. Sánchez Cerro finally visited the club on September 8, accompanied by his brother, by Flores, and by other UR notables. This meeting attracted members from other nearby clubs, including the women's Sánchezcerrista clubs of Magdalena del Mar and Miramar.[30]

29. These minutes books ended up—after being confiscated from a political prisoner, probably in 1936 (Drinot 2001, 334)—in the Interior Ministry holdings of Peru's national archives (AGN/MI), where I had access to them. Drinot 2001 is a micro-history of this group, based on the minutes books and membership rolls, and is the only study to have exploited this valuable source material.

30. Not only were women important in UR organizations, they were also central to a rhetorical strategy that posited APRA aggression toward women and perversion of the youth. In numerous articles, *La Opinión* denounced the alleged Aprista actions against women. As one headline read: "For the first time in Peru's political history, one political band preys on women, abdicating the gentlemanly sentiment of respect toward the feminine sex" (*La Opinión*, September 30, 1931, 4).

Only on September 22—just three weeks before the election—did UR request that the club elect members to be representatives before the Casa Política and compile an "honor roll" (*cuadro de honor*) of those members who had most distinguished themselves in fulfilling their obligations.

The rate of club formation rose sharply with the founding of Unión Revolucionaria on July 30, but even those clubs formed after this date did so mostly independently. A large proportion of the 155 clubs counted by Stein (1980) were formed only around the time of Sánchez Cerro's return from exile and the formation of the UR. The greatest number were formed in June and July (Stein 1980, 122), although the newspapers for August and September 1931 are similarly replete with the news of the formation of new clubs (multiple clubs daily), right up until election day. There is strong evidence that in most cases Unión Revolucionaria learned of the birth of a new club only on their presentation of tribute to the candidate, usually by public announcement in a periodical and by sending a delegate to present the news to Sánchez Cerro or a secondary party leader.[31] As Stein (1980, 102) put it, Sánchez Cerro "transformed an originally amorphous group of working class sympathizers into an effective political force." Essentially, what Unión Revolucionaria did was to recognize and then develop a system for channeling the independent organizing efforts of the Sánchezcerrista clubs. This facilitated their coordinated political action, aided in aligning the clubs with UR aims and strategies, and incorporated club members into the greater party.

All of the foregoing discussion has focused on the Sánchezcerrista clubs of Lima and the surrounding areas (such as Callao, Miraflores, and Chorillos). As was the case with APRA, incorporative organizing efforts appear to have been the strongest in this area, although our knowledge of the extent to which this is the case is complicated by the fact that data are quite limited on the real numbers and relative importance of Sánchezcerrista clubs operating in provincial urban centers and rural areas. The little evidence that exists suggests that by October 1931, a remarkable number of Sánchezcerrista political clubs were operating throughout Peru, in provincial cities and towns, and that the Unión Revolucionaria leadership treated these as relevant to the campaign. In an announcement that Unión Revolucionaria published in *El Comercio* on August 18, 1931 (quoted in Molinari Morales 2006, 45–46), the party claimed to have constituted provincial and departmental committees throughout Peru—as a reflection of its decentralist agenda—although it noted that some

---

31. My analysis of the minutes book for the Sánchezcerrista club of the neighborhood of Magdalena del Mar, which informed the party of its formation immediately thereafter, supports this point. See also Stein 1980, 122.

departmental delegates had yet to be designated. This same announcement listed sixty-five departmental delegates, designated to represent the departments in UR's Comité Central Directivo in Lima.[32] Sánchezcerrista Carlos Miró Quesada (1946:156) boasts that "numerous electoral organizations" were formed in the southern provinces, and of the presence of strong support in the south (in the departments of Puno, Cuzco, Arequipa, Moquegua, Ayacucho, Apurímac, and Ica), in the central highlands (in Junín and San Martín), and up the north coast (in Piura, Ancash, and Tumbes)—although in this recollection, Miró Quesada remains vague as to whether this support was organized via popular organizations.[33] Pedro Ugarteche, Sánchez Cerro's personal secretary through most of his political career, calls attention to the formation of Sánchezcerrista electoral organizations by military personnel at outposts in some of the most remote parts of the country (1969, 2:xlii). Still, there is good reason to believe that the UR network of popular organizations was by far the most extensive in Lima, where a dense network of civic associations had slowly developed over the past thirty years.

Thus, both Haya de la Torre and Sánchez Cerro oversaw the rapid organization of hierarchical political parties meant to coordinate and incorporate

32. The extent to which this schema actually became a reality and was undergirded by actual local clubs is more difficult to know. In one instance, we do know that there was a party head of UR in the district of Yaután, Province of Casma, Ancash department, because he encouraged the writing of a letter to the subprefect of Santa province that denounced the Aprista organizing there (see letter to César Pazos, September 28, 1931, AGN/PL, Legajo 3.9.5.1.15.1.14.2, Presos Políticos y Sociales, Asuntos Políticos, 1931–1945).

33. It is possible that there could have been support in certain regions without this having been organized through popular organizations. Or, it is possible that it could have been organized through entirely disconnected groups. For example, Pike (1967, 250) notes that a "rapidly growing organization calling itself the Youth of Cuzco (*Juventud del Cuzco*) saw in Sánchez Cerro the man who would inaugurate the reforms that the Andean political leaders had been advocating for over twenty years." Ugarteche's (1969, 2:xlvi–liii) account of Sánchez Cerro's campaign through the southern provinces in early August records connections at the level of leadership, as well as the participation of popular sectors in political rallies; but if popular clubs were central to UR's organizing strategy in the provinces at this time, there is little indication of it in Ugarteche's account. In Arequipa, for example, Ugarteche (1969, 2:xlvii–xlviii) describes widespread popular support on Sánchez Cerro's arrival, but does not describe the means of this mobilization. He mentions don Clemente J. Revilla as the director of Sánchez Cerro's campaign for the city. He also lists Juan Manuel Chávez Bedoya, the Chirinos Pacheco family, the Lozada Benavente family, and the Corso Masías family as the "bases of action" in the city, along with Manuel Mujica Gallo (who the campaign dropped off in the city along the way, to oversee organizing and link the Arequipenos with the Comité Central Directiva in Lima). But it is only through anecdotal and vague evidence such as this that the presence of UR popular organizations in the provinces can be assessed.

grassroots support. In doing so, each was aided by a small but tightly knit inner circle of dedicated supporters who formed an elite corps at the top of a hierarchical party structure. In both cases, these groups played an important role in coordinating grassroots incorporation through dense networks of party-affiliated popular organizations. But APRA and UR incorporated their grassroots organizational bases in different ways. Haya de la Torre and his party leadership did so from the top down: they mapped out and attempted to create a web of organizations that reached deep into society, doing their best to integrate these tightly into APRA's hierarchical structure as they did so. Sánchez Cerro and his party leadership allowed for a more bottom-up dynamic to play itself out. Most pro-Sánchez Cerro popular organizations were formed independently by the figure's supporters, in part out of ongoing gratitude for his anti-Leguía coup. While UR eventually made efforts to coordinate and channel these grassroots activities, its popular organizations remained only loosely integrated into the party hierarchy. But despite these variations in party structure and integration dynamics, the grassroots incorporative organizing projects of both APRA and Unión Revolucionaria shared a fundamental goal: to incorporate popular sectors into the parties. In practical terms, much of the "incorporation"—the building of new party loyalties, solidarities, and social relationships—took place in the popular clubs, cells, and committees, regardless of how these suborganizations were linked into the broader party. In the end, popular organizations were not only about membership, but about *active participation* in organizational activities. The organizations were ultimately effective both at inculcating loyalties and at coordinating the political activities of adherents, and much of this success is attributable to clubs' abilities to get adherents participating in the regular organizational life of the clubs.

Staging Contentious Displays of Strength

In addition to their development of infrastructures for grassroots organization, both candidates and their parties staged mass rallies and marches that were unprecedented in their scale and contentious implications. Indeed, in both Lima and to a lesser extent in the provinces, they made such contentious displays of strength a cornerstone of their campaigns. Each candidate organized multiple mass rallies in Lima; and each structured his tours to the periphery around smaller rallies in provincial cities and towns. Such mass political rallies provided an opportunity for supporters to demonstrate their enthusiasm to crowds of spectators in the hopes of gaining new adherents. But they also had less obvious functions. They served as a demonstration of strength *to opponents*. And perhaps most important, they provided an opportunity for supporters to participate jointly in the social production of a spectacle, demonstrating *to themselves* their own strength and virtues.

Such events did not represent a spontaneous eruption of popular enthusiasm, nor were they evoked simply by the persuasive powers of populist leaders. Rather, they required detailed planning and organization by both party elites and the rank-and-file. A significant amount of unseen labor and organization went into the production of such performances—before any actors actually took to the stage—and continued throughout the event.[34] The events were carefully choreographed and staged, attendance was preplanned and synchronized, and the post-hoc framings of the event were carefully controlled. Regardless of the specific styles of marching or modes of organizing, the production of these events was a social accomplishment.

Rallies bring a set of social actors out from their semi-private meeting spaces onto the highly visible public stage of avenues, promenades, parks, and plazas. Here, they come face to face with their leaders, with curious spectators, with their opponents (sometimes including the state's forces of "public order"), and—perhaps most important—with each other. In the streets, by virtue of their public visibility, ordinary social actors become *political* actors. On the public stage, they coordinate their (often pre-scripted) activities to perform a meaningful (and "readable") political ritual before a range of audiences. In so doing, they rely on various props: banners, flags, costumes, automobiles, audio and lighting equipment—even the occasional pistol. The performance itself is typically segmented into a series of narrative acts, of which the giving of a public speech by a dynamic leader is only one of many—albeit often the climax. Finally, as will be discussed in the next section of this chapter, the post-event framing of a rally, by both sympathetic and antagonistic propagandists, can be in some respects even more important than the event itself.

While the charismatic leader is the star of the production, he is backed by a large supporting cast. Typically, a range of party leaders and notable supporters also give speeches and participate in the rallying of the crowd, while other elements of the party leadership work backstage, coordinating the event. The members of the crowd attending the event are also active participants.

---

34. This labor and organization is rarely the focus of scholarly attention because the eyes of scholars and spectators alike are usually fixed on the same thing: the populist speaker. Also, populists themselves have an interest in deflecting attention from the organizational underpinnings of their events. Political rallies are supposed to be *alive*, to pulse, to be energetic; a well-produced rally is one in which the behind the scenes organization is not the focus of attention indeed, where the event appears to be the result of the organic, spontaneous, and overwhelming support of the people.

The crowd should not be viewed as an undifferentiated mass "audience"; it is rather constituted by individuals with varying degrees of preexisting political commitment to the candidate and integration into social and organizational units that participate in the event *as* units. Many, if not most, people in the 1931 crowds were already committed to the candidate and participated as members of political clubs or organizations. Others were unaffiliated sympathizers, some even uncommitted spectators. All actively and jointly participated in enacting the spectacles of collective enthusiasm to which they were witness, by chanting, singing, cheering, parading, and generally coordinating their activities with seemingly like-minded consociates—sometimes even in the face of opposition. That is, the "audience" members were actors in the performance as much as was the political leader. It may be that what happens onstage is secondary to what goes on in the street itself, which can be just as energizing and transformative as the reception of rousing oratory broadcast from the podium. It may also be that the horizontal ties forged among the rank-and-file participants are as important—if not more—than the vertical, leader-led relationship.

If the crowds in 1931 were in large part not passive audiences, but constituted by active—often already sympathetic—participants, then who was the true audience for these political rallies? Two audiences may be identified beyond the limits of the active crowd. These rallies put on a show for sympathetic spectators and for opponents alike. They were quite literally "demonstrations," in that they claimed to be—and were often taken as—evidence of the extent and intensity of support for a candidate. As such, they could attract new supporters by creating an impression of strength and inevitability; likewise, for the same reasons, they served as a threat to political adversaries (and an inducement either to compromise or to stand down entirely). In 1931, the prominence of the two nontraditional candidates already posed a threat to social and political elites; but seeing swarms of their supporters filing through the city's most distinguished avenues and plazas made that threat all the more palpable—sometimes provoking violent responses. Politically neutral or potentially sympathetic spectators were less likely to be found at the center of the gathered crowd than on the periphery—in the balconies or on rooftops along the parade route, or at the margins of the crowd. Many would not even be present at the event itself, but nonetheless were influenced by later media representations or street gossip after the fact. Similarly, unless they were able to pass as spectators, or were there to actively harass the crowd, opponents were not responding to direct experience of the event *itself*, but rather to later framings of it.

Seen from this perspective, political rallies are clearly complex, choreographed, and meaningful affairs. The moment of speech making matters, of course, as the highlight of the event; and so rallies are indeed, at least in part, vehicles for political rhetoric. At the same time, however, they are demonstrations of political support directed at multiple audiences, both sympathetic and antagonistic. Finally, the *practice* of rallying is *itself* significant, apart from the speech-making function of the event. Participation in ritualized rallying practices with others can be incredibly energizing, contributing to renewed commitment to the group and to ongoing mobilization efforts.

Neither APRA nor the group that would become Unión Revolucionaria staged public events like this in the early months of campaigning, when they were more focused on organizing their party leadership, setting up grassroots political organizations, and disseminating their message through printed propaganda. But once the candidates returned from exile to find their supporters waiting for them, in late July, they began to incorporate rallying into their political practices.

Among the first things that each candidate did on returning was to undertake extensive campaigns to the provinces. This was unusual for Peruvian politicians, who in the past had tended to focus their efforts on Lima (and only work through correspondence with their allies in other cities). But both Haya and Sánchez Cerro understood that personal appearances throughout the country would help them to win support from ordinary Peruvians who had never before received such attention from national political figures. Smaller rallies were the cornerstone of these provincial tours in July and early August, as well as later in the campaigning (see figure 5.1). But the contentious displays of strength heated up in August. As rallies became more central to APRA's strategy, UR followed suit. In his biography of Haya de la Torre, Aprista writer Felipe Cossío del Pomar (1977, 1:341) claims, for example, that on hearing of a successful Aprista march on August 15, Sánchez Cerro declared, "These swine have deceived me! They've lied in assuring me that such Aprismo didn't exist!" Sánchez Cerro then made sure that his own rally the following weekend would be larger still. Haya de la Torre then dispatched his close confidant, Luis Alberto Sánchez, on the afternoon of Sánchez Cerro's August 22 rally, to report back on what took place there.[35] Such one-upmanship played a critical role in amplifying the theatrics of the rallies.

---

35. As Luis Alberto Sánchez recalled in his memoir: "In the late afternoon, Víctor [Raúl Haya de la Torre] called me aside and said, 'I beg you to go in person to see what this rally is like; getting in will be risky, but I trust your objectivity'" (Sánchez 1969, 355).

FIGURE 5.1. Supporters of Sánchez Cerro rally in Arequipa.
Source: Ugarteche 1969, 2:160.

The rallies held in Lima on the weekend of August 22 and 23, 1931, are often singled out—by participants and scholars alike—as having been the most important of the candidates' respective campaigns.[36] They were dramatic and symbolically significant events held at the height of the electoral contest. On the weekend itself, the city center was overtaken for two consecutive days by throngs of partisans and spectators from all corners of the city. In what contemporary observers described as an atmosphere charged with anticipation and excitement, tens of thousands took to the streets in support of their candidates—and thousands more looked on from the sidelines and the balconies above. These spectacles centered around mass public gatherings in which a series of charismatic speakers enthralled crowds with lofty populist rhetoric; and both involved mass processions down similar routes through the capital city, past symbolically important sites and centers of social and political life. In the wake of the rallies, the print media were filled with competing depictions of and claims about the events.

On August 22, 1931, Sánchez Cerro staged a mass rally in commemoration of the one-year anniversary of his overthrow of Leguía. The so-called "Hero of Arequipa" took full advantage of the timing of this anniversary, billing the

36. On the importance of the Sunday rally for APRA, see Basadre 1999, 13:3190–91.

PRACTICING POPULIST MOBILIZATION 175

rally as a national event of utmost importance for "all patriotic citizens."[37] This occasion, which drew an estimated 50,000 people (Basadre 1999, 13:3196), provided an opportunity to remind Peruvians of their supposed debt to their emancipator, which many believed ought to be repaid by awarding him the presidency.[38] Thus, while not officially billed as a campaign rally, the Saturday event was clearly intended to build support for Sánchez Cerro's candidacy.[39] And it was on this day that Sánchez Cerro published his political program (Molinari Morales 2006, 47). The day after Sánchez Cerro's public commemoration of his Revolution of Arequipa, Haya de la Torre staged a mass rally of his own (see figure 5.2). Its purpose was to outline the APRA party's official program for the public. This was a momentous and long-awaited event, both for the Aprista leadership and for the rank-and-file.

That both candidates scheduled important mass rallies for the same weekend was not accidental. It was no secret that Sánchez Cerro's support could be attributed in large measure to the popularity of his overthrow of Leguía. Given the symbolic significance of his coup of the year before, it is reasonable to assume that the candidate had planned well in advance on making its commemoration an important fulcrum for his campaign. The APRA leadership likewise had to have been aware of the importance that August 22 would hold for the UR campaign. Even without detailed knowledge of UR plans, they could reasonably assume that the day would be slated for a raft of opportunistic commemorative activities. The APRA leadership chose the Saturday *before* Sánchez Cerro's event (August 15) to stage Haya de la Torre's long-anticipated return to Lima from eight years of exile; and they waited until the Sunday *after*

---

37. *El Comercio*, August 22, 1931, 1.

38. The argument that the Peruvian people ought to grant Sánchez Cerro the presidency as a token of their gratitude was widespread, both before and after elections were announced. See, for example, the circular calling for the election of Sánchez Cerro—and explaining how to cast a ballot for him—reproduced in Ugarteche 1969 (2: unpaginated plate following 210). As this bulletin explains, "Comandante Sánchez Cerro destroyed the Leguía dictatorship and returned public freedom to Peru, in the glorious campaign of Arequipa of August 22, 1930. The Peruvian people have the obligation to preserve and defend this treasure, and to make sure that the fruits of the Revolution are not lost to the ambitions and intrigues of the bad citizens."

39. It was clear that this was in reality a partisan event. As the *West Coast Leader* (August 25, 1931, 19) reported: "The official commemoration of the day was limited to a salute of 21 guns and the hoisting of the national flag on public buildings. There was a complete absence of any sign of general rejoycings. No business houses and few private residences hung out banners in honour of the occasion. This was probably due to the fear that such an act might be interpreted as expression of political sympathies. The desire to make party capital out of the anniversary was visible in the [Sánchezcerrista] manifestation."

FIGURE 5.2. Supporters of Haya de la Torre rally in Lima on August 23, 1931. "Apristas marched last night with uncontainable enthusiasm from the Plaza de Acho to the Plaza La Victoria, to the chant of: 'Apristas cannot be bought, not for rum, not for three *soles* [Peruvian currency].'"
Source: *La Tribuna*, August 24, 1931, 3.

Sánchez Cerro's event (August 23) to outline APRA's political program at a second mass rally. Both Aprista events were important: the latter was significant for its political content, the former for the even larger crowds that it drew.[40] There is no way to know for sure how far in advance—or with what type of speculation about the opposition's plans—the decision was made to bookend Sánchez Cerro's most predictable day in the sun with mass Aprista events. All that can be known is the fact of the chosen dates—and that Haya's gradual return from exile through the northern port of Talara (rather than the more conventional choice of Lima) and six-week tour of northern departments timed out quite conveniently. Still, the lack of specific evidence should not lead to the presumption that the decision was arbitrary or the events under-planned, as this would be entirely inconsistent with Haya's demonstrated history of strategic acumen.

40. APRA claims the August 15 event to have drawn some 80,000 people—double their claims for the event of the twenty-third (*La Tribuna*, August 17, 1931, 2). While these numbers are likely inflated, it is reasonable to expect that they give an accurate sense of the *relative* size of the two events.

Each party devoted significant time and resources—at both elite and grassroots levels—to preparation in advance of this weekend of rallies. The anticipation of the events by party leaders conditioned their political practice during the preparatory period—with Sánchez Cerro planning his southern campaign itinerary to build up to the Lima rally and Haya de la Torre spending his week before the event meeting with Aprista grassroots organizations and staging preliminary local rallies. At the same time, Sánchezcerrista and Aprista grassroots organizations met more frequently than usual, coordinated with other party organizations, discussed and planned their participation, painted signs, and rehearsed their chants in the lead up to the rallies. Of course, these actions were all undertaken toward the end of pulling off impressive public performances. But it is reasonable to assume that it was precisely this common purpose that rendered the preparation more than prologue, in that it infused the involved coordinated actions with a sense of consequentiality and shared meaning that could jump-start the wheels of solidarity- and antagonism-building well before the first bodies hit the streets.

At the same time, the meaningful activities surrounding the events were far from over when the crowds began to disperse. First, demobilization itself was a temporally extended social process in which participants continued to interact with each other—and in some cases with their opponents (see figure 5.3). Second, it was only after the manifestations had ended that party leaders and their opponents began the equally (or perhaps even more) important work of narrating the event to audiences who had not been present, as well as to those who were.

Each party also relied heavily on the grassroots organizations described above to mobilize, energize, and organize supporters for their rallies. The role of the two parties' organizations followed from the main differences outlined in the previous section. The Sánchezcerrista clubs were highly decentralized and did much of the mobilizing work on their own, without the assistance of Unión Revolucionaria. Indeed, the clubs coordinated more laterally with each other than vertically with the central party. APRA's mobilizing structure was more highly centralized. Meetings took place at central locations, and the central party set the agenda for meetings, coordinated visiting speakers, and met regularly with the club secretaries. Despite these differences, however, both parties managed to turn out tens of thousands of participants and to organize their participation through the network of grassroots clubs. In neither case was participation an individualized matter; in both cases, participation was channeled through clubs and maintained according to this organizational structure over the course of the event.

FIGURE 5.3. Cartoon depicting conflict between supporters of Sánchez Cerro and Haya de la Torre. *Source*: *Variedades*, October 14, 1931, 35.

Nor were the gathering sites and parade routes left to chance—they were both symbolically important in various respects and evidenced thoughtful planning. Although starting from different locations in Rímac, both Unión Revolucionaria and APRA began their processions in this working class district that had once been the home of the city's elite social life. The promenade and the bull ring were both hubs of working class public leisure activities, but both also held a meaningful place in the city's history. Each party made its way from its respective starting point to the historic stone bridge—the Puente de Piedra—which formed the main link between Rímac and the city center.

PRACTICING POPULIST MOBILIZATION 179

Each shared the route from the bridge, through the Plaza de Armas, along the Jirón de la Unión to the Plaza San Martín (see figure 5.4). This route passed by the most important centers of government, commerce, culture, and social life, and traced the path from the old city center to the new center of civic life at the Plaza San Martín. Sánchez Cerro ended his procession here, on this

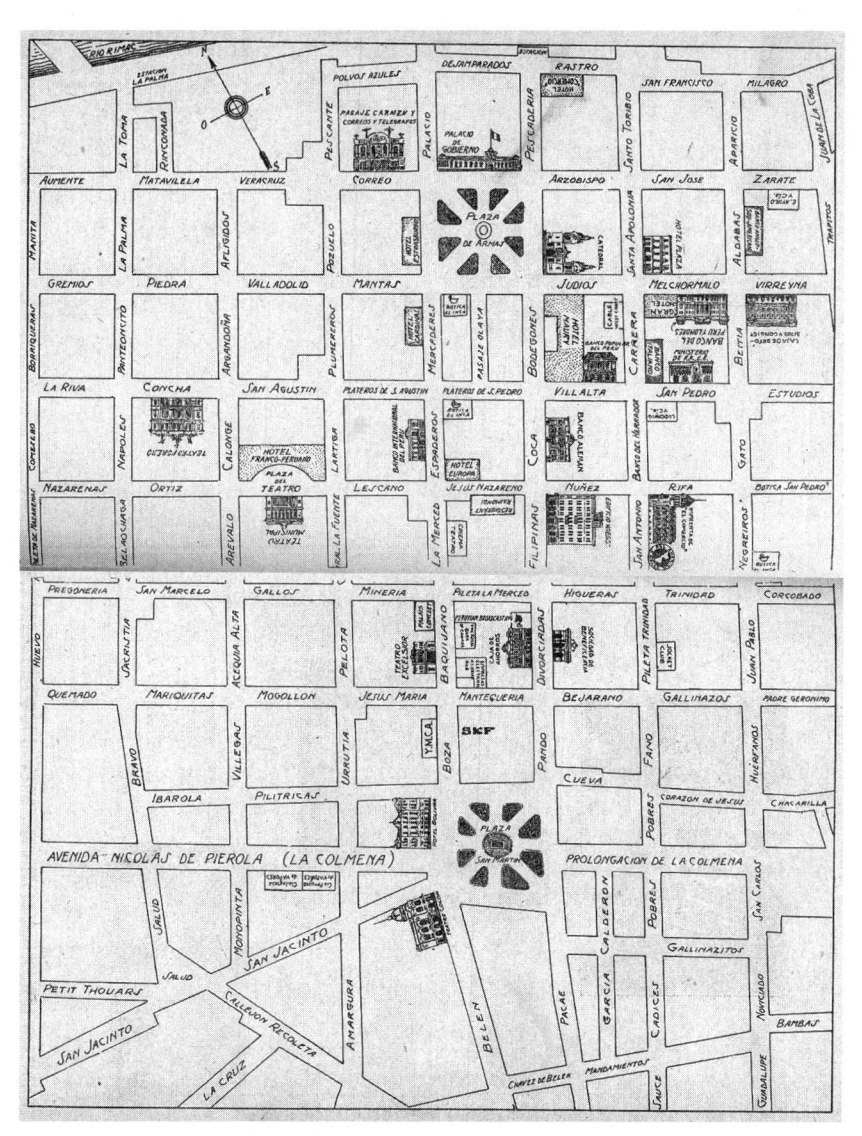

FIGURE 5.4. Map of central Lima (c. 1925), from the Plaza de Armas (top) to the Plaza San Martín (bottom).
Source: Laos 1928, 78–79.

grand plaza, while Haya de la Torre pushed his even further, past the new apartment developments and municipal offices south of the Plaza San Martín, past the APRA party headquarters, past the new statue of the Incan leader Manco Capac, and into the Aprista-friendly working class neighborhood of La Victoria. These routes, for both candidates, were not arbitrary. They were well thought out and symbolically meaningful.

At the same time, there were considerable differences in how participants in the two events conducted themselves and in the meanings that they and their audiences attached to this difference. The Sánchezcerrista procession, while loosely organized, took on a somewhat carnivalesque atmosphere. Indeed, the directorate of Unión Revolucionaria often received notices from the Prefecture of Lima asking it to better control its members during demonstrations (Drinot 2001, 344).[41] The Aprista procession, by contrast, was much more orderly and disciplined. The differences in style extended beyond the realm of discipline and decorum while parading, however, to a fundamental difference in the structuring of the two events. For Sánchez Cerro's Saturday event, the initial assembly and march through the city was in many ways the central feature. It was capped by Sánchez Cerro's speech at the Plaza San Martín, but this speech was relatively short. For Haya de la Torre's Sunday event, by contrast, the series of speeches at the Plaza de Acho lasted for upwards of three hours and was billed as the most important happening of the day. This difference is indicative of a pattern that would hold throughout the campaign.

Overall, the staging of contentious displays of strength like those of the twenty-second and twenty-third were central to each party's project of populist mobilization. They capitalized on the organizational infrastructure of small grassroots clubs that each party had built, and they provided critical sites for fomenting solidarity among adherents and generating contentious antagonism with opponents. At the same time, they transmitted the populist rhetoric that each candidate was in the process of developing.

Propagating Populist Rhetoric

All of the practical activities discussed so far in this chapter were infused with the candidates' newly formulated populist rhetoric. The rallies were of course

41. It appears that Unión Revolucionaria at least *tried* to control its members via the political clubs. When the Club Sánchez Cerro de Magdalena del Mar asked Unión Revolucionaria if it could stage a counter demonstration against Haya de la Torre's visit to that district, in the week before the rallies, the party emphasized in its response that the club must enforce order among its members and keep the event from turning violent ("Club Sánchez Cerro de Magdalena del Mar No. 1," AGN/PL, Legajo 3.9.5.1.15.1.14.2, Presos Políticos y Sociales, Asuntos Políticos, 1931–1945, 15).

organized around the delivery of political speeches, but they also provided occasions for the dissemination of pamphlets, fliers, and other forms of party propaganda. The meetings of the grassroots political organizations, while also accomplishing other functions, likewise included time for speeches by party notables and involved the dissemination of propaganda to members (in many cases with the intent that they would in turn disseminate it further). In addition to the rhetoric conveyed through meetings and rallies, both candidates had outlets through newspapers and the printing of pamphlets and fliers, and occasionally engaged in polemics with opponents in other venues as well.

But before exploring the details of these rhetorical practices, it is important to remember what I mean by populist rhetoric. In chapter 1, I defined it as an anti-elite, nationalist rhetoric that valorizes ordinary people. On the one hand, this definition highlights a particular vision of social solidarities and divisions. Populist rhetoric emphasizes the natural social unity of the national people—in a way that traverses at least some traditionally politicized social divides (like class, ethnicity, or region)—emphasizing similarities and downplaying differences at the popular level. Horizontal antagonisms are replaced by vertical antagonisms: the most important social distinction is posited to be between the national people and an exclusive elite oligarchy. On the other hand, the definition suggests that the main problem facing the nation stems from the nature of this vertical antagonism. The nation's principle problem is that the antipopular elites have been parasites on the inherently virtuous national people. While Haya de la Torre and Sánchez Cerro differed somewhat in the specific content of their claims, their rhetoric converged in expressing these basic populist principles.

The use of the term "converged" here is important, as the candidates only came to elaborate a similar mode of populist rhetoric as the political moment unfolded. As Manuel Castillo Ochoa (1990) has explained, the socio-political crisis that emerged with the fall of Leguía produced two parallel currents: one that tried to overcome the crisis by superseding the oligarchy and transforming the social order (that aligned with APRA), another that tried to do so by affirming order and countering the forces of antipatriotism (that which fell in behind Sánchez Cerro). That is, it must be remembered that the two nontraditional candidates did not come from the same ideological place. Haya de la Torre's rhetoric had already been moving in a populist direction prior to 1931, as he developed his ideas through writing while in exile. But Sánchez Cerro's rhetoric only crept in an increasingly populist direction between the Augusts of 1930 and 1931, from the xenophobic nationalism, paternalism, and anti-*Leguiísmo* of his August 22 (1930) Manifesto of Arequipa (released at the time of his coup) to the decidedly pro-popular and anti-elite sentiments expressed in his August 22 (1931) speech on the Plaza San Martín (delivered at the high-water mark of his presidential campaign).[42] That is, the populist direction of Sánchez Cerro's rhetoric was reinforced over the course of the campaign, as APRA's mounting successes upped the ante. As each candidate elaborated populist claims that differed in the specifics of their content, each attempted to undermine the populist credentials of the other. Over time, a veritable war of populist framings emerged, with each party claiming that its own practices were the only true expression of popular virtue.[43] This was a war that was perhaps most visible in the public rallies, but that was also carried out through the writing, printing, and distribution of party propaganda.

The differing ways in which Haya de la Torre and Sánchez Cerro elaborated what was in the end similarly populist rhetoric can be grasped most clearly by examining the competing speeches that they gave on the weekend of their dueling rallies in late August 1931, in the context of the political programs that they released late in their campaigns.

Sánchez Cerro's rally came first, on Saturday, August 22. While he released the entirety of his 1931 platform on that same day, he did not elaborate it in detail in his speech, but rather made it available in the form of a forty-eight-page pamphlet (see Sánchez Cerro 1931). While his political program itself was quite detailed, the speech was relatively short, and somewhat vague.

The speechmaking on the Plaza San Martín opened with remarks from a handful of the candidate's prominent supporters and advisors. Dr. Francisco Lanatta spoke first.[44] Leaving no doubt as to the real purpose of the day's events—that it was indeed a campaign rally, and not just a national commemoration—he began by drawing a direct line from the support for the overthrow of Leguía that was presently being demonstrated on the plaza to Sánchez Cerro's presidential candidacy. Lanatta likened Leguía to other recently ousted dictators in Venezuela and Guatemala, denounced his financial mismanagement as a "despicable attack" on the public finances, criticized his ceding of national territory in the north, and condemned the Conscripción Vial for having "resuscitated the slavery of the Indian." Sánchez Cerro's political opponents were sellouts, APRA no less so than Leguía. In contrast, Lanatta praised Sánchez Cerro's coup, and especially his abolition of the con-

42. For the full text of the 1930 manifesto, see Ugarteche 1969, 1:113–17. For the 1931 speech, see Ugarteche 1969, 2:178–81.
43. See Cossío del Pomar 1977, 1:342; Miró Quesada Laos 1947, 157; *La Tribuna*, August 24, 1931, 3.
44. For the full text of Lanatta's speech, see *El Comercio*, August 23, 1931, 5.

scription act as a triumph for worker liberty—and for the indigenous people of Peru in particular.

The other preliminary speakers then proceeded to lead the crowd on a whirlwind tour through recent Peruvian history. They detailed the evils of the former dictatorship and the "eclipse of democracy" that Leguía's reign had represented; they emphasized that "an act of force had been necessary" to "restore freedom" for all Peruvians. They reminded the crowd that the Revolution of Arequipa—the patriotic action that had answered the "honorable protests of the people"—had earned Sánchez Cerro the "gratitude of the nation." They noted the high points of what the figure had done on behalf of Peru's workers and indigenous peoples during his short tenure as head of the military junta. They made clear that Sánchez Cerro had the interests of the nation in mind when he then stepped down from this powerful position (arguing that he had done so to avoid further bloodshed and noting that he had been the first in the history of the country to so resign). They argued that he was now charged with defending the nation again, as he had done in the past. They said that, with his understanding of the needs of the people and the social ills of inequality, Sánchez Cerro was destined to become the savior of the fatherland. And they reminded the crowd that the Peruvian people still owed an "honorable debt of gratitude" to the man who had "reclaimed for us the dignity of free beings." Dr. Wieland concluded his remarks by leading the crowd in singing the national anthem.[45]

Sánchez Cerro then addressed the crowd in a "thunderous voice" (Ugarteche 1969, 2:lvi), gesticulating and speaking in a way that was uniquely his (Molinari Morales 2006, 27). He began by announcing, "My heart throbs with gratitude and is intimately thrilled by this great demonstration, with which the people of Lima and Callao have received me and offered their support and assistance." The "eleven years of night" under Leguía had turned the country's moral values upside down, he argued. The Leguiístas had made themselves rich off of politics, he said, and were blind to the ruin that they brought to Peru in the process; and the Apristas, he continued, were their "present day accomplices," also conspiring against the nation. But a "material and spiritual perfecting of the country" was still possible. Through his "program of national reconstruction"—and with the efforts and sacrifice of Peru's "virtuous citizens"—Sánchez Cerro promised to reverse the harm that had been done

---

45. For Wieland's speech, see *El Comercio*, August 23, 1931, 5. (This Sunday edition of *El Comercio* failed to reproduce Nariu's speech alongside the others, although the Saturday edition announced the fact that he would be speaking [ibid., August 22, 1931, 15].)

by "*un*virtuous citizens" and the conspirators against the nation. "The two most urgent necessities of the present moment," he went on to explain, "are the defense of our democratic institutions and the need to meet the just demands of the proletarian classes." Speaking further to the concerns of workers, he continued:

> I love the people, with gratitude and conviction. I want your betterment and your wellbeing; and I hope to secure these—in a fully democratic fashion—by spreading the culture of the [ordinary] people, by developing and perfecting the existing worker's legislation, by raising the proletariat's standard of living, and by opening up for them opportunities to achieve as much as their abilities will permit. In this, I have here the honorable, just, and effective way to protect the working classes.

Concluding with a strong "Compatriots! *Viva* Peru!," Sánchez Cerro ended his speech.[46] Compared with the Aprista speeches of the following day, the Sánchezcerrista remarks on the Plaza San Martín were concise and somewhat vague. But although Stein (1980, 110) has said that Sánchez Cerro "mounted a campaign in which the consideration of the issues received little attention," this was more true of his speeches than of his written rhetoric.

The political program that Sánchez Cerro released that same day was considerably more elaborate, and his populist themes emerge more clearly in that text. Rarely distinguishing between classes or groups at the popular level, the program uses inclusive language to bring all virtuous Peruvians into the national family. One distinction in particular that the document attempts to break down is between whites and mestizos, on the one hand, and the indigenous population on the other:

> I consider the indigenous problem the nourishing mother of my revolutionary governing program. We cannot resolve this basic problem of nationality without changing the spiritual attitude of the white and *mestizo* inhabitants toward our indigenous brothers (Sánchez Cerro 1931, 34).

The document goes on to say that this will only be possible if whites abandon their paternalist and superior attitudes and accept the indigenous people (ibid., 34–35). It also makes the point that the leaders of Unión Revolucionaria are not party men, pursuing partisan interests, but good nationalists, whose power emanates from the people (ibid., 4–5). The former supporters of Leguía are singled out as the parasitic elite who have been harming the virtuous nation. The program argues that a small number of "impure people" had "illicitly captured" the government, "silencing all of the citizenry's organs

---

46. For the full text of Sánchez Cerro's speech, see Ugarteche (1969, 2:178–81).

of expression" (ibid., 9). It warns that the people's newly discovered liberties can still be lost (ibid., 4); and it implies that APRA (like Leguía) represents an antidemocratic tendency, because it aspires to a single-party political system that would exclude all opposition from the government (ibid., 12–13).

In response to these problems, the program proposes a number of political solutions. Rather than waging class struggle, or interest group, family, or individual politics, Sánchez Cerro says that his only political enemies are those who commit crimes against the fatherland (Sánchez Cerro 1931, 11). Much of the document is then devoted to outlining proposals to respond to the social and economic hardships facing ordinary Peruvians. These include proposals for better availability of credit, the establishment of an agricultural bank, agrarian reform, a social security system, the building of infrastructure to combat hunger in the interior, better labor legislation, the elimination of unemployment, and the establishment of a ministry of Work and Indigenous Questions (ibid., 20, 23–24, 27–32, 35–36). The program also promises that all could become property owners (ibid., 28–29, 31). Finally, echoing Sánchez Cerro's corporatist vision of society and paternalist approach to the maintenance of social order, the document argues for the development of corporate labor union associations that would guarantee "just relations between capital and workers, creating between them the harmony necessary for national progress," and eliminating the need for purposeless strikes and protests (ibid., 30).

APRA did not release its political program on the day of its rally, as Sánchez Cerro had, but rather waited until late September. Since at least December 1930, the party leadership had been urging Haya to release its official platform, arguing that APRA would never be able to generate adequate public support until he did so. Haya de la Torre had long before published APRA's *general* political agenda, known as its Programa Máximo. As APRA was initially conceived as an international party, this Programa Máximo contained the party agenda for Latin America as a region. But how this abstract, international agenda would translate into concrete proposals for Peru remained, until relatively late in the campaign, a source of speculation, excitement, and concern.

But APRA's Programa Mínimo was, in the end, much more schematic than Sánchez Cerro's Programa de Gobierno. With little sustained social or political analysis, the document was more a laundry-list style program that enumerated all of the things that APRA would do to modernize the country and satisfy the needs of nearly all constituents (apart from the oligarchy) once the party attained power. Main themes included the modernization of the economy, the restructuring of public administration to eliminate patrimonialism and nepotism, land and labor reforms, and the development of laws to protect the indigenous population (APRA [1931] 1984, 14, 18–19, 21–24)—all proposals that reflect a general interest in the social and economic betterment of ordinary citizens. But topics in the platform ran the gamut, from international relations, to state structure, to education, to public works, to relations with the military. But while reflecting the populist principles that Haya de la Torre had developed in his writings over the recent years, the document itself is not particularly compelling rhetorically.

Much more important for the Aprista campaign was Haya de la Torre's speech at the Plaza de Acho the day after Sánchez Cerro's on the Plaza San Martín. Haya de la Torre's speeches tended to be much more elaborate and ideological than those of Sánchez Cerro, and it was in this speech that Haya developed the social and political framework against which the APRA program should be read. The speech also introduced important political and social questions that received little or no analysis in the printed program itself.

In his speech, Haya portrayed himself as a knowledgeable leader, but also as a humble man in touch with the difficulties faced by ordinary Peruvians. Drawing on his extensive ideological apparatus, Haya sketched a vision of Peruvian society that was much more specific than that of Sánchez Cerro. The indigenous peasantry, in its current state of development, was incapable of ruling itself; the proletariat remained incipient, because Peru's industrialism was incipient; the middle class (consisting of small proprietors, shopkeepers, miners) was growing, and perhaps the majority class (Haya de la Torre [1931] 1984, 62–64). But the indigenous people should be incorporated into the nation (ibid., 71) and the worker should be elevated. All three classes have historically been excluded from the government, which has long been controlled by the oligarchy (ibid., 58, 66). The APRA party is a united front, "formed to solve the problems of the three classes" by retaking the state from the oligarchs and returning it to the majority of the nation (ibid., 64, 66). Haya de la Torre emphasized that APRA should be the moral backbone of the country, and that Apristas should be honest, sincere, and self-sacrificing (Basadre 1999, 13:3192; Haya de la Torre [1931] 1984, 77). But he also emphasized that APRA's plan was a *national* plan, not just a party plan (Haya de la Torre [1931] 1984, 69).

The nation's key problem, quite simply, was with the country's traditional oligarchy. Haya's analysis linked the rulers with state capacity, national cohesion, and national prosperity. National prosperity requires a cohesive national body; national cohesion can only be facilitated by a capable state; a capable state must be built by competent rulers; but Peru's traditional oligarchy is made up of incompetent opportunists interested only in their own gain. It is thus the oligarchy that has so far made the good life (citing Aristotle) impossible for the ordinary Peruvian (Haya de la Torre [1931] 1984, 58). Haya grants that it was the creole landowning class that emancipated Peru from Spain, but this class, lacking its own ideology, did not consolidate a democratic-republican system (ibid., 57). Thus, "the state appears not as a representative instrument of a national entity or class, but only as the instrument of an oligarchy" (ibid., 58). The solution to this national problem—in addition to the modernizing and inequality-reducing measures outlined in the program and elaborated in the speech—was fundamentally for APRA, as representative of the united front of (indigenous) peasants, workers, and the middle class, to retake the government from the oligarchy.

Haya and Sánchez Cerro's rhetoric in the programs and speeches differed in some respects. Haya filled his speech with social and political analysis, while Sánchez Cerro kept his speeches short and saved the analysis for his printed program. APRA's printed program was relatively short on analysis, but looked much more like a built-out party platform than did Sánchez Cerro's. Sánchez Cerro's construction of the category of the national people was more vague and traditionalist, whereas Haya's was quite specific in its vision of a united front of the peasantry, workers, and the middle class. And Haya identified as the elite target the traditional landed oligarchy, while Sánchez Cerro identified it as the body of Leguiísta bureaucrats and associates. But both figures promised themselves as solutions. Sánchez Cerro promised loyalty, revolutionary credentials, order, and constructiveness. Haya promised a humble intellectual who felt for the needs of the common Peruvian. Both suggested a litany of programs designed to help ordinary working people (even if Sánchez Cerro's solutions were more cautious, Haya's more radical). And both attempted to tar the other with an antipopular brush. Haya associated Sánchez Cerro with the traditional oligarchy, Sánchez Cerro associated Haya with the Leguiístas.

But the rhetorical significance of the political programs and rally speeches did not end when the crowds dispersed. Indeed, the framings of the rhetoric and rallies after the fact were at least as important as the events themselves. Of course, each party framed its own event in a positive light—in terms of turnout, the conduct of its supporters, the enthusiasm of its spectators, the charisma of its leader, and the overall significance of the event. For example, a telling comic depicts the "game" of competing mass rallies as a soccer match, and portrays Unión Revolucionaria's claim to have bested APRA (presumably in terms of turnout) with its two major Lima rallies of the campaign (see figure 5.5). In this comic, a strong soccer player (portrayed with indigenous features) kicks two successful goals (identified as the first and second Sánchezcerrista marches) past a soft, childlike goalkeeper (labeled as the Partido Aprista Peruano [PAP]).

FIGURE 5.5. Cartoon depicting the electoral competition. Sánchez Cerro scores two goals against the Partido Aprista Peruano, with soccer balls signifying his Lima rallies of August 22 and October 4, 1931. *Source*: *La Opinión*, October 6, 1931, 1.

The two sides also used the differences in their ideological sophistication and speaking styles as grounds for attack. APRA claimed that UR lacked any kind of coherent program. Sánchez Cerro, in turn, criticized Haya de la Torre for his stodgy, professorial ways, suggesting that actions are more important than lofty ideas. In one cartoon image published in the UR party organ *La Opinión*, APRA is depicted as a sickly intellectual imp, toting the dim lanterns of its Programa Máximo and Programa Mínimo (mere words); UR is represented in the strong body of a worker, illuminating the scene by the bright torchlight of its Revolution of Arequipa (a definitive deed).[47]

Each party also prided itself on its own conduct in demonstrations and was critical of that of its opponent. At least as spun by the party leadership, Sánchezcerristas were proud of marching in a way that they argued was unpretentious and authentically Peruvian, rather than in a style imported from abroad. As UR leader Carlos Miró Quesada (1947, 157) put it, the Sánchezcerrista way of marching was "developed in the climate of traditional Peru. The columns of citizens marched under the Peruvian flag, as they had marched in the times of Salaverry, Castilla, Vivanco, Cáceres, Piérola, and Guillermo Billinghurst. They were the authentic people, with their emotions and illusions." The Unión Revolucionaria leadership contrasted this way of marching with what they argued was APRA's internationally influenced, fascist or Communist style (see Klarén 2000, 273; Stein 1980, 112, 125). Unión Revolucionaria leader Pedro Ugarteche (1969, 2:liv), for example, in describing the Aprista march of August 15, claimed that Haya de la Torre's "followers had marched through the streets of the city imitating the Italian fascists and the German Nazis, in squadrons in military formation, as if they were a civil army." Sánchezcerristas also contrasted their own "Peruvian" style of marching with APRA's flying of Aprista flags and singing of their own party hymn, the "Marseilles Aprista" (with its obvious foreign influence), rather than the national anthem. In its headline describing the Sánchezcerrista rally of August 22, *El Comercio* stated emphatically that there were no flags flown other than the Peruvian, no songs sung other than the national anthem. The APRA leaders, in contrast, prided themselves on the orderliness and discipline of their followers. This theme comes up time and again in Aprista writings. For Apristas, the discipline of their ranks demonstrated that their followers—many from the so-called "popular classes"—were not rabble, but dignified and responsible citizens (see *La Tribuna*, August 24, 1931, 3). The APRA leadership contrasted their own style with those of the Sánchezcerristas, whose demonstrations the Apristas characterized as disorganized and rowdy, its marchers as drunken and violent. Thus, the parties did differ in how they conducted themselves at public events—indeed they claimed these characterizations with pride. The disagreement was over which manner of marching was the most noble, the most authentic, and the best representation of the character and political importance of ordinary Peruvians.

47. *La Opinión*, September 10, 1931, 1.

Conclusion

By election day 1931, populist mobilization had crystalized as a coherent mode of political practice in Peru. It had been developed by Haya de la Torre and his APRA party, and by Sánchez Cerro and his Unión Revolucionaria party, through six months of intense campaigning. In the end, while the parties and their agendas may have been different, the situationally constituted leadership of both the APRA and Unión Revolucionaria parties responded to their perceptions of a problem situation in 1931 in ways that were quite similar. Each transcended routine and stitched together bits and pieces from a wide range of influences to construct a new package of political ideas and practices that can be reasonably understood as populist mobilization. Thus, through astute perception, savvy assessment, and audacious creativity these collective political actors converged in developing a new mode of political practice in 1931; and the iterative and interactional dynamics of the parties in the second half of campaigning added fuel to the fire. But this did not mean that the new practice would stick and have a legacy as an established part of the Peruvian political repertoire. That outcome is the subject of the next chapter.

6

The Routinization of Political Innovation
Resonance, Recognition, and Repetition

By election day 1931, the political parties of Haya de la Torre and Sánchez Cerro had developed a mode of political practice that had not been seen before in Peru, or even elsewhere in Latin America. They arrived at this practical modality over time through trial and error—through recognition of and adaptation to social and political opportunities and challenges, and in competitive interaction with one another—both innovating, but neither having set out with a blueprint for a new political strategy. By the end of the electoral saga, however, populist mobilization had been practiced for the first time in Peru.

But just because something new had been done did not mean that the Peruvian political repertoire was bound to incorporate it going forward. The innovation could have been ephemeral. Had the new practice failed to resonate with audiences, the repertoire would have remained unchanged. Similarly, even if the practice had resonated, if other political actors had failed to recognize this fact, it would not have made its way into the established repertoire. Finally, even if the practice had resonated and been recognized, if other political actors had lacked the willingness, means, or ability to repeat it, the old repertoire would have persisted unchanged. That is, for it to change repertoires, political innovation must become *routinized*.

Populist mobilization did become routinized in this way. First, it resonated. It was appropriate to (indeed, appealing in the face of) the social and political realities of the moment; and while representing something new, the package of ideas and practices was close *enough* to previous ones so as not to appear totally foreign to the setting. Second, its successes were recognized. The strategies and tactics were largely visible and recognizable by other (and future) political actors. In Peru, ordinary people and politicians alike responded (both positively and negatively) to populist mobilization; and the set of practices generated enough opposition that it became solidified as a threat in the minds of opponents. Third, it was repeated. The reasons why it was understood to have worked were transposable to future situations; and political actors came along who were willing and able to deploy it in these situations. It was this that led populist mobilization to become an established part of the political repertoire in Peru, changing the terrain of future political possibilities. Furthermore, the audiences who witnessed or later became aware of what happened in Peru in 1931 were not just Peruvians. Other Latin American politicians (albeit to greater and lesser degrees) also recognized the successes that this new mode of practice brought to those who first developed it. Whether they saw it as representing a new opportunity for or a new threat to themselves, they would now have to take it into account when charting their own strategic courses. This fact would play an important role in the larger (and admittedly more complicated) story of how populist mobilization was deployed in localized political struggles in other parts of Latin America.

To substantiate these claims, this chapter will first discuss how and why populist mobilization resonated in Peru in 1931. It will then explore the issues of recognition and repetition by examining the immediate and longer-term consequences of populist mobilization in Peru in the wake of the election. Finally, it will conclude by sketching some of the impacts of these outcomes beyond the Peruvian case.[1]

Why Populist Mobilization Resonated

The new mode of political practice developed by the Apristas and Sánchezcerristas over the course of the 1931 campaigns could have fallen flat with Peruvian audiences for any number of reasons, but it did not.[2] Rather, it resonated amongst the key groups whose loyalties these candidates were attempting to engage. The candidates' populist rhetoric spoke to contemporary social and political problems as ordinary Peruvians understood and were experiencing

---

1. To explore fully any of these particular issues—how ordinary Peruvians of various stripes felt about and responded to the candidates' populist mobilization projects, the consequences of the development of new practices in the 1931 election, or the linkages between the elaboration of a Latin American style of populist mobilization in Peru in 1931 and the deployment of this package of practices in other Latin American countries throughout the twentieth century—would require a book of its own. This chapter presumes only to gesture toward the importance of these issues, and to sketch out some preliminary evaluations in broad strokes.

2. Indeed, some fifty years later, a Mexican sociologist recalled that, during the 1930s, "Peru developed the most vigorous popular movement in the continent" (Alimonda 1982, 1325).

them; and it also shared some affinities with (while still diverging from) familiar political ideas that had already been circulating in Peru. At the same time, the mobilizing practices validated the political action of ordinary Peruvians in ways that felt to them both legitimate and significant.

Nothing makes this resonance clearer than the fact that those who practiced populist mobilization in Peru in 1931 enjoyed dramatically more success at the polls than those who did not. Sánchez Cerro won the election handily, with 152,149 votes (51 percent) to Haya's 106,088 votes (35 percent) (Tuesta Soldevilla 2001, 607). But what is more important for our purposes is the fact that this means that 86 percent of the votes cast in the election went to a candidate who relied heavily on populist mobilization. The nonpopulist candidates were thoroughly trounced, garnering between them just 14 percent of the vote. Clearly, populist mobilization resonated well enough to compel the vast majority of voters.

The new set of practices did not need to resonate across the board, but only with targeted groups. As discussed in chapter 3, suffrage—while it had expanded rapidly—remained quite limited. Women were excluded, as were indigenous language speakers who were not literate in Spanish. The newly enfranchised were largely working and middle class urban males. This fact also had implications for the distribution of voting across the country. Lima was by far the most important department, with 100,186 registered voters; the next three most important were Junín (34,299 voters), Cajamarca (31,957 voters), and Haya de la Torre's home department of La Libertad (32,838 voters) (República del Perú 1933, 230). That is, the populist message and mobilization only had to resonate amongst certain groups in particular areas—and especially in Lima.

Workers overwhelmingly responded to the mobilization efforts of the two nontraditional candidates. Some responded more strongly to Haya de la Torre, some to Sánchez Cerro. As Steve Stein (1980, 185) has shown, the more organized the working class group was, the more they seemed to support Haya. Most of the top labor leaders supported APRA in the election.[3] Sánchez Cerro's support came from "the more numerous urban *lumpenproletariat*" (Stein 1980, 187). But what matters for our purposes is that the practices of both of these candidates resonated generally with the urban working class.

The populist rhetoric elaborated by the two nontraditional candidates conveyed an understanding of the changing social conditions that were impacting the lives of ordinary Peruvians. Peru in 1931 was a country in transition, from being an underdeveloped, traditionalist society dominated by regional strongmen, to one that was industrializing, modernizing, urbanizing, and

---

3. For a list of unions that supported APRA, see Sabroso Montoya 1934 (122–24).

liberalizing. With this transition came opportunities, but also hardships. Rural-to-urban migration—driven by industrialization and modernization in the cities, poverty in the highlands, and infrastructural expansion—produced a growing sector of urban workers with ties to the provinces, and with hopes for a better life. And these processes, along with the expansion of the state bureaucracy under Leguía, also produced a growing sector of middle- and lower-middle-class white collar workers who had tasted modest prosperity for the first time. The Depression of 1929 hit both groups hard, just as things had seemed to be looking up. These same groups, which had been socially marginalized and politically excluded for so long, were also on the cusp of political inclusion. The populist rhetoric of the campaigns spoke to these concerns in a way that other Peruvian politicians had not, and in terms that were familiar to ordinary people and conveyed an understanding of their life circumstances.

Because the populist rhetoric of Haya de la Torre and Sánchez Cerro drew in part on preexisting currents of social thought, it did not appear entirely foreign. For an idea or practice to resonate, it does not have to be entirely familiar, mapping one hundred percent onto preexisting ideas and practices—if it did, no political innovation would ever be possible. But it does require some kind of correspondence with, or appropriateness to, the broad strokes of what is going on in a society. And it requires some kind of first-stage recognizability, or at least partial correspondence to things that are more familiar. In this way, the populist ideas developed by the two actors resonated with other preexisting ideas. The populist thought of Haya de la Torre was not itself purely socialist, or anarcho-syndicalist, or indigenist, or modernist, or Andeanist, or anti-imperialist, or nationalist. But it drew on all of these currents (and extended them further, or otherwise modified them). The result was that when Haya introduced his populist rhetoric into the Peruvian context, although it was new, it did not entirely feel that way. The same was the case with Sánchez Cerro, who expanded on nationalist tropes and addressed indigenous themes. The latter were particularly important for both candidates; even though the vast majority of the highland indigenous population was not eligible to vote in the election, the newly enfranchised urban workers had close ties to their highland roots, and so these themes mattered to them. The feeling of familiarity was helped along (indeed, made possible) by the fact that earlier movements had already elaborated the other strains of thought already mentioned, and that these movements had developed some momentum by the 1920s.

The populist mobilizing practices, likewise, had a sense of familiarity about them. The rallies took on a quasi-religious form, with their processions and elevation of the leader. This form would be very familiar to Catholic Peruvians.

The grassroots organizations had similarities to an earlier generation of political clubs (although operating by a different logic) and to the growing terrain of civic associations in Peru. Another significant continuity was in similarities that populist mobilization shared with a historical culture of patrimonialism and clientelism in Peru—what Stein (1980, 203–17) identifies as the "politics of personal dependence." As he explains:

> Elite groups for generations had used clientelistic mechanisms to hold society together through the absorption or cooptation of other power contenders, rising middle sector individuals, and even upstart peasants. But in the mass society of the 1930s patronage could no longer proceed solely on a one-to-one basis. The populist movements that replaced the single patrons involved a whole series of clientelistic relations in which lesser party officials such as the Sánchezcerrista *capituleros*, as well as the top leaders, distributed rewards to "deserving" followers. (Stein 1980, 205)

The point in all of this is *not* to say that populist mobilization was not novel—indeed it was, in all of the ways that the book has emphasized thus far. But it was a novel *combination*—of ideas, claims, argumentation, tactics, and practices—some of which had been imported from other contexts, but some of which had domestic origins. The source of the sense of familiarity was in the latter, which made it possible to assimilate the former.[4] People who had been exposed to various other movements and strains of thought could see in APRA and UR an extension of existing tendencies, and see their own particular worldviews—or at least familiar and sympathetic worldviews—represented, while either seeing any less familiar influences less clearly or, if seeing them, being open to entertaining what they represented.

One example of this is apparent in the anarcho-syndicalists' general support for the Aprista movement. The Peruvian labor movement was dominated by anarcho-syndicalism in the 1910s and 1920s; and APRA was distinctly not an anarcho-syndicalist party. Yet APRA's rhetoric and practices resonated strongly with anarcho-syndicalists in 1931. This cannot be seen more clearly than in the case of the anarcho-syndicalist labor organizer turned staunch

---

4. This task of assimilation was not without its difficulties, since APRA and UR were cautious to disassociate themselves from past political parties, even as they claimed to speak for a historic national identity. For example, when the Communist newspaper *La Noche* accused Sánchez Cerro's new government of being "clearly Civilista," the UR paper, *La Opinión*, snapped back with rhetorical acrobatics: "This is completely false. Civilismo in reality does not exist, just like the Democratic and Liberal parties don't exist. All those groups . . . were extinguished by Leguía during the first years of the dictatorship" (*La Opinión*, December 10, 1931, 5).

Aprista, Arturo Sabroso Montoya. Sabroso was an anarcho-syndicalist well before APRA came on the scene. He encountered Haya de la Torre through his early struggles in the 1920s, and found much to sympathize with in his thought and actions. Sabroso grew closer to Haya, and by 1931 was a key Aprista leader. But he did not feel that supporting APRA meant abandoning his anarcho-syndicalist roots. Indeed, he saw no contradiction. That is, while Haya was not himself an anarcho-syndicalist, for someone like Sabroso, it was perfectly reasonable to see Haya's thought and political project as an extension of those of anarcho-syndicalism. The points of familiarity provided something to hang on to, a point of entry, a reason for affiliation. It was in this way that Haya's populist ideas resonated with Sabroso's anarcho-syndicalist thought—and in this way that other domestic influences on the populist rhetoric and practices of the two outsider candidates lent these a sense of familiarity.

One group amongst whom APRA's message did *not* resonate was the military. While the party went into the 1931 election with the support of some significant elements within the armed forces, many officers came to fear that its mobilization of workers and the middle class posed a threat to the armed forces as an institution—and that its "rigid organizational framework" made this threat even more "imposing" (Masterson 1991, 46). But as suggested above, populist mobilization did not have to resonate in all quarters to be effective.

Thus, the populist mobilization—both ideas and practices—elaborated by Haya de la Torre and Sánchez Cerro, via their respective parties and supporters, resonated at a grassroots level amongst the sectors that mattered most in 1931. Other rhetoric or practices that these nontraditional candidates might have developed, had they been exposed to different sets of experiences or encountered different decision-making dynamics within their own parties, could have fallen flat—as populist mobilization itself did in some sectors. But populist mobilization proved incredibly appropriate to the context of action for which it was developed.

Particularly revealing, the strategies of populist mobilization resonated with members of the two outsider parties themselves, who made concerted efforts to expand populist rhetoric outside the electoral context and to consolidate and formalize the party infrastructures that emerged during the election cycle. The expansion of populist rhetoric past the electoral context took different forms for each party given the changes to their respective political contexts. For APRA, extending populist mobilization meant challenging the election results as fraud, while for UR, consolidating its position of populist leadership meant curtailing competing populist claims by treating them as treasonous against the true representatives of the popular will. As one UR publication put it a few weeks after the election: "The APRA party continues to incite rebellion that could have bloody consequences.... Alarmist public notices [not unlike those common during the election] constitute true crimes against public tranquility."[5] As both parties moved to translate populist rhetoric into their new political contexts, they also took deliberate steps to consolidate and formalize their organizational structures. This is particularly revealing in the case of UR, for which party formalization emerged out of its competitive struggle with the deliberately structured APRA party. In the months after the election, UR party officials took steps to discipline the Sánchezcerrista clubs by requiring the vetting of public speakers at meetings and, in November 1931, requesting that Sánchezcerrista clubs register as Unión Revolucionaria locals.[6] In a 1932 public announcement of the restructuring and formalization of the party, UR leaders justified the move in populist terms: "The ideological purpose of the PLAN OF PARTY ORGANIZATION is no other than to stimulate and support the patriotic nationalist trend... that is predominant among PERUVIANS, proven by the grand and historic civic act of October 11 of the past year."[7] APRA leaders too expressed the need to maintain and expand the party infrastructure in populist terms. As a November 4, 1931, Lima police dispatch from an APRA local meeting recounted:

> Cornejo [an Aprista leader] announced that the party local would remain open as was customary, because the party cannot die; the party is not an organism born on the eve of the elections to end after these; the party is something more, an institution that must keep progressing every day and reinforcing itself to exercise control over the government; [the party] should keep operating as before in relation to the aspirations of the sovereign people.[8]

Thus, the forces of both APRA and UR both continued to play the populist game well after the polling places had closed.

Recognition and Repetition: The Consequences of Populist Mobilization in Peru

The 1931 election was extremely conflictual. It resulted in an unprecedented level of social and political polarization, which manifested in an elite backlash and ultimately translated into a virtual civil war between the military and the defeated APRA party that would define the contours of Peru's political-institutional

---

5. *La Opinión*, November 15, 1931, 6.

6. *La Opinión*, November 28, 1931, 3.

7. "Reorganización de la Unión Revolucionaria," AGN/PL, Legajo 3.9.5.1.15.1.14.2, Folder 8, Presos Políticos y Sociales, Asuntos Políticos, 1931–1945.

8. "Doy cuenta a Ud. que anoche a horas 9 ...," AGN/PL, Legajo 3.9.5.1.15.1.16.50, Folder 10, Subprefectura de Lima, 1931.

landscape for years to come. Along the way, the success of populist mobilization was recognized—becoming a go-to strategy for some and something to oppose for others. Repeated by others, it became a recurring feature of the Peruvian political landscape. Through recognition and repetition, the mode of practice ultimately became routinized.

During the period of campaigning itself, the candidates' new way of practicing politics reinforced and reconfigured social and political cleavages, polarizing loyalties and patterns of sociability in politically incorporated regions of the country. Populist mobilization politicized the populace and infused politics with a moralistic charge. As described above, supporters were not atomized voters, but were actively involved in intimate local organizations. The act of organizing and participating in face-to-face organizational life builds social connections and identities with candidates and among co-participants alike. Participating on a regular basis in mundane organizational activities—like painting placards, meeting to vote on club policies, and so on—in the service of a morally charged purpose can itself play a key role in building deep solidarities. But with solidarities come antagonisms, in this case fueled by the rhetorical battles that the parties waged with one another. For Apristas and Sánchezcerristas alike, political participation—and political opposition—became a regular part of daily life. Because the localized political organizations often mapped onto existing identities and groups, many neighborhoods and factories became clearly identified with one party or the other—leaving residents or workers at these locations who identified with the wrong side to fear for their personal safety. This dynamic naturally spilled over into the contentious demonstrations that each side made so central to their campaigning. Political rallies often drew violent attacks from opponents, occasionally even involving the discharge of firearms.[9] Overall, popular participation, in grassroots political organizations and in enacting contentious rallies, had a politicizing and ultimately polarizing effect on many parts of Peruvian society.

The months following the election remained incredibly contentious. The conflict between APRA and Unión Revolucionaria continued, and even intensified, as APRA refused to concede defeat and its members became increasingly implicated in violent behavior—culminating in a major insurrection in July 1932 in the city of Trujillo. And the election spurred an immediate, elite-supported

9. The antagonism between the opposing parties manifested itself in sometimes violent confrontations. Newspapers of the time were filled with dispatches written by local party members accusing adherents of the opposing party of violence and hostility. The examples are numerous, but see *La Opinión*, September 30, 1931, 8 ["Be on Alert, Peruvian Mothers!"]; *La Opinión*, October 3, 1931, 3 ["At Gunpoint, Aprista and Police Officers Assaulted a Sánchezcerrista Rally"]. See also Giesecke (1978, 81), *La Tribuna*, September 1, 1931, 8, and *La Tribuna*, September 28, 1931, 3.

military backlash against APRA, as the opposition of elites to the practices of both candidates grew. One historian has referred to the conflicts that emerged after the election as a "virtual civil war"—even as "the bitterest social discord in [the country's] history" (Pike 1967, 250).

After the election, the defeated APRA party alleged fraud.[10] It then began a campaign of open opposition to the Sánchez Cerro regime, which the newly elected president reciprocated.[11] In early December, Haya de la Torre gave a speech in the Aprista stronghold of Trujillo calling for continued struggle; at the same time, in an effort to block Sánchez Cerro's inauguration, APRA staged a series of small-scale uprisings (Giesecke 1992; Pike 1967, 262). Competing counts estimate that between seven to eleven disruptions or "insurrections" led by APRA members took place in early December 1931 (Giesecke 2010, 234–35). Notably, these failed insurrections show how, outside of the constrained and uniquely competitive context of the election, elements of populist mobilization became intertwined with the insurrectionary tactics of the past. Many of the small-scale insurrections used party infrastructure and populist rhetoric to mobilize participants who felt the "popular will" had been cheated by electoral fraud. As Margarita Giesecke (2010, 209–10) explains: "In all the insurrections, the militant groups marched through the streets toward their target—telegraph offices, municipal headquarters, police stations, etc.—hurling slogans that expressed their intentions and loyalties. . . . In all instances they shouted 'Viva APRA!' and 'Death to el Mocho [Sánchez Cerro's nickname].'" On seizing their targets, some only for a few hours, the insurrectionaries borrowed again from old repertoires by delivering and distributing revolutionary manifestos, not unlike Sánchez Cerro's widely distributed Manifesto of Arequipa. Blending the populist rhetoric that emerged over the

---

10. Claims of electoral corruption were widespread after the election. APRA alleged fraud in at least three cities: Cajamarca, Yangas, and Huaytara (*La Opinión*, October 19, 1931, 2; *La Opinión*, October 21, 1931, 4). Ultimately, only one of these would be deemed a legitimate case of fraud (*La Opinión*, November 23, 1931, 2).

11. APRA continued to organize marches and allegedly incited violence against the newly elected government. The consequence of this mutual hostility was widespread paranoia. After a six-hour blackout in Lima on the night of December 6, UR's *La Opinión* quickly interpreted the event as a botched revolutionary plot: "an incessant revolutionary propaganda has spread through the assemblies of local APRA clubs and at the frequent gatherings outside the capital, [and] groups had been organized to strike at the proper moment [the blackout]" (*La Opinión*, December 6, 1931, 4–5). There is ongoing debate as to which oppositional Aprista actions were officially sanctioned and which represented the independent actions of rogue elements. But to the extent that some of these actions were not initiated or endorsed by the party, this only reinforces the claim that the 1931 election produced deep antagonisms that extended beyond the bounds of the party apparatus.

course of the election with old political practices, one manifesto delivered during a failed Aprista insurrection in Cerro de Pasco explained:

> Public opinion has been cheated despite APRA's victory, in the secret ballot, by the scandalous inflation of voter registrations and duplicate ballots, the absolute partiality of the Electoral Board, and the indifference demonstrated by the National Junta.... All the towns of Peru, its armed forces: the marines, police, military and air force, conscious of their historic responsibility, have risen from this imposition to save the nation once and for all from the nefarious actions of *civilismo*.... The APRA party ... calls all its affiliates and the conscious people of Cerro de Pasco, which cannot forget its past suffering, to sacrifice what is necessary, to fulfill their duty to defend the Peruvian flag. (Giesecke 2010, 212)

And the conflict would only continue from there.

Later in December, police invaded the APRA party headquarters in Trujillo, wounding several party members (Masterson 1991, 48). In January and February, Sánchez Cerro established martial law and arrested and exiled all twenty-three newly elected Aprista members of the constituent assembly (ibid.). In March, an Aprista wounded Sánchez Cerro in a botched assassination attempt (Masterson 1991, 48; Pike 1967, 264–65). In May, Haya de la Torre was arrested, Aprista naval officers staged a mutiny and were promptly executed, and preparations began for the Aprista rebellion in the northern coastal town of Trujillo (Masterson 1991, 48–49; Scheina 1987, 107–16). The events of July 1932 cemented the antagonism between APRA and the army. On July 7, the party staged a rebellion and successfully held Trujillo for two days. When the army finally regained control, it discovered that the Apristas had executed thirty-five military prisoners. It retaliated by massacring hundreds of Aprista men and boys at the pre-Incan ruins of Chan Chan, just outside of town.[12] Nine months later, another Aprista revolt broke out in which an APRA-allied army officer led his three-hundred-man Cajamarca regiment in revolt (Masterson 1991, 52). Finally, a month later, Sánchez Cerro was assassinated by a seventeen-year-old Aprista—who was promptly killed by the crowd. At that point, APRA was definitively driven underground.

The dynamics that developed in the wake of the election contributed to populist mobilization becoming established in the Peruvian political repertoire. Its strategic potential could not be ignored once demonstrated. The mode of practice crystalized at this time in the minds of opponents as something to

---

12. The best historical study of this episode—indeed, the only one, apart from a few clearly partisan accounts—is Giesecke 2010.

oppose. At the same time, its demonstrated success solidified commitment to the approach amongst those who had practiced it. The very fact that populist mobilization quickly became so polarizing is itself evidence that it had been recognized as a potentially useful go-to strategy by at least some political actors. The result was that, by the end of this conflictual period, it was clearly recognized—both as having been successful and as something that others might attempt. Thus, the election provided models of populist rhetoric and practice, while establishing the viability of populist strategies in a way that later politicians would be unable to ignore.

This was a game changer for Peruvian politicians. Thenceforth, the majority of successful democratic candidates (and even some military dictators) would at least toy with the strategy at one time or another (Stein 1999; Stepan 1978). And those conservative politicians who remained opposed to populist mobilization—of whom there were still many—would increasingly have to rely on military rather than democratic means for securing power (Masterson 1991). Indeed, the history of Peruvian politics from 1931 until at least the early 1980s can be characterized as a series of back and forth alternations between projects of populist mobilization and reactive responses (Collier and Collier 1991; Klarén 2000, 255–76; Villanueva Valencia 1972, 1975). And the democratic opening of the 1980s unleashed yet another wave of populist mobilization that has continued off and on into the present. Populist mobilization became a recurring strategy in Peru, and opposition to it a regular response. In the end, as populist mobilization became routinized, it became an established part of the Peruvian political repertoire.

Conclusion

Populist mobilization became routinized in Peru in the wake of the 1931 election, revolutionizing that country's political repertoire. The new mode of practice represented a distinct departure from previous ways of doing politics in the country up until that point. Still, novel as it was, it resonated with the most important audiences, was broadly recognized as having been successful, and was repeated over the years in various contexts by quite different political actors. 1931 thus marked a critical turning point in Peruvian political history.

But the election also marked a critical turning point in the political history of Latin America as a region. The Peruvian case would be the first in what has come to be known as the "classic" era of Latin American populism, in the middle years of the twentieth century. By the definition used in this book, seven other Latin American countries experienced at least one sustained episode of populist mobilization before 1955.[13] The highest profile of these episodes are certainly those spearheaded by Lázaro Cárdenas in Mexico, Juan Domingo Perón in Argentina, and Getúlio Vargas in Brazil. But populist mobilization also made an appearance in Bolivia, Colombia, Ecuador, and Venezuela during this period. The Peruvian case was thus the first of many, as the practice became routinized throughout the region, just as it had been routinized in Peru.

Populist mobilization was certainly not endemic. Notably, it did not appear in Chile, Uruguay, or Paraguay during the classic period. Nor was it chronic: even in countries that experienced populist mobilization, it remained episodic (as it was in Peru). The success of the Cuban revolution in 1959 introduced yet another new strategy into the repertoire for those on the left side of the political spectrum—the *foco* model of guerilla warfare—that was itself appealing in its own ways to the socially and politically excluded who desired change (Wickham-Crowley 1992). One consequence of the introduction of this Cuban model was increased state repression and the rise of authoritarian regimes, which at the same time foreclosed avenues for the practice of populist mobilization. But as Latin American countries redemocratized in the 1980s, in an era in which socialist revolution had become increasingly discredited, populist mobilization again became a widely practiced option—initiating a wave of neo-populism throughout the region. After 1931, populist mobilization was a regular—if certainly not constant—occurrence throughout Latin America.

Thus, the consequences of the development of populist mobilization in Peru in 1931 rippled throughout Latin America. Once the mode of practice had crystalized and been demonstrably successful in the Peruvian context, it appeared on the radars of and so became available to other Latin American politicians facing comparable conditions. Later actors in other Latin American countries, aware of what had happened in Peru, could now pick up this package of practices and modify it, here and there, in minor ways to fit similar (but not entirely the same) circumstances. And even those who would not themselves undertake populist mobilization now had to consider the very real possibility that others might. As historian James Malloy (1977, 7) observed, "In one manner or another, all political forces from left to right have been forced to structure their behavior in response to the populist challenge." In this way, populist mobilization became a part of the region's political culture.

All of this said, a simple diffusion argument—as appealing as it might be—is unlikely to prove adequate, at least on its own, for explaining the spread

---

13. Not including cases in Central America, the Caribbean, and the Guianas.

of populist mobilization across the region in the second half of the twentieth century. It would be going too far to suggest that the development of populist mobilization in Peru was the principal cause of its later development in other Latin American countries. And it would certainly be going too far to suggest that populist mobilization would not have emerged elsewhere in Latin America during the 1940s and 1950s—let alone in the 1990s and 2000s—if it had not first emerged in Peru in 1931. I am not claiming that all future Latin American politicians were equally familiar with the events that took place in Peru in 1931, nor am I discounting the possibility that some might have been entirely unaware. Not only would it be foolhardy to make such strong claims, but it would be counter to this book's central argument about how to explain political action. This book has argued that as political actors with different reservoirs of experience encounter problem situations in concrete contexts of action, they craft lines of action in response to those situations—sometimes more out of habit, sometimes more creatively, depending on their perceptions and understandings. In most cases, political action tends to be fairly routine, drawing on established repertoires; and when it is not, it cannot be explained by reading action off of structural conditions, identities, or ideologies in any straightforward way. This applies as much to later populist cases as it does to Peru in 1931. It would be anathema to such a situated-actor-based approach to explain political action in the other Latin American cases by the blunt force of exogenous imposition. Thus, the mode of analysis demonstrated here complicates any simplistic application of diffusion models to explain the emergence of populist mobilization in other Latin American cases.

Such an undertaking would require conducting analyses similar to the one demonstrated here. The key difference would be that, for the later cases, and for at least some of the later actors, populist mobilization would have already been a part of the existing repertoire. So the question would no longer be one of political innovation, but of how political actors in a given situation choose from one set of tools in the toolkit over others. That is, it would be a question of strategy *selection*. It is likely that, in examining how this played out, the precedent of Peru would at least be a part of the contextual experience shaping the actors' deliberations. And so the Peruvian case is critical, but in this specific way. Still, it remains reasonable to suggest that explanations of the later cases, or of the importance of populist mobilization in the region more generally, must take the prior existence of the Peruvian case into serious consideration—something that has rarely been done thus far.

CONCLUSION

Peru's 1931 presidential election was a critical turning point in that country's political history. Prior to this event, the repertoire of go-to political practices included political militarism (including *caudillo* politics, coup d'état, and authoritarian rule), the activation of clientelistic obligations, formal and informal strategies of disenfranchisement, electoral corruption, and the brokering of deals amongst political elites. While the country had seen brief episodes of bottom-up insurrection, as well as limited experiments in top-down popul*ar* mobilization (based largely on clientelism rather than a valorization of "the people" as such), nothing like populist mobilization had been practiced on a national scale to seek elected office. After this event, populist mobilization became a tried-and-true practical modality that would be repeated time and again by those aspiring to secure or maintain political power and legitimacy. Explaining this shift has been the principal aim of this book. Ultimately, I have argued that populist mobilization entered into the Peruvian political repertoire in 1931 because organized outsider political actors—constituted as such and contingently empowered by the changing dynamics of the political field—recognized the limitations of routine political practice and had the socially and experientially conditioned understanding, vision, and capacities to modify, transpose, invent, and recombine practices that matched up with the changing social and political context of action. The product of this situated political innovation was a distinctly Latin American style of populist mobilization—a mode of practice that became increasingly routinized after the fact.

While the rise of populist mobilization in Peru was decidedly not an automatic byproduct of social-structural or political conditions, the social and political contexts of action impinged on the innovative moment in critical ways. As shown in chapter 2, changing social conditions (economic development

CONCLUSION 205

and depression, the expansion of transportation and communication infrastructures, internal migration and urbanization, the disruption of traditional social relationships, working class formation, and the rise of new forms of civic association) produced new grievances, made new groups of potential supporters both politically available and logistically reachable, and laid the social groundwork for political organization and mobilization. This created new possibilities for political action, especially to outsider political actors who were disposed by necessity to seek out and recognize the novel opportunities afforded by these changes. At the same time, as shown in chapter 3, four distinct periods of reconfiguration of the political field resulted in the crystallization of at least semi-organized collectivities around the charismatic figures of Víctor Raúl Haya de la Torre and Luis M. Sánchez Cerro. While occupying outsider positions, the forces of Aprismo and Sánchezcerrismo were also contingently empowered to act in innovative and potentially efficacious ways coming into 1931 (by their enjoyment of broad popular support, their exposure to practices from outside the traditional Peruvian repertoire, and the political opportunities afforded by the changing field—most notably, Leguía's disempowering of the traditional political elite and the professionalized military's positive stance toward democratization).

Still, while they played critical roles in shaping and channeling the possibilities for political innovation, these social and political realities did not render it inevitable, nor did they determine what the new mode of practice would look like. Rather, as shown in chapter 4, populist mobilization only emerged when the forces of Haya de la Torre and Sánchez Cerro confronted and recognized a crisis in the applicability of routine practice to the changing social and political context of action. That they would do so was not a foregone conclusion. Other political actors facing the same situation—on the right, the fragmented remnants of the elite parties, and on the left, the doctrinaire leadership of the Partido Comunista Peruano—either failed to recognize it as problematic (in the pragmatist sense) or, in the cases of those who did recognize it as such, were unable to envision any acceptable alternative response to it. But the nontraditional political experiences of the Aprista and Sánchezcerrista leadership, which were a contingent result of their earlier political marginalization and particular paths to prominence, enabled them to develop savvy understandings of how changing conditions were unsettling their political routines, and then to cobble together novel packages of practices that were appropriate to the new context of action. As the two candidates began to enjoy increasing success from their early experiments in populist mobilization, their relational focus shifted from the adversaries who had most preoccupied them previously (for Haya, the Communists; for Sánchez

Cerro, the rightist elites and military junta) to one another. As shown in chapter 5, a competitive dynamic developed between the forces of APRA and Unión Revolucionaria, in which continued experimentation, imitation, and one-upmanship pushed them to amplify their practices right up to election day. It was through these processes that strikingly different political actors ended up converging to elaborate what can now be recognized as populist mobilization in Peru in 1931.

While Sánchez Cerro won the election by a significant margin, what mattered most for the history of political practice in Peru was that populist mobilization had produced impressive results for both candidates. As discussed in chapter 6, the practice resonated with popular audiences and decidedly trumped the practical approaches of all others who had tried to take advantage of the political moment. This fact was recognized by Haya de la Torre and Sánchez Cerro, but also by later Peruvian politicians, who would go on to repeat the practice in new situations. Populist mobilization became routinized—not in the sense that it became chronic, but in the sense that it became something that *could* reasonably be done, and done successfully. Through this process, the Peruvian political repertoire was revolutionized.

Distillation of a Pragmatist Approach to Repertoire Change

In the introductory chapter, I sketched out the intellectual scaffolding for a pragmatist approach to repertoire change based on the concept of *situated political innovation*. Now, at the conclusion of what has been an extended exercise in theoretically informed historical explanation, it is worth taking a moment to distill the lessons learned more schematically. I have suggested that it is useful to understand repertoire change in a particular way: as a product of the elaboration and routinization of a new mode of political practice. This understanding of the outcome suggests certain imperatives for the explanatory framework. It must be able to account for the elaboration of a new practice, for why that practice looked as it did and not otherwise, and for why that practice became routinized. In what follows, I will address each of these points in turn, doing my best to specify clearly what I take to be the abstract steps of my theoretical argument.

First, how to account for the elaboration of a new political practice? Clearly creativity is involved—but not the sort of romantic and highly individualized genius that is so often attributed to the artistic, scientific, and technological savants of the world (cf. Becker 1982; De Nora 1997; Lamont 1987). Creativity is a universal human endowment, even if habit is a common human response to situations (Joas 1996). The question is not *who* is exceptionally creative, but rather *what prompts social actors to respond in creative rather than habitual ways to particular situations?* The pragmatist approach outlined in the introductory chapter suggests that political innovation happens when habitual responses to a given situation fail to yield adequate results for political actors, producing a problem situation. But this must be unpacked and extended a bit.

It is not enough for a habitual response to fail. If it is to trigger a shift to creative action, this failure must be recognized as such, and its reasons must be attributed to the inadequacy of the habitual response to the situation. That is, the failure and its reasons must be recognized and understood. At the same time, it is not always necessary for things to come to the point of *actual* failure. Because human action is often undertaken with a view to the future, in anticipation of possible outcomes, a shift from habit to creativity can also be occasioned by a *projection* that routine action is likely to fail in the face of a given situation. Of critical note here is that the emergence of a habit-disrupting problem situation requires recognition, understanding, and future projection, all of which are conditioned not by an individual's cognitive capacities alone, but also by his or her socially shaped experiences and experiential learning; and this is all the more the case when the actor in question is a collective one, in which pooled experiences are brought to bear in processes of deliberation.

Once a problem situation has emerged for a collective political actor, novel ways of responding to it must be discovered through creative understanding, projection, and experimentation. This can involve modifying routine practices, transposing practices from other times and places (from sometimes more, sometimes less, analogous situations), transposing practices from nonpolitical domains, or inventing new practices out of whole cloth. Unless an entire strategic package is imported wholesale from another context (in which case, we would no longer be speaking of innovation per se), the modified, transposed, or invented practices must be recombined in a way that gives at least the impression of internal consistency and is appropriate to the situation at hand. All of this emerges through a self-corrective process of trial and error over time and requires creativity, flexibility, and a savvy understanding of the practice-situation relationship. Again, it is not special cognitive abilities or inexplicable genius that enable successful creativity of this kind, but experience, exposure, knowledge, and discernment that are products of the social trajectories and relational positionings of those making the strategic decisions.

But it is not enough to come up with alternatives in the face of a habit-disrupting situation. For a new political practice to emerge, it must be executed. This requires both autonomy of action and the resources to act.

Internal and external constraints—such as strategic disagreements amongst party leaders, subservience to external organizations, problems of coordination with allies in the political field, and legal rules or procedures—can undermine a political collectivity's autonomy of action. At the same time, a lack of social, organizational, and material resources can impede that collectivity's ability to carry out the line of action that it envisions. Only with the autonomy and resources to act can a collective political actor elaborate a new mode of practice through creative experimentation in response to a habit-disrupting problem situation.

The second imperative of the explanatory framework is that it be able to account for why the new political practice looked as it did. It is important to be clear that the characteristics of a new practice are not *dictated* by the nature of the problem situation (let alone by more general social or political conditions), as different actors might come up with any number of creative readings of and responses to a set of disruptions and opportunities. To explain why a new practice looked as it did, it is necessary to trace the social sources of experiential influence conditioning how specific political actors made sense of the context of action and generated a set of practical alternatives to match it. In the case of a collective actor, this means tracing the personal trajectories, worldviews, and social locations of all individuals who were in a position to impact the group's strategic decision making, as well as understanding the deliberative dynamics of the group and how these shaped its choices about what lines of action to pursue. Ultimately, what we must investigate if we are to explain the characteristics of a new practice is how the combined stock of social experience of a body of individuals shaped their understanding of the social and political realities of the situation, their conception of the set of possible new actions on which they might draw or which they might modify to fit that situation, their assessment of the reasons for the success or failure of their own actions (past and present), their readings of how their opponents were acting or were likely to act, and their future projections of the likely outcomes of various possible lines of action, given the nature of the situation.

Third, what does it take for a new political practice to become routinized? New practices are often—perhaps even typically—ephemeral. If political innovation is spurred by desperation in the face of a problematic situation, and shaped by desperate searching for *un*tried yet hopefully still true solutions in the face of it, it only stands to reason that its product would often be inadequate or otherwise unappealing to others. For a political practice to become routinized, it must match up with the situation in a way that produces results (even if not unqualified success). It must resonate, at least to some extent, with the intended audience. This resonance must then be recognized by others and understood as a mark of promise—as an indication that the practice might yield favorable results in future analogous scenarios. Finally, the practice must be repeated. As it is reapplied to new situations by the original or other actors, it develops a track record and becomes increasingly familiar, thinkable, doable. If this happens, the practice can be said to have entered into the political repertoire, and the repertoire can be said to have changed.

These are the nuts and bolts of my explanatory approach, but it is also critical to consider how the broader social and political environment impinges on these processes. Here, my thoughts have been particularly shaped by my engagement with the events of the Peruvian election, which is a specific type of case in a number of respects (an instance of rapid repertoire change, rippling out from a centralized rather than diffuse point of origin, in the unsettled times of a poorly institutionalized context), and so must be taken as provisional. What I am most confident in suggesting is simply *that* any study of repertoire change undertaken from a pragmatist perspective must come up with systematic ways to take broader social and political realities seriously, or risk placing too much explanatory weight on the backs of a few individuals.

I suggest that social and political conditions matter for political innovation not because of what they compel (very little), but for what they make possible. Social realities can enable certain practical options and foreclose others. For the question of innovation, changes in these conditions—especially rapid ones, even if they remain small in absolute terms—can be particularly consequential, as political actors seeking responses to problem situations may recognize and latch onto them. Such changes do not force innovation, but they afford opportunities to those seeking them. Similarly, political realities matter for how they empower, disempower, and position actors vis-à-vis one another in the field of political contention, as well as for how they establish the potential applicability of various political tools to a situation. While not automatically producing an innovative response, let alone determining the nature of that response, political realities can set the stage for situated political innovation. In these ways—and likely many others—the social and political contexts of action impinge, even if indirectly, on the innovative moment.

Finally, if there is any concrete, explanatory lynchpin to all of this, it is the importance that I have discovered, through engagement with the Peruvian case, of the status of being a *contingently empowered outsider*. Those at the margins of the political field are more likely to perceive the shortcomings of routine practice, to feel themselves compelled to take strategic risks, and thus to seek out and identify opportunities in the social and political context that more central actors have not yet recognized or accepted as necessary. Such outsiders are also more likely to have experience with nontraditional political practices, through exposure to and engagement with politics outside the boundaries of what more central political actors routinely encounter in the course of conducting their more traditional political business. And they are more likely to enjoy a measure of autonomy in their strategic choices, as they are less beholden to powerful interests, affiliates, and allies. Rarely are such outsiders in a position to act—or at least to act successfully. But at moments when contingencies in the dynamics of the political field elevate marginal political actors to positions from which they might feasibly make a go of it, they are particularly well situated to act in innovative ways. If they are successful, such contingently empowered outsiders can be the engines of rapid repertoire change.

Implications of the Approach

This approach to repertoire change, derived largely from pragmatist theories of action and foregrounding processes of situated political innovation, differs from the prevailing macro-historical approach, pioneered by Charles Tilly and advanced by others, in at least three respects. The first of these has to do with the pace of repertoire change. In his work on the development of modern protest repertoires in France and Great Britain, Tilly (1986, 1995, 2006, 2008) was engaged in explaining repertoire change that transpired gradually, over the course of decades. But as the Peruvian case illustrates, while repertoires may often change gradually, they can also be transformed through dramatic moments of radical innovation. Sidney Tarrow (1995) recognized this fact nearly two decades ago and suggested the need for more careful qualitative studies of such moments, but his call fell largely on deaf ears. I have attempted to answer Tarrow's call not only by focusing on a case of rapid change, but also by offering an approach that might be useful in explaining similar cases. Second, studies of gradual repertoire change have also typically, because of the nature of their cases, been focused on change that unfolds in a relatively diffuse way—that is produced by multiple actors responding independently to similarly structured situations. But repertoire change can also ripple out from a more socially centralized point of origin. In Peru, it was instigated by relatively small groups of political leaders responding to one another on the national stage. While similar processes of creative recognition and adaptation are no doubt involved either way, variation in the focal breadth of the overall change process arguably impinges on these in critical respects. Third, a focus on gradual and diffuse repertoire change predisposes the researcher to search for slow-moving and macro-level explanations, which inevitably shifts the lens away from localized and eventful interactions and processes toward broader structural factors. The approach advanced here suggests that it is necessary to attend to the situational processes by which structural conditions translate into action, as such conditions are not in themselves sufficient for producing new political practices. Rather, new practices are the result of constrained yet innovative action undertaken at moments when the reproduction of old practices no longer suffices for the situation at hand.

More generally, by showing that the rise of populist mobilization in Peru was neither the automatic result of changing social or political conditions, nor a natural outgrowth of the ideological orientations, institutional affiliations, or social origins of those who first practiced it, this study challenges approaches in political sociology whose implicit or explicit theories of action have assumed otherwise. I have made the case that political practice is neither wholly determined by structural conditions nor idiosyncratically contingent. While at least relatively autonomous from structural conditions, it remains patterned in distinct ways and so requires explanation on its own terms. Through zeroing in on how political actors work through their strategic options in relationally and processually unfolding situations, it becomes clear that social and cultural experiences condition their understandings of these situations, shape their habits and routines, color their senses of the strategic options, and provide materials for creative action that can have truly significant consequences. In this way, this book can be understood as specifying one mechanism by which culture channels political processes and outcomes—thus playing a critical role in the balancing act between political stability and change (see Sewell 2005, 318–72). At the same time, it suggests the importance of attending to how socially patterned but still autonomous social action in eventful situations can play a critical role in producing macro-historical outcomes (ibid., 1996).

This argument resonates with recent work in comparative-historical sociology and the study of contentious politics that recommends increased attention be paid to event sequences (Abbott 1983), path dependence (Mahoney 2000), turning points and critical junctures (Abbott 1997, Collier and Collier 1991, Mahoney 2001), and the temporality of historical processes generally (Pierson 2003). In particular, it joins with others who have emphasized the need to understand the internal dynamics of critical situations or events when endeavoring to explain (at least some types of) macro-historical stability and change (Abbott 2001; Ermakoff 2008 and 2015; Gould 1995; Kurzman 2004; Sewell 2005; Wagner-Pacifici 2010). Such an emphasis should not be interpreted as a blanket call to shift the focus entirely from macro-historical to micro-historical sociology, but rather as a reminder that each must inform the other through the careful and systematic integration (indeed, even analytical dissolution) of these levels of analysis. This enterprise requires, among other things, a careful consideration of our views about social action.

My own response to this imperative has been to develop a pragmatist approach to situated political innovation that I believe provides a critical set of tools for understanding the internal dynamics of eventful moments of political change. One of my broader goals in so doing has been to demonstrate the utility of pragmatist theories of action for historical research on politics. As a few have recently argued, such theories hold great promise for comparative-historical sociology (Biernacki 2005; Gross 2010; Schneiderhan 2011), but this potential has yet to be fully realized. Most likely, this is because pragmatism is often assumed to deny the power, even the relevance, of those structural conditions that the subfield has long regarded as critical to historical explanation. But this book stands as evidence that embracing a pragmatist perspective does not have to mean giving short shrift to the broader social and political realities that shape specific contexts of action. In transposing pragmatist theories for use in explaining macro-historical outcomes, however, some creative adaptation is required. We must think seriously about how to understand the relationship between broader social and political conditions and more localized contexts of action, about how to move from the level of the individual to that of organized collective actors, and about how access to resources and the characteristics of the institutional environment impinge on interactions between collective actors differently than they do on interactions between individuals. I have been wrestling with these questions over the course of writing this book, and my answers remain provisional at best; yet I remain optimistic that pragmatism has much to offer to scholars of historical change and contentious politics. In particular, given its emphases on habit and human creativity, it seems to me uniquely poised to enhance our explanations of political stability and change.

Whither Populism Studies?

I have thus far avoided explicit discussion of "populism" per se. This choice may have disappointed some who would have liked me to have engaged more explicitly with the perennially vexing "problem of populism." But there are only so many directions a book can take without distracting from its main argument. Still, the apparent resurgence of populism (however defined) on the world stage compels me to close this book with a few more general comments. In Latin America, it has been patently clear for more than two decades now that populism is not a relic of an earlier developmental stage, but rather an important and persistent feature of the political landscape (see de la Torre and Arnson 2013). With some Latin American neo-populists advancing neoliberal agendas (Weyland 1996), and others being associated with the region's political "left turn" (Cameron and Hershberg 2010), populism shows no signs of fading away in the region. At the same time, the term "populist" has been increasingly used to describe right wing politicians in Western Europe—such as France's Jean-Marie Le Pen and Italy's Silvio Berlusconi—as well as a range of xenophobic political movements in Eastern Europe and the former Soviet republics (Berezin 2004; Betz 1994; Held 1996; Jagers and Walgrave 2007; Rydgren 2006; Taggart 2004; Učeň 2007; Weyland 1999). It is even coming back into use in descriptions of U.S. politicians, from various "Tea Party" candidates to Bernie Sanders to Donald Trump. While recent political developments in Latin America and elsewhere should not be assumed to be similar simply because the same term has been applied to them, the times clearly call for a reinvigoration of comparative populism studies.

I have made the case for the advantages of approaching populism from the perspective of practice, under the rubric of populist mobilization, and think that doing so has a few advantages. It sidesteps persistent debates about whether populism *is* fascist or socialist, reactionary or progressive, authoritarian or democratic, militarist or civilian, urban or rural, and so on, by recognizing that politicians of various stripes can employ populist mobilization in the pursuit of a wide range of social, political, and economic agendas. It also opens up a new set of research questions. This book has focused on explaining the rise of populist mobilization in a specific context. But once the practice has been assimilated into a given political repertoire, what explains why some politicians take it up at certain points in time while others do not—especially if the practice is not necessarily tied to any particular ideological stance or policy agenda? How does it get implemented in various concrete settings, how is it organized, and what are the consequences of different ways of practicing it? Finally, what are the social and political consequences (intended and unintended) of populist mobilization *as* a practice? Might it, for example, lead to outcomes like social polarization or institutional destabilization that are independent of—and possibly unrelated to—whether the practice is driven by leftist or rightist agendas?

But rather than making the case that scholars should stop talking about "populism" and start talking about "populist mobilization" (I have presented a limited version of this argument elsewhere, see Jansen 2011), I would plead humbly for more conceptual precision especially in empirical case studies and comparative research—regardless of the definition on which one ultimately settles. Populism stands alongside nationalism and fascism as notoriously difficult to conceptualize.[1] As Ernesto Laclau (1977, 143) explained long ago, "few [terms] have been defined with less precision. . . . We know intuitively to what we are referring when we call a movement or an ideology populist, but we have the greatest difficulty in translating the intuition into concepts." This problem remains a thorn in the side of the literature. Populism is often identified, at the most basic level, as a regime or movement in which leaders claim some affinity with "the people" (Knight 1998, 226). Indeed, this is the journalistic sense of the word. But as this definition might apply to virtually any modern regime—ever since the idea that legitimacy ascends from "the people" superseded the notion that it descends by divine or natural right (Calhoun 1997, 70)—it is hardly a sufficient conceptual foundation. The term has been used to describe a wide array of historical phenomena, from Maoism to fascism to Peronism. It has been used to describe movements, regimes, leaders, ideologies, policies, and state structures. Most historical case studies use the concept as little more than a generic label. Worse still, in such studies, most cases end up being treated as exceptional—a rhetorical move that, in stressing the uniqueness of individual populist experiences, creates the false impression of their incomparability. This inhibits both systematic attempts at comparison (of which we are in dire need) and the development of cumulative theoretical knowledge more generally. If we cannot agree on a definition, let us at least be clear about what we are explaining before we explain it.

Perhaps such clarity would help bring political sociologists back around to studying the phenomenon. While some of the most prominent early populism scholars were sociologists, few have engaged the topic in recent years.[2] Most broad studies of political forms fail to incorporate populist cases.[3] The most striking example of this omission may be McAdam, Tarrow, and Tilly's much heralded *Dynamics of Contention* (2001): although wide-ranging in its treatment of contentious politics, this work does not include a single populist

---

1. On the difficulties of conceptualizing populism, see de la Torre 2000; Ionescu and Gellner 1969b, 1–3; and Stein 1980, 9. Of nationalism, Minogue (1969, 199) writes that, "in the course of two centuries, a great variety of radically different movements have come to shelter under the broad conceptual umbrella;" Brubaker (2004, 132) similarly describes how nationalism "has been marked by deep ambivalence and intractable ambiguity." Likewise, Mann (2004, x, 4–5) notes that fascism has often been used in a loose sense and that conflicting idealist and materialist accounts have failed to produce an adequate theory.

2. The only exception seems to be the U.S. case, which has received a modest share of attention from political sociologists (see, for example, Bonikowski and Gidron 2016; Braunstein 2015; Gerteis 2003 and 2007; Redding 1992; Schwartz 1976; and Soule 1992). Mabel Berezin (2009) and Carlos de la Torre (2000) are among the few sociologists to have recently engaged with international cases.

3. Lipset's *Political Man* (1960) is a rare exception.

case among its fifteen core examples. The most significant impediment for political sociology has probably been a general suspicion of the slipperiness of the concept, and so an uncertainty about how populist cases should be incorporated into broader comparative frameworks. Such caution, as just noted, has been warranted. But it is also lamentable, in that it has meant that political sociology has systematically neglected a phenomenon that is now reasserting itself in a significant way on a global scale. Sociologists engaged in the study of contentious politics should take notice.

Appendix A: Chronology

Before the 1931 Election

1914   FEBRUARY: Sánchez Cerro, at age twenty-four, participates in the coup d'état that ousts Guillermo Billinghurst. He sustains serious injuries while leading the raid on the Palacio de Gobierno.

1918   DECEMBER: Textile workers strike in Lima. Their action escalates in January into a general strike for an eight-hour workday, in which twenty-three-year-old Haya de la Torre plays a pivotal role as chief negotiator.

1919   JULY: Leguía assumes the presidency through coup d'état on July 4, resulting in the collapse of the Aristocratic Republic (1895–1919) and marking the beginning of his eleven-year rule. That same month, he institutes a patronage system governing military promotions.

1920   MARCH: Haya de la Torre presides over the first national congress of the Federación de Estudiantes del Perú.

         MAY: Leguía authorizes the Conscripción Vial (Highways Conscription Act), an unpopular compulsory labor program that places a particular burden on the indigenous population.

         JUNE: Leguía contracts a U.S. mission to modernize the Peruvian Navy, in an attempt to undermine the relative influence of the Army.

1921   JANUARY: The Federación de Estudiantes del Perú, under Haya de la Torre's leadership, opens the first popular university in central Lima.

         APRIL: Leguía authorizes a Spanish mission to train and restructure the Guardia Civil. Funding for this police force—which reports directly to Leguía—will increase threefold during his administration, even as the army's budget will stagnate.

1922   AUGUST: Sánchez Cerro is involved in a foiled plot to oust Leguía, in which he is seriously wounded.

1923   MAY: Under Haya de la Torre's leadership, students and workers protest Leguía's attempt to consecrate Lima to the Sacred Heart of Jesus. The protest is successful but results in Haya's deportation in October. Haya, who will not return to Peru until 1931, leaves domestic political activities in the hands of José Carlos Mariátegui and other close associates.

1924 MAY: Haya de la Torre founds his APRA party, envisioned at the time as a pan-continental movement, in Mexico City.

SEPTEMBER: Leguía's undermining of the traditional political parties—especially the Partido Civil—culminates in the imprisonment of Rafael Belaúnde Diez-Canseco, the grandson of a former president and brother of a prominent intellectual who strongly opposes Leguía.

1925 Leguía allows the government's contract with French military advisors to expire, alienating professionally trained army officers—many of whom are already critical of the favoritism driving promotions under Leguía.

1926 SEPTEMBER: Mariátegui begins publication of *Amauta*, a radical journal of cultural and literary criticism.

OCTOBER: Haya de la Torre introduces his party to European leftists through the publication of an article ("What is APRA?") in a British labor journal.

1928 OCTOBER: Mariátegui establishes the Partido Socialista del Perú (which will become the Partido Comunista del Perú on his death in April 1930).

1929 AUGUST-SEPTEMBER: Haya de la Torre and Mariátegui split over growing disagreements about political strategy.

1930 AUGUST: Sánchez Cerro overthrows Leguía and is acclaimed as a hero for ending the widely despised dictatorship. He imprisons Leguía, assumes leadership of the governing junta, and consolidates his popular support by abolishing the Conscripción Vial.

SEPTEMBER: Communist-led unions organize a general strike against the Cerro de Pasco Copper Corporation.

SEPTEMBER: The Partido Aprista Peruano (Peruvian branch of the APRA party) is founded.

NOVEMBER: Martial law is declared in Lima and Junín. Sánchez Cerro intensifies his persecution of Apristas and Communists.

DECEMBER: Sánchez Cerro's Comité de Saneamiento y Consolidación Revolucionaria sentences Leguía and his three sons to pay reparations, while continuing its purge of alleged Leguiísta sympathizers.

1931 JANUARY: The Comité de Saneamiento y Consolidación Revolucionaria nominates Sánchez Cerro to the presidency (he accepts) before elections are formally stipulated. That same month, the Partido Comunista issues a resolution affirming an "objectively revolutionary situation" and advocates strikes and worker insurrection rather than participation in electoral politics.

FEBRUARY: Unrest breaks out among the armed forces in Callao and various provinces, in response to Sánchez Cerro's presidential aspirations. After southern insurrectionaries declare a second junta in Arequipa, headed by David Samanez Ocampo, members of the Lima junta pressure Sánchez Cerro to renounce his presidential bid.

MARCH: Sánchez Cerro resigns from the Lima junta (on March 1) and departs for Europe (on March 7). Samanez Ocampo assumes leadership of a new conciliatory junta, but Gustavo Jiménez retains de facto control. After Apristas are released from prison, the Partido Aprista Peruano reconstitutes its executive committee and registers as a party in Lima.

APRIL: Elite leaders announce their Concentración Nacional initiative, a proposal to circumvent the party system through a committee-negotiated presidential nomination process. Sánchez Cerro supports the initiative from exile, viewing it as an avenue for political relevance, but later retracts his support, citing the junta's reluctance to allow him to return to Peru.

MAY: An omnibus strike results in a call for a general strike by the Confederación General de Trabajadores del Perú. As social unrest continues, the junta announces that it will not allow Sánchez Cerro to return to Peru. Although Haya de la Torre remains in exile, Apristas in Peru found a party newspaper (*La Tribuna*) and organize a May Day rally in Lima's Teatro Apolo.

1931 Election

MAY 26: Elections are declared for September 13, electoral reforms are promulgated, and martial law is lifted to facilitate the electoral process. Shortly thereafter, Sánchez Cerro disobeys the junta and departs from France to Panama without authorization.

JUNE 12: From Panama, Sánchez Cerro issues a public ultimatum, demanding that the junta allow him to return to Peru and giving them a deadline of June 22 by which to act.

JULY 2: Sánchez Cerro arrives in Callao, Peru, but remains docked, after a chaotic clash breaks out between the large crowd awaiting his return, on one side, and soldiers and policemen, on the other. He disembarks on July 3.

JULY 12: Haya de la Torre arrives at the port of Talara, Peru, and begins campaigning.

JULY 13: Sánchez Cerro officially announces his candidacy.

JULY 26: Apristas stage a mass rally in Trujillo, on Haya de la Torre's return to his hometown.

JULY 29: Apristas hold a rally in Lima's central Plaza San Martín, which is reported to have been filled to overflowing.

JULY 30: Unión Revolucionaria is officially formed.

AUGUST 1: Sánchez Cerro and his party officials leave on a tour of the south.

AUGUST 14: The junta postpones the election from September 13 to October 11.

AUGUST 15: Haya de la Torre arrives in Lima and gives a speech at the Plaza San Martín, in which he accepts his party's nomination for the presidency.

AUGUST 19: Sánchez Cerro and his party officials return to Lima.

AUGUST 22: In celebration of the one-year anniversary of his Revolution of Arequipa, Sánchez Cerro stages a mass rally in Lima and releases his "Programa de Gobierno."

AUGUST 23: APRA holds a mass rally in Lima, in direct competition with Sánchez Cerro's of the previous day.

SEPTEMBER 19: An internal APRA election nominates a slate of candidates for the constituent assembly (including Arturo Sabroso, Luis Alberto Sánchez, and Manuel Seoane).

SEPTEMBER 20: APRA releases its "Programa Mínimo."

OCTOBER 4: Sánchez Cerro holds his second major Lima rally, which one sympathetic publication estimates to have attracted 100,000 attendees.

OCTOBER 7: Sánchezcerristas rally in Arequipa, with their party claiming 25,000 in attendance.

OCTOBER 8: Haya de la Torre speaks at a major Lima rally, with his party claiming 27,000 in attendance.

OCTOBER 11: Election Day.

NOVEMBER 28: The Jurado Nacional de Elecciones declares Sánchez Cerro the legal winner of the presidential election.

DECEMBER 4–6: A series of small and unsuccessful APRA-affiliated insurrections break out across the country, including a major botched attempt in Lima that results in a city-wide blackout. This marks the beginning of a period of clandestine activity and violent contention that will culminate in the Aprista-led Trujillo rebellion of July 1932—and ultimately in Sánchez Cerro's assassination on April 30, 1933.

DECEMBER 8: Sánchez Cerro is inaugurated. Haya de la Torre holds a mass meeting in Trujillo and gives a speech urging continued struggle. The constituent assembly begins sessions.

Appendix B: Population, Suffrage, and Exclusion

The discussion of the Estatuto Electoral in chapter 3 introduces data on the composition of the Peruvian electorate in 1931. Because statistics from this period are spotty, the data come from a number of sources and, in some cases, are only estimates. Table B.1 gives a fuller picture of these data; and this appendix describes the sources and methods that were used to produce them.

The first column of the table presents my population estimates for each Peruvian department in 1931.[1] Unfortunately, the contest between Sánchez Cerro and Haya de la Torre came toward the end of a sixty-four-year censual drought. The country had not conducted a national census since 1876; and it would not do so again until 1940. It is thus necessary to rely on estimated figures for 1931.

Most studies of the period have invoked an estimate that was produced—using unspecified methods—by the Sociedad Geográfica de Lima, which placed the 1927 national population at around 6,147,000 (República del Perú 1939, 14).[2] While this figure is better than nothing, the authors of the official report on the 1940 census found it to be implausibly inflated for a number of reasons (República del Perú 1941, 34–44). As an alternative, made possible by the availability of new data from 1940, the authors of the report interpolated by second-degree polynomial from the censuses of 1940, 1876, and 1862 (the first national census to yield relatively reliable results) to produce a more

---

1. Departments (now called "regions") are Peru's largest administrative unit. Each department is subdivided into provinces, which in turn contain districts. Note that in 1931, Callao, Moquegua, and Tumbes were not departments per se, but rather stand-alone provinces not subsumed within any department (the "Provincia Constitucional del Callao," the "Provincia Litoral de Moquegua," and the "Provincia Litoral de Tumbes").

2. Indeed, I have myself used the 1927 estimate in previous work (Jansen 2016).

TABLE B.1. Population, suffrage, and exclusion

Department	Population	Adult Male Population	Eligible to Vote	Percentage of Adult Males Eligible to Vote	Percentage of Adult Males Excluded from Voting	Percentage of Population Indigenous	Illiteracy Rate	Percentage of Population No Formal Schooling	Percentage of Population Monolingual in Indigenous Language
Amazonas	58,505	12,128	4,727	39.0	61.0	20.4	57.8	55.9	5.3
Ancash	397,776	80,430	25,340	31.5	68.5	55.8	69.9	68.6	54.9
Apurímac	225,300	51,256	6,588	12.9	87.1	70.0	87.2	87.4	86.2
Arequipa	247,121	56,615	23,902	42.2	57.8	26.4	41.8	38.5	17.2
Ayacucho	288,381	60,272	10,782	17.9	82.1	75.9	85.5	85.3	82.4
Cajamarca	443,250	87,764	31,957	36.4	63.6	12.3	68.4	64.0	1.1
Callao	70,141	20,098	13,003	64.7	35.3	5.0	11.5	6.6	0.0
Cuzco	432,403	109,658	13,992	12.8	87.2	71.7	82.3	81.8	79.4
Huancavelica	208,876	45,054	7,708	17.1	82.9	78.7	84.7	83.2	78.8
Huánuco	198,487	44,084	7,802	17.7	82.3	63.5	75.2	72.2	52.6
Ica	121,176	30,452	13,053	42.9	57.1	29.2	30.5	23.6	1.8
Junín	379,211	85,740	34,299	40.0	60.0	60.9	62.4	59.6	31.7
La Libertad	333,229	76,576	32,838	42.9	57.1	12.9	54.6	50.0	0.2
Lambayeque	183,035	44,624	15,661	35.1	64.9	30.1	47.0	39.8	2.8
Lima	695,143	189,009	100,186	53.0	47.0	15.3	20.1	15.4	2.4
Loreto	134,616	29,360	7,720	26.3	73.7	38.2	54.4	50.8	13.5
Madre de Dios	4,340	1,204	357	29.7	70.3	25.9	46.4	46.8	5.4
Moquegua	33,740	7,770	2,671	34.4	65.6	46.2	59.5	56.0	24.3
Piura	343,560	75,411	19,801	26.3	73.7	37.8	63.1	58.3	0.0
Puno	494,856	111,639	10,341	9.3	90.7	92.4	87.0	85.8	83.4
San Martín	84,944	16,241	4,936	30.4	69.6	25.0	45.8	42.3	12.5
Tacna	34,723	9,275	3,029	32.7	67.3	52.2	43.4	41.7	16.1
Tumbes	21,802	4,899	1,670	34.1	65.9	1.5	43.7	34.3	0.0
NATION	5,434,617	1,249,559	392,363	31.4	68.6	41.2	57.5	54.3	28.4

modest estimate for 1927 of 5,173,675 (see República del Perú 1941, 41; on estimating populations by interpolating from three censuses, see United Nations 1952:31–32).

I used this same method to produce intercensal estimates at the department level for 1931.[3] Drawing on departmental population figures from the censuses of 1862, 1876, and 1940 (República del Perú 1939, 12–14; República del Perú 1941, 52), I calculated independent parabolic growth curves for each department and used these to generate 1931 estimates. Then, following current U.S. Census Bureau practice (see United States Census Bureau 2012), I controlled the departmental estimates to a national one (produced using data from República del Perú 1939, 12–14 and República del Perú 1941, 52). As the Amazonian department of Madre de Dios was omitted from the censuses of 1862 and 1876, this department required a more crude estimation procedure.[4] Based on my estimates for population growth at the national level between 1931 and 1940, and between 1919 and 1931, I extrapolated backward from the department's 1940 population of 4,950 (República del Perú 1941, 52) to produce the figure that appears in the table. Finally, as we have an actual 1931 head count for the province of Callao (from the census of the provinces of Lima and Callao undertaken in that year to assess the impact of the worldwide Depression on the metropolitan region), I have replaced my Callao estimate with this count (Departamento de Lima 1931, 99).

The second column of the table presents the numbers of males aged twenty and above residing in each department in 1931. Again, as no proximate census data are available, estimation was necessary. The first step was to estimate the share of the population with these characteristics for each department. Given that the two available censuses were the 1940 national census and the 1931 Lima-Callao census, the two options were either to use the 1940 department-specific rates (which requires assuming that the age and gender distributions in each department were stable between 1931 and 1940) or to use the 1931 Lima rate for all other departments. As Lima's population was both older (by about 4.8 percent) and more male (by about 3.6 percent) than the national average

---

3. I thank my colleagues Rachel Best and Deirdre Bloome for their counsel and assistance in producing these estimates. Any errors in method or execution are entirely my own.

4. This data problem is fairly trivial, as Madre de Dios was the least populous department at the time and as the 1940 census figures for Amazonian regions were already suboptimal (because the census administrators did not adequately count the sparse and dispersed indigenous populations of the lowland rainforest). Nevertheless, I dropped Madre de Dios when calculating the national-level growth curve to avoid any minor skewing of this function—something that the authors of the 1940 census report did not do.

(calculations based on figures reported in República del Perú 1941, 52–54), I chose the first option. I thus used data from the 1940 census (República del Perú 1941, 52–54) to calculate the percentages of males age twenty and above. I then estimated the absolute size of each department's adult male population by multiplying these percentages by the 1931 population estimates discussed above.[5] The one exception is again the province of Callao, for which I used the actual 1931 count (Departamento de Lima 1931, 99).

The third column presents the actual number of people registered to vote in the 1931 election, by department. These data come from the statistical report on voter characteristics in the 1931 election (República del Perú 1933, 230). As voting was obligatory, I use the number of registered voters as a proxy for the number eligible to vote.

The fourth and fifth columns show the great variation across departments in the share of the adult male population that was eligible to vote (or was excluded from voting) in 1931. Column four, which lists the percentages of males age twenty and above who were eligible to vote in the 1931 election, was calculated by dividing the absolute numbers of eligible voters (column three) by the estimated adult male populations of each department (column two). Column five lists the percentages of males age twenty and above who were excluded (and is simply the inverse of the results presented in column four).

The sixth column presents the share of the population of each department that was identified as indigenous in the 1940 census (República del Perú 1941, 65). As noted in chapter 3, such ethnicity statistics should be interpreted cautiously, given the slipperiness of the *Indio* and mestizo categories and the fact that the vast majority of ethnic identifications were made by the census enumerators. In the again exceptional case of Callao, an actual percentage is available and was used (Departamento de Lima 1931, 93).

The last three columns relate to the issue of Spanish-language literacy (a necessary requirement for voting in 1931). Column seven presents rates of illiteracy, by department, for individuals above the age of five. I calculated these rates using data from the 1940 census (República del Perú 1944, 170, 260), again with the exception of Callao, for which we have 1931 data (Departamento de Lima 1931, 159). Column eight presents the percentage of the

---

5. Since the reason for estimating these figures was to calculate rates of electoral exclusion (see below), it would have been preferable to use data on the male population twenty-*one* or older. But the Peruvian censuses of the time demarcated age groups at twenty. Of course, the population of males twenty-one or older would have been slightly smaller than the population of those twenty or older.

population above the age of fifteen in each department who received no formal schooling. These rates were also calculated using data from the 1940 census (República del Perú 1944, 189). Finally, column nine presents the percentage of the population of each department who were monolingual in an indigenous language (and thus did not speak Spanish). These rates are reported in the 1940 census and are for individuals above the age of five (República del Perú 1944, 163).

References

Archival Collections

ADLP Archivo Digital de la Legislación del Perú (available online at http://www.congreso.gob.pe/ntley/default.asp)
AGN Archivo General de la Nación
    /PL Prefectura de Lima
    /MI Ministerio del Interior
PUCP Pontificia Universidad Católica del Perú, Sala de Colecciones Especiales, Centro de Documentación de Ciencias Sociales
    /AASM Archivo Arturo Sabroso Montoya
    /AI Archivo Imperialismo
    /CMAP Colección Moisés Arroyo Posadas

Newspapers and Periodicals

Amauta	*Claridad*	*Libertad*	*La Prensa*	*Variedades*
APRA	*El Comercio*	*La Noche*	*La Tribuna*	*West Coast Leader*

Government Publications

Departamento de Lima (Junta Departamental de Lima Pro-Desocupados). 1931. *Censo de las provincias de Lima y Callao levantado el 13 de noviembre de 1931*. Lima: Imprenta Torres Aguirre.

———. 1935. *Memoria. (Acción social y obras ejecutadas por la Junta Departamental de Lima Pro-Desocupados, 1931–1934)*. Lima: Imprenta Torres Aguirre.

República del Perú. 1901. *Ley electoral dada por la legislatura extraordinaria de 1896*. Lima: Imprenta del Estado.

República del Perú (Dirección Nacional de Estadística). 1933. *Extracto estadístico y censo electoral de la República*. Lima: Linotipía.

República del Perú (Ministerio de Hacienda y Comercio, Departamento de Censos). 1941. *Censo nacional de 1940, resultados generales: Primer informe oficial*. Lima.

República del Perú (Ministerio de Hacienda y Comercio, Dirección Nacional de Estadística).
1939. *Extracto estadístico del Perú, 1939*. Lima: Imprenta Americana.
———. 1944. *Censo nacional de población y ocupación, 1940*. Vol. 1. Lima.

Published Primary and Secondary Sources

Abbott, Andrew. 1983. "Sequences of Social Events: Concepts and Methods for the Analysis of Order in Social Processes." *Historical Methods* 16:129–49.
———. 1997. "On the Concept of Turning Point." *Comparative Social Research* 16:85–105.
———. 2001. *Time Matters: On Theory and Method*. Chicago: University of Chicago Press.
Abel, Christopher, and Marco Palacios. 1991. "Colombia, 1930–58." In *Latin America Since 1930: Spanish South America*, edited by Leslie Bethell, 587–627. Cambridge: Cambridge University Press.
Adams, Julia, Elisabeth S. Clemens, and Ann Shola Orloff. 2005. "Introduction: Social Theory, Modernity, and the Three Waves of Historical Sociology." In *Remaking Modernity: Politics, History and Sociology*, edited by Julia Adams, Elisabeth S. Clemens, and Ann Shola Orloff, 1–72. Durham, NC: Duke University Press.
Adrianzén, Alberto. 1990. "Introducción: Continuidades y rupturas en el pensamiento político." In *Pensamiento político Peruano, 1930–1968*, edited by Alberto Adrianzén, 15–28. Lima: DESCO.
Alexander, Jeffrey C., Bernhard Giesen, and Jason L. Mast, eds. 2006. *Social Performance: Symbolic Action, Cultural Pragmatics, and Ritual*. Cambridge: Cambridge University Press.
Alexander, Robert J. 1973. *Aprismo: The Ideas and Doctrines of Víctor Raúl Haya de la Torre*. Kent: Kent State University Press.
Alimonda, Héctor. 1982 "Paz y administración: 'Ordem e progresso': Notas para un estudio comparativo de los estados oligárquicos argentino y brasileño." *Revista Mexicana de Sociología* 44:1323–50.
Aljovín de Losada, Cristóbal. 2000. *Caudillos y constituciones: Perú, 1821–1845*. Lima: Pontificia Universidad Católica del Perú, Instituto Riva-Agüero.
———. 2005. "Sufragio y participación política: Perú 1808–1896." In *Historia de las elecciones en el Perú: Estudios sobre el gobierno representativo*, edited by C. Aljovín de Losada and Sinesio López, 19–74. Lima: Instituto de Estudios Peruanos.
Aljovín de Losada, Cristóbal, and Sinesio López. 2005. *Historia de las elecciones en el Perú: Estudios sobre el gobierno representativo*. Lima: Instituto de Estudios Peruanos.
Alzamora, Carlos. 2013. *Leguía, la historia oculta: Vida y muerte del Presidente Augusto B. Leguía*. Lima: Titanium Editores.
Anderson, Benedict. 1991. *Imagined Communities*. London: Verso.
Anderson, Perry. 1974. *Lineages of the Absolutist State*. London: Verso.
APRA (Alianza Popular Revolucionaria Americana). (1931) 1984. "Plan de acción inmediata, o programa mínimo." In *Obras completas*, edited by Luis Alberto Sánchez. Vol. 5, 11–29. Lima: Juan Mejia Baca.
Arroyo Reyes, Carlos. 2005. *Nuestros años diez: La Asociación Pro-Indígena, el levantamiento de Rumi Maqui y el incaismo modernista*. Argentina: Libros en Red.
Auyero, Javier. 2007. *Routine Politics and Violence in Argentina: The Gray Zone of State Power*. Cambridge: Cambridge University Press.

REFERENCES

Balbi, Carmen Rosa. 1980. *El Partido Comunista y el APRA en la crisis revolucionaria de los años treinta*. Lima: G. Herrera.

Bargheer, Stefan. 2011. "Moral Entanglements: The Emergence and Transformation of Bird Conservation in Great Britain and Germany, 1790–2010." PhD diss., University of Chicago.

Basadre, Jorge. 1961–64. *Historia de la República del Perú*. 5th ed. 10 vols. Lima: Ediciones "Historia."

———. 1980. *Elecciones y centralismo en el Perú: Apuntes para un esquema histórico*. Lima: Universidad del Pacífico.

———. 1999. *Historia de la República del Perú: 1822–1933*. 8th ed. 13 vols. Santiago: La República / Universidad Ricardo Palma.

Becker, Howard. 1982. *Art Worlds*. Berkeley: University of California Press.

Beissinger, Mark R. 2002. *Nationalist Mobilization and the Collapse of the Soviet State*. Cambridge: Cambridge University Press.

Berezin, Mabel. 1997. *Making the Fascist Self: The Political Culture of Inter-War Italy*. Ithaca, NY: Cornell University Press.

———. 2004. "Re-asserting the National: The Paradox of Populism in Transnational Europe." Paper presented at the annual meeting of the American Sociological Association, San Francisco, California, August 14–17.

———. 2009. *Illiberal Politics in Neoliberal Times: Culture, Security and Populism in the New Europe*. Cambridge: Cambridge University Press.

Berk, Gerald, and Dennis Galvan. 2009. "How People Experience and Change Institutions: A Field Guide to Creative Syncretism." *Theory and Society* 38:543–580.

Betz, Hans-Georg. 1994. *Radical Right-Wing Populism in Western Europe*. New York: St. Martin's Press.

Biernacki, Richard. 2005. "The Action Turn? Comparative-Historical Inquiry beyond the Classical Models of Conduct." In *Remaking Modernity: Politics, History, and Sociology*, edited by Julia Adams, Elisabeth S. Clemens, and Ann Shola Orloff, 75–91. Durham, NC: Duke University Press.

Blanchard, Peter. 1977. "A Populist Precursor: Guillermo Billinghurst." *Latin American Studies* 9:251–73.

———. 1982. *The Origins of the Peruvian Labor Movement, 1883–1919*. Pittsburgh: University of Pittsburgh Press.

Bloom, Joshua. 2015. "The Dynamics of Opportunity and Insurgent Practice: How Black Anticolonialists Compelled Truman to Advocate Civil Rights." *American Sociological Review* 80:391–415.

Bonikowski, Bart, and Noam Gidron. 2016. "The Populist Style of American Politics: Presidential Campaign Discourse, 1952–1996." *Social Forces* 94:1593–1621.

Bonilla, Heraclio. 1974. *Guano y burguesía en el Perú*. Lima: Instituto de Estudios Peruanos.

Bourricaud, Francois. 1970. *Power and Society in Contemporary Peru*. New York: Praeger.

Braunstein, Ruth. 2015. "The Tea Party Goes to Washington: Mass Demonstrations as Performative and Interactional Processes." *Qualitative Sociology* 38:353–74.

Bromley, Juan, and Jose Barbagelata. 1945. *Evolución urbana de la ciudad de Lima*. Lima: Editorial Lumen.

Brubaker, Rogers. 1996. *Nationalism Reframed: Nationhood and the National Question in the New Europe*. Cambridge: Cambridge University Press.

———. 2004. *Ethnicity Without Groups*. Cambridge, MA: Harvard University Press.

Brubaker, Rogers, and David Laitin. 1998. "Ethnic and Nationalist Violence." *Annual Review of Sociology* 24:423–52.

Brumley, Krista. 2010. "Understanding Mexican NGOs: Goals, Strategies, and the Local Context." *Qualitative Sociology* 33:389–414.

Burga, Manuel, and Alberto Flores Galindo. 1979. *Apogeo y crisis de la república aristocrática: Oligarquía, aprismo y comunismo en el Perú, 1895–1932.* Lima: Ediciones "Rikchay" Perú.

Cáceres Arce, Jorge Luis. 2006. "Haya de la Torre estudiante peregrino." In *Vida y obra: Víctor Raúl Haya de la Torre*, edited by Luis Alva Castro. Vol. 3, 15–149. Lima: Instituto Víctor Raúl Haya de la Torre.

Calhoun, Craig. 1991. "The Problem of Identity in Collective Action." In *Macro-Micro Linkages in Sociology*, edited by Joan Huber, 51–75. New York: Sage.

———. 1997. *Nationalism*. Minneapolis: University of Minnesota Press.

Cameron, Maxwell A. 1994. *Democracy and Authoritarianism in Peru: Political Coalitions and Social Change*. New York: St. Martin's Press.

Cameron, Maxwell A., and Eric Hershberg, eds. 2010. *Latin America's Left Turns: Politics, Policies, and Trajectories of Change*. Boulder: Lynn Reinner.

Campbell, Angus, Philip E. Converse, Warren E. Miller, and Donald E. Stokes. 1960. *The American Voter*. Chicago: University of Chicago Press

Capuñay, Manuel A. 1952. *Leguía: Vida y obra del constructor del gran Perú*. Lima: Compañía de Impresiones y Publicidad, Enrique Bustamante y Ballivián.

Castillo Ochoa, Manuel. 1990. "El populismo conservador: Sánchez Cerro y la Unión Revolucionaria." In *Pensamiento político Peruano, 1930–1968*, edited by Alberto Adrianzén, 45–76. Lima: DESCO.

Castro Pozo, Hildebrando. 1924. *Nuestra comunidad indígena*. Lima: El Lucero.

Chanamé, Raul. 2006. "Haya de la Torre y Las Universidades Populares." In *Vida y obra: Víctor Raúl Haya de la Torre*, edited by Luis Alva Castro. Vol. 1, 19–111. Lima: Instituto Víctor Raúl Haya de la Torre.

Chang-Rodríguez, Eugenio. 2007. *Una vida agónica: Víctor Raúl Haya de la Torre. Testimonio de parte*. Lima: Fondo Editorial del Congreso del Perú.

Chiaramonti, Gabriella. 1995. "Andes o nación: La reforma electoral de 1896 en Perú." In *Historia de las elecciones en Iberoamérica, siglo XIX*, edited by A. Annino, 315–346. Buenos Aires: FCE.

———. 2000. "Construir el centro, redefinir al ciudadano: Restricción del sufragio y reforma electoral en el Perú de finales de siglo XIX." In *Legitimidad, representación y alternancia en España y América Latina: Las reformas electorales (1880–1930)*, edited by C. Malamud, 230–61. México: FCE-Colegio de México.

———. 2005. *Ciudadanía y representación en el Perú (1808–1860): Los itinerarios de la soberanía.* Translated by J. R. Rehren. Lima: Fondo Editorial de la Universidad Nacional Mayor de San Marcos.

Ciccarrelli, Orazio A. 1969. "The Sánchez Cerro Regimes in Peru, 1930–1933." PhD diss., University of Florida.

———. 1973. "Militarism, Aprismo and Violence in Peru: The Presidential Election of 1931." Working paper, SUNY-Buffalo Council on International Studies.

Clemens, Elisabeth S. 1997. *The People's Lobby: Organizational Innovation and the Rise of Interest Group Politics in the United States, 1890–1925.* Chicago: University of Chicago Press.

Collier, David. 1976. *Squatter Settlements and the Incorporation of Migrants into Urban Life: The*

Case of Lima. Cambridge: Migration and Development Study Group, Center for International Studies, MIT.

Collier, Ruth Berins, and David Collier. 1991. *Shaping the Political Arena: Critical Junctures, the Labor Movement, and Regime Dynamics in Latin America*. Princeton, NJ: Princeton University Press.

Compañía Anónima La Victoria. 1924. *Fábrica Nacional de Tejidos de Algodón "La Victoria," 1899-1924*. Lima: Sanmartí.

Conaghan, Catherine M. 2005. *Fujimori's Peru: Deception and the Public Sphere*. Pittsburgh: University of Pittsburgh Press.

Conniff, Michael L. 1982. "Populism in Brazil, 1925-1945." In *Latin American Populism in Comparative Perspective*, edited by Michael L. Conniff, 67-91. Albuquerque: University of New Mexico Press.

———. 1999. "Introduction." In *Populism in Latin America*, edited by Michael L. Conniff, 1-21. Tuscaloosa: University of Alabama Press.

Cossío del Pomar, Felipe. 1977. *Víctor Raúl: Biografía de Haya de la Torre*. 2 vols. 2nd ed. Lima: Ediciones: Enríque Delgado Valenzuela.

Cyr, Jennifer, and James Mahoney. 2012. "The Enduring Influence of Historical-Structural Approaches." In *Routledge Handbook of Latin American Politics*, edited by Peter Kingstone and Deborah J. Yashar, 433-46. New York: Routledge.

Davies, Thomas M., Jr. 1971. "The Indigenismo of the Peruvian Aprista Party." *Hispanic American Historical Review* 51:626-45.

———. 1974. *Indian Integration in Peru: A Half Century of Experience, 1900-1948*. Lincoln: University of Nebraska Press.

Dalton, Benjamin. 2004. "Creativity, Habit, and the Social Products of Creative Action: Revising Joas, Incorporating Bourdieu." *Sociological Theory* 22:603-22.

de la Cadena, Marisol. 2000. *Indigenous Mestizos: The Politics of Race and Culture in Cuzco, Peru, 1919-1991*. Durham, NC: Duke University Press.

de la Torre, Carlos. 2000. *Populist Seduction in Latin America: The Ecuadorian Experience*. Athens: Ohio University Center for International Studies.

———, ed. 2015. *The Promise and Perils of Populism: Global Perspectives*. Lexington: University Press of Kentucky.

de la Torre, Carlos, and Cynthia J. Arnson, eds. 2013. *Latin American Populism in the Twenty-First Century*. Washington DC: Woodrow Wilson Center Press.

Delaune, E. and Er. Dumas-Vorxet. 1930. "Colombie, Venezuela, Ecuador" (map). David Rumsey Map Collection. Accessed July 19, 2016. http://www.davidrumsey.com/luna/servlet/detail/RUMSEY~8~1~36567~1201122:Colombie,-Venezuela,-Ecuador-#.

De Nora, Tia. 1997. *Beethoven and the Construction of Genius: Musical Politics in Vienna, 1792-1803*. Berkeley: University of California Press.

Derpich, Wilma, José Luis Huiza, and Cecilia Israel. 1985. *Lima años 30: Salarios y costo de vida de la clase trabajadora*. Lima: Fundación Friedrich Ebert.

de Soto, Hernando. 1989. *The Other Path: The Invisible Revolution in the Third World*. New York: Harper & Row.

Deustua Carvallo, José, Steve Stein, and Susan C. Stokes. 1984. "Soccer and Social Change in Early Twentieth Century Peru." *Studies in Latin American Popular Culture* 3:17-27.

———. 1986. "Soccer and Social Change in Early Twentieth Century Peru, Part II." *Studies in Latin American Popular Culture* 5:68-77.

———. 1987. "Entre el offside y el chimpún: Las clases populares limeñas y el fútbol, 1900–1930." In *Lima obrera, 1900–1930*, edited by Steve Stein. Vol. 2, 119–62. Lima: El Virrey.

Deustua, José, and José Luis Rénique. 1984. *Intelectuales, indigenismo y descentralismo en el Perú, 1897–1931*. Cusco: Centro de Estudios Rurales Andinos "Bartolomé de las Casas."

Deutsch, Karl. 1954. *Nationalism and Social Communication: An Inquiry into the Foundations of Nationality*. Cambridge: Massachusetts Institute of Technology Press.

———. 1963. "Social Mobilisation and Political Development." In *Comparative Politics*, edited by Harry Eckstein and David E. Apter, 582–603. New York: Free Press.

Dewey, John. 1922. *Human Nature and Conduct: An Introduction to Social Psychology*. New York: Henry Holt.

———. 1925. *Experience and Nature*. Chicago: Open Court.

Di Tella, Torcuato S. 1965. "Populism and Reform in Latin America." In *Obstacles to Change in Latin America*, edited by Claudio Veliz, 47–74. Oxford: Oxford University Press.

———. 1990. *Latin American Politics: A Theoretical Approach*. Austin: University of Texas Press.

Dobyns, Henry E., and Paul L. Doughty. 1976. *Peru: A Cultural History*. New York: Oxford University Press.

Drinot, Paulo. 2001. "El Comité Distrital Unión Revolucionaria de Magdalena del Mar: Un ensayo de micro historia política." *Revista del Archivo General de la Nación* 23:333–51.

———. 2005. "Food, Race and Working-Class Identity: 'Restaurantes Populares' and Populism in 1930s Peru." *The Americas* 62:245–70.

———. 2011. *The Allure of Labor: Workers, Race, and the Making of the Peruvian State*. Durham, NC: Duke University Press.

Eguiguren, Luis Antonio. 1933. *En la selva política para la historia, 1930–1933*. Lima: San Martí.

Emirbayer, Mustafa, and Chad Alan Goldberg. 2005. "Pragmatism, Bourdieu, and Collective Emotions in Contentious Politics." *Theory and Society* 34:469–518.

Emirbayer, Mustafa, and Ann Mische. 1998. "What Is Agency?" *American Journal of Sociology* 103:962–1023.

Emirbayer, Mustafa, and Erik Schneiderhan. 2013. "Dewey and Bourdieu on Democracy." In *Bourdieu and Historical Analysis*, edited by Philip S. Gorski, 131–57. Durham, NC: Duke University Press.

Ennis, James G. 1987. "Fields of Action: Structure in Movements' Tactical Repertoires." *Sociological Forum* 2:520–33.

Enríquez, Luis Eduardo. 1951. *Haya de la Torre: La estafa política más grande de América*. Lima: Ediciones del Pacífico.

Enríquez, Luis Eduardo, Manuel Seoane, and Carlos Manuel Cox. 1930. *Sánchez Cerro al desnudo (Texto fidedigno de una entrevista histórica)*. Lima: Imprenta "El Globo."

Ermakoff, Ivan. 2008. *Ruling Oneself Out: A Theory of Collective Abdications*. Durham, NC: Duke University Press.

———. 2015. "The Structure of Contingency." *American Journal of Sociology* 121:64–125.

Fantasia, Rick. 1988. *Cultures of Solidarity: Consciousness, Action, and Contemporary American Workers*. Berkeley: University of California Press.

Faulkner, Robert R., and Howard S. Becker. 2009. *"Do You Know . . . ?" The Jazz Repertoire in Action*. Chicago: University of Chicago Press.

Federación de Trabajadores en Tejidos del Perú. 1921. *Declaración de principios y reglamento*. Lima: "Imprenta Proletaria" Malambo.

REFERENCES

Fligstein, Neil, and Doug McAdam. 2011. "Toward a General Theory of Strategic Action Fields." *Sociological Theory* 29:1–26.

Forment, Carlos A. 2003. *Democracy in Latin America, 1760–1900.* Vol. 1, *Civic Selfhood and Public Life in Mexico and Peru.* Chicago: University of Chicago Press.

French, John D. 1989. "Industrial Workers and the Birth of the Populist Republic in Brazil, 1945–1946." *Latin American Perspectives* 16:5–27.

Frye, Margaret. 2012. "Bright Futures in Malawi's New Dawn: Educational Aspirations as Assertions of Identity." *American Journal of Sociology* 117:1565–1624.

Fundación Augusto B. Leguía. (1935) 2007. *Lima 1919–1930: La Lima de Leguía.* Lima: Editorial San Marcos.

Gamson, William A. 1975. *The Strategy of Social Protest.* Homewood: The Dorsey Press.

Ganz, Marshall. 2000. "Resources and Resourcefulness: Strategic Capacity in the Unionization of California Agriculture, 1959–1966." *American Journal of Sociology* 105:1003–1062.

———. 2009. *Why David Sometimes Wins: Leadership, Organization, and Strategy in the California Farm Worker Movement.* New York: Oxford University Press.

Garavito Amézaga, Hugo. 1989. *El Perú liberal: Partidos e ideas políticas de la ilustración a la República Aristocrática.* Lima: Ediciones el Virrey.

García-Bryce, Iñigo. 2004. *Crafting the Republic: Lima's Artisans and Nation Building in Peru, 1821–1879.* Albuquerque: University of New Mexico Press.

Garrett, Gary R. 1973. "The Oncenio of Augusto B. Leguía: Middle Sector Government and Leadership in Peru, 1919–1930." PhD diss., University of New Mexico.

Gellner, Ernest. 1983. *Nations and Nationalism.* Ithaca, NY: Cornell University Press.

Germani, Gino. 1963. *Política y sociedad en una época de transición: De la sociedad tradicional a la sociedad de masas.* Buenos Aires: Editorial Paidos.

———. 1978. *Authoritarianism, Fascism, and National Populism.* New Brunswick, NJ: Transaction.

Gerteis, Joseph. 2003. "Populism, Race, and Political Interest in Virginia." *Social Science History* 27:197–227.

———. 2007. *Class and the Color Line: Interracial Class Coalition in the Knights of Labor and the Populist Movement.* Durham, NC: Duke University Press.

Giesecke, Margarita. 1978. *Masas urbanas y rebelión en la historia. Golpe de estado: Lima, 1872.* Lima: CEDHIP.

———. 1992. "The Trujillo Insurrection, the APRA and the Making of Modern Politics." PhD diss., University of London (Birkbeck College).

———. 2010. *La insurrección de Trujillo: Jueves 7 de julio de 1932.* Lima: Fondo editorial del Congreso del Perú.

Godbersen, Guillermo. 2012. *Augusto B. Leguía en la historia del Perú.* Lima: Editora Huellas del Universo.

Gonzales, Michael J. 1984. *Plantation Agriculture and Social Control in Northern Peru, 1875–1933.* Austin: University of Texas Press.

———. 1991. "Planters and Politics in Peru, 1895–1919." *Journal of Latin American Studies* 23:515–42.

Gonzáles, Osmar. 2005. *El gobierno de Guillermo E. Billinghurst: Los orígenes del populismo en el Perú, 1912–1914.* Lima: Mundo Nuevo.

González Prada, Manuel. 1966. *Páginas libres.* Lima: Fondo de Cultura Popular.

Goodwin, Jeff. 2001. *No Other Way Out: States and Revolutionary Movements, 1945–1991.* Cambridge: Cambridge University Press.

Gootenberg, Paul. 1989. *Between Silver and Guano: Commercial Policy and the State in Postindependence Peru*. Princeton, NJ: Princeton University Press.

———. 1993. *Imagining Development: Economic Ideas in Peru's Fictitious Prosperity of Guano, 1840–1880*. Berkeley: University of California Press.

———. 1997. *Caudillos y comerciantes: La formación económica del estado peruano, 1820–1860*. Cuzco, Peru: Centro Bartolomé de Las Casas.

Gorski, Philip S. 2003. *The Disciplinary Revolution: Calvinism and the Rise of the State in Early Modern Europe*. Chicago: University of Chicago Press.

Gould, Roger V. 1995. *Insurgent Identities: Class, Community, and Protest in Paris from 1848 to the Commune*. Chicago: University of Chicago Press.

Grompone, Romeo. 1998. *Fujimori, Neopopulismo y Comunicación Política*. Lima: Instituto de Estudios Peruanos.

Gross, Neil. 2007. "Pragmatism, Phenomenology, and Twentieth-Century American Sociology." In *Sociology in America: A History*, edited by Craig Calhoun, 183–224. Chicago: University of Chicago Press.

———. 2008. *Richard Rorty: The Making of an American Philosopher*. Chicago: University of Chicago Press.

———. 2009. "A Pragmatist Theory of Social Mechanisms." *American Sociological Review* 74:358–79.

———. 2010. "Charles Tilly and American Pragmatism." *American Sociologist* 41:337–57.

Haya de la Torre, Víctor Raúl. (1928) 1984. "El antimperialismo y el Apra." In *Obras completas*, edited by Luis Alberto Sánchez. Vol. 4, 73–213. Lima: Juan Mejia Baca.

———. (1931) 1984. "Discurso—programa." In *Obras completas*, edited by Luis Alberto Sánchez. Vol. 5, 53–82. Lima: Juan Mejia Baca.

———. 1957. *Haya de la Torre: Su vida y sus luchas*. Lima: Editorial Andimar.

———. 1984. *Obras completas*, edited by Luis Alberto Sánchez. 3rd ed. 7 vols. Lima: Editorial Juan Mejía Baca.

Haya de la Torre, Víctor Raúl, and Luis Alberto Sánchez. 1982. *Correspondencia, 1924–1976*. 2 vols. Lima: Mosca Azul Editores.

Held, Joseph, ed. 1996. *Populism in Eastern Europe: Racism, Nationalism, and Society*. New York: Columbia University Press.

Hennessy, Alistair. 1969. "Latin America." In *Populism: Its Meaning and National Characteristics*, edited by Ghiţa Ionescu and Ernest Gellner, 28–61. New York: Macmillan.

Heysen, Luis E. 1931. *El Comandante del Oropesa*. Cuzco, Peru: Editorial H. G. R. SC.

———. 1933. "Prólogo." In *Por el APRA (en la cárcel, al servicio del P.A.P.)*, edited by Romulo Meneses, 13–31. Lima: Atahualpa.

Hirsch, Steven Jay. 1997. *The Anarcho-Syndicalist Roots of a Multi-Class Alliance: Organized Labor and the Peruvian Aprista Party, 1900–1933*. PhD diss., George Washington University.

Hobsbawm, Eric. 1983. "Introduction: Inventing Tradition." In *The Invention of Tradition*, edited by Eric Hobsbawm and Terence Ranger, 1–14. Cambridge: Cambridge University Press.

Horowitz, Joel. 1999. "Populism and Its Legacies in Argentina." In *Populism in Latin America*, edited by Michael L. Conniff, 22–42. Tuscaloosa: University of Alabama Press.

Hunt, Shane. 1973. *Growth and Guano in 19th Century Peru*. Princeton, NJ: Woodrow Wilson School of Public and International Affairs, Princeton University.

Huntington, Samuel P. 1991. *The Third Wave: Democratization in the Late Twentieth Century*. Norman: University of Oklahoma Press.

REFERENCES

———. (1968) 1996. *Political Order in Changing Societies.* New Haven, CT: Yale University Press.
Ibáñez Avalos, Víctor Manuel. 2006. "La influencia de la Revolución Mexicana en la formación ideológica y doctrinaria del aprismo." Pp. 75–126 in *Vida y obra: Víctor Raúl Haya de la Torre,* edited by Luis Alva Castro. Vol. 6. Lima: Instituto Víctor Raúl Haya de la Torre.
Ionescu, Ghiţa, and Ernest Gellner, eds. 1969a. *Populism, Its Meaning and National Characteristics.* New York: Macmillan.
———. 1969b. "Introduction." In *Populism: Its Meaning and National Characteristics,* edited by Ghiţa Ionescu and Ernest Gellner, 1–5. New York: Macmillan.
Itzigsohn, José, and Matthias vom Hau. 2006. "Unfinished Imagined Communities: States, Social Movements, and Nationalism in Latin America." *Theory and Society* 35:193–212.
Jacobsen, Nils. 2005. "Public Opinions and Public Spheres in Late-Nineteenth-Century Peru." In *Political Cultures in the Andes, 1750–1950,* edited by Nils Jacobsen and Cristóbal Aljovín de Losada, 278–300. Durham, NC: Duke University Press.
Jagers, Jan, and Stefaan Walgrave. 2007. "Populism as Political Communication Style: An Empirical Study of Political Parties' Discourse in Belgium." *European Journal of Political Research* 46:319–45.
James, Daniel. 1988. *Resistance and Integration: Peronism and the Argentine Working Class, 1946–76.* Cambridge: Cambridge University Press.
James, William. 1975. *Pragmatism.* Cambridge, MA: Harvard University Press.
Jansen, Robert S. 2011. "Populist Mobilization: A New Theoretical Approach to Populism." *Sociological Theory* 29:75–96.
———. 2016. "Situated Political Innovation: Explaining the Historical Emergence of New Modes of Political Practice." *Theory and Society* 45:319–60.
Jasper, James. 1997. *The Art of Moral Protest: Culture, Biography, and Creativity in Social Movements.* Chicago: University of Chicago Press.
———. 2004. "A Strategic Approach to Collective Action: Looking for Agency in Social-Movement Choices." *Mobilization* 9:1–16.
Jenkins, Craig J. 1983. "Resource Mobilization Theory and the Study of Social Movements." *Annual Review of Sociology* 9:527–53.
Jenkins, Richard. 1997. *Rethinking Ethnicity: Arguments and Explorations.* London: Sage.
Joas, Hans. 1985. *G.H. Mead: A Contemporary Re-examination of his Thought.* Translated by Raymond Meyer. Cambridge: Polity Press.
———. 1993. *Pragmatism and Social Theory.* Chicago: University of Chicago Press.
———. 1996. *The Creativity of Action.* Chicago: University of Chicago Press.
Karno, Howard Laurence. 1970. "Augusto B. Leguía: The Oligarchy and the Modernization of Peru, 1870–1930." PhD diss., University of California, Los Angeles.
Kenney, Charles D. 2004. *Fujimori's Coup and the Breakdown of Democracy in Latin America.* Notre Dame, IN: University of Notre Dame Press.
Klaiber, Jeffrey L. 1975. "The Popular Universities and the Origins of Aprismo, 1921–1924." *Hispanic American Historical Review* 55:693–715.
Klarén, Peter F. 1973. *Modernization, Dislocation, and Aprismo: Origins of the Peruvian Aprista Party, 1870–1932.* Austin: University of Texas Press.
———. 2000. *Peru: Society and Nationhood in the Andes.* Oxford: Oxford University Press.
Knight, Alan. 1998. "Populism and Neo-Populism in Latin America, Especially Mexico." *Journal of Latin American Studies* 30:223–48.
Kornhauser, William. 1959. *The Politics of Mass Society.* Glencoe, IL: Free Press.

Kurzman, Charles. 2004. *The Unthinkable Revolution in Iran*. Cambridge, MA: Harvard University Press.

Laclau, Ernesto. 1977. *Politics and Ideology in Marxist Theory: Capitalism, Fascism, Populism*. London: NLB.

Laitin, David D. 1985. "Hegemony and Religious Conflict: British Imperial Control and Political Cleavages in Yorubaland." In *Bringing the State Back In*, edited by Peter Evans, Dietrich Rueschemeyer, and Theda Skocpol, 285–316. Cambridge: Cambridge University Press.

Lamont, Michèle. 1987. "How to Become a Dominant French Philosopher: The Case of Jacques Derrida." *American Journal of Sociology* 93:584–622.

Laos, Cipriano A. 1928. *Lima: 'La ciudad de los virreyes' (El libro peruano). Bajo el alto patronato del Touring Club Peruano, 1928–1929*. Lima: Editorial Perú.

El libro de oro: Directorio Social de Lima, Callao y Balnearios para el año 1927. 1927. Lima: Guía Lascano.

Linz, Juan J., and Alfred Stepan, eds. 1978. *The Breakdown of Democratic Regimes*. Baltimore: Johns Hopkins University Press.

Lipset, Seymour M. 1960. *Political Man: The Social Bases of Politics*. New York: Doubleday.

Lomnitz, Claudio. 2001. *Deep Mexico, Silent Mexico: An Anthropology of Nationalism*. Minneapolis: University of Minnesota Press.

Lynch, John. 1992. *Caudillos in Spanish America, 1800–1850*. Oxford: Clarendon Press.

Mahoney, James. 2000. "Path Dependence in Historical Sociology." *Theory and Society* 29: 507–48.

———. 2001. *The Legacies of Liberalism: Path Dependence and Political Regimes in Central America*. Baltimore: Johns Hopkins University Press.

———. 2010. *Colonialism and Postcolonial Development: Spanish America in Comparative Perspective*. Cambridge: Cambridge University Press.

Mahoney, James, and Kathleen Thelen, eds. 2010. *Explaining Institutional Change: Ambiguity, Agency, and Power*. Cambridge: Cambridge University Press.

Mallon, Florencia E. 1983. *The Defense of Community in Peru's Central Highlands: Peasant Struggle and Capitalist Transition, 1860–1940*. Princeton, NJ: Princeton University Press.

———. 1995. *Peasant and Nation: The Making of Postcolonial Mexico and Peru*. Berkeley: University of California Press.

Malloy, James, M. 1977. "Authoritarianism, Corporatism and Mobilization in Latin America: The Modal Pattern." In *Authoritarianism and Corporatism in Latin America*, edited by James M. Malloy, 3–19. Pittsburg: University of Pittsburg Press.

Mann, Michael. 1984. "The Autonomous Power of the State: Its Origins, Mechanisms and Results." *Archives Europeennes De Sociologie* 25:185–213.

———. 2004. *Fascists*. Cambridge: Cambridge University Press.

Manza, Jeff, and Clem Brooks. 1999. *Social Cleavages and Political Change: Voter Alignments and U.S. Party Coalitions*. Oxford: Oxford University Press.

Manza, Jeff, Michael Hout, and Clem Brooks. 1995. "Class Voting in Capitalist Democracies Since World War II: Dealignment, Realignment, or Trendless Fluctuation?" *Annual Review of Sociology* 21:137–62.

Mariátegui, José Carlos. (1928) 1995. *Siete ensayos de interpretación de la realidad peruana*. Lima: Biblioteca "Amauta."

———. 2005. *Invitación a la vida heroica: José Carlos Mariátegui, textos esenciales*. Lima: Fondo Editorial del Congreso del Perú.

Martínez de la Torre, Ricardo. 1947. *Apuntes para una interpretación marxista de historia social del Perú*. 4 vols. Lima.

Martín, José Carlos. 1963. *El gobierno de don Guillermo Billinghurst, 1912–1914: Apuntes para la historia del Perú*. Lima: CIP.

Marx, Karl. (1852) 1969. *The Eighteenth Brumaire of Louis Bonaparte*. New York: International.

———. (1871) 1968. *The Civil War in France: The Paris Commune*. New York: International.

Masterson, Daniel M. 1991. *Militarism and Politics in Latin America: Peru from Sánchez Cerro to Sendero Luminoso*. New York: Greenwood Press.

McAdam, Doug. 1982. *Political Process and the Development of Black Insurgency, 1930–1970*. Chicago: University of Chicago Press.

McAdam, Doug, Sidney Tarrow, and Charles Tilly. 2001. *Dynamics of Contention*. Cambridge: Cambridge University Press.

McCarthy, John D., and Mayer N. Zald. 1977. "Resource Mobilization and Social Movements: A Partial Theory." *American Journal of Sociology* 82:1212–41.

McClintock, Cynthia, and Abraham F. Lowenthal, eds. 1983. *The Peruvian Experiment Reconsidered*. Princeton, NJ: Princeton University Press.

McEvoy, Carmen. 1997. *La utopía republicana: Ideales y realidades en la formación de la cultura política peruana (1871–1919)*. Lima: Fondo Editorial de la Pontificia Universidad Católica del Perú.

———. 1999. "Estampillas y votos: El rol del correo político en una campaña electoral decimonónica." In *Forjando la nación. Ensayos sobre historia repúblicana*, edited by Carmen McEvoy, 119–68. Lima: PUCP.

Mead, George Herbert. 1932. *The Philosophy of the Present*. Chicago: Open Court.

———. 1934. *Mind, Self, and Society: From the Standpoint of a Social Behaviorist*. Chicago: University of Chicago Press.

Melucci, Alberto. 1989. *Nomads of the Present*. London: Hutchinson Radius.

Méndez, Cecilia. 1992. "República sin indios: La comunidad imaginada del Perú." In *Tradición y modernidad en los Andes*, edited by Henrique Urbano, 15–41. Lima.

———. 1996. "Incas Sí, Indios No: Notes on Peruvian Creole Nationalism and Its Contemporary Crisis." *Journal of Latin American Studies* 28:197–225.

Michels, Robert. (1915) 1999. *Political Parties: A Sociological Study of the Oligarchical Tendencies of Modern Democracy*. New Brunswick, NJ: Transaction.

Miller, Rory. 1982. "The Coastal Elite and Peruvian Politics, 1895–1919." *Journal of Latin American Studies* 14:97–120.

Mills, C. Wright. 1956. *The Power Elite*. Oxford: Oxford University Press.

Minogue, Kenneth. 1969. "Populism as a Political Movement." In *Populism: Its Meaning and National Characteristics*, edited by Ghiţa Ionescu and Ernest Gellner, 197–211. New York: Macmillan.

Miró Quesada Laos, Carlos. 1947. *Sánchez Cerro y su tiempo*. Buenos Aires: Librería "El Anteneo" Editorial.

———. 1961. *Autopsia de los partidos políticos*. Lima: Ediciones "Páginas Peruanas."

Mische, Ann. 2009. "Projects and Possibilities: Researching Futures in Action." *Sociological Forum* 24:694–704.

Molinari Morales, Tirso. 2006. *El fascismo en el Perú: La Unión Revolucionaria, 1931–1936*. Lima: Fondo Editorial de la Facultad de Ciencias Sociales, Universidad Nacional Mayor de San Marcos.

Morris, Aldon D. 1984. *The Origins of the Civil Rights Movement: Black Communities Organizing for Change.* New York: Free Press.

Mudde, Cas, and Cristóbal Rovira Kaltwasser, eds. 2012. *Populism in Europe and the Americas: Threat or Corrective for Democracy?* Cambridge: Cambridge University Press.

Mücke, Ulrich. 2001. "Elections and Political Participation in Nineteenth-Century Peru: The 1871–72 Presidential Campaign." *Journal of Latin American Studies* 33:311–46.

———. 2004. *Political Culture in Nineteenth-Century Peru: The Rise of the Partido Civil.* Pittsburgh: University of Pittsburgh Press.

Oberschall, Anthony. 1973. *Social Conflict and Social Movements.* Englewood Cliffs: Prentice-Hall.

O'Donnell, Guillermo, and Philippe C. Schmitter. 1986. *Transitions from Authoritarian Rule: Tentative Conclusions About Uncertain Democracies.* Baltimore: Johns Hopkins University Press.

Pareja Pflucker, Piedad. 1978. *Anarquismo y sindicalismo en el Perú (1904–1929).* Lima: Ediciones "Rikchay" Perú.

Parker, David S. 1998. *The Idea of the Middle Class: White-Collar Workers and Peruvian Society, 1900–1955.* University Park: Pennsylvania State University Press.

Peirce, Charles S. (1878) 1992. "How to Make Our Ideas Clear." In *The Essential Peirce. Selected Philosophical Writings.* Vol. 1, *1867–1893*, edited by Nathan Houser and Christian Kloesel, 124–41. Bloomington: Indiana University Press.

Peloso, Vincent C. 1996. "Liberals, Electoral Reform, and the Popular Vote in Mid Nineteenth Century Peru." In *Liberals, Politics and Power: State Formation in Nineteenth Century Latin America*, edited by V. C. Peloso and B. Tenenbaum, 186–211. Athens: University of Georgia Press.

———. 2001. *Reformas electorales liberales y el voto popular durante la época del guano en el Perú.* Lima: Instituto de Estudios Peruanos.

Peralta, Víctor. 2005. "Los vicios del voto: El proceso electoral en el Perú, 1895–1929." In *Historia de las elecciones en el Perú: Estudios sobre el gobierno representativo*, edited by Cristóbal Aljovín de Losada and Sinesio López, 75–107. Lima: Instituto de Estudios Peruanos.

Pierson, Paul. 2003. "Big, Slow-Moving, and . . . Invisible: Macrosociological Processes in the Study of Comparative Politics." In *Comparative Historical Analysis in the Social Sciences*, edited by James Mahoney and Dietrich Rueschemeyer, 177–207. Cambridge: Cambridge University Press.

Pike, Fredrick B. 1967. *The Modern History of Peru.* New York: Praeger.

———. 1986. *The Politics of the Miraculous in Peru: Haya de la Torre and the Spiritualist Tradition.* Lincoln: University of Nebraska Press.

Polletta, Francesca. 2002. *Freedom is an Endless Meeting.* Chicago: University of Chicago Press.

Posada-Carbó, Eduardo, ed. 1996. *Elections before Democracy: The History of Elections in Europe and Latin America.* New York: St. Martin's Press.

Przeworski, Adam. 1977. "Proletariat into a Class: The Process of Class Formation from Karl Kautsky's The Class Struggle to Recent Controversies." *Politics and Society* 7:343–401.

Quijano, Anibal. 1968. "Tendencies in Peruvian Development and Class Structure." *Latin America: Reform or Revolution?*, edited by James Petras and Maurice Zeitlin, 289–328. Greenwich: Fawcett.

Ramos Tremolada, Ricardo. 1990. "La democracia de Haya e el país incomprendido." In *Pensamiento político Peruano, 1930–1968*, edited by Alberto Adrianzén, 93–112. Lima: DESCO.

Ravines, Eudocio. 1952. *La gran estafa (La penetración del Kremlin en Iberoamérica).* México, D.F.: Libros y Revistas, S.A.

Redding, Kent. 1992. "Failed Populism: Movement-Party Disjuncture in North Carolina, 1890–1900." *American Sociological Review* 57:340–52.

Riley, Dylan. 2010. *The Civic Foundations of Fascism in Europe: Italy, Spain, and Romania, 1870–1945*. Baltimore: Johns Hopkins University Press.

Roehner, Bertrand M., and Tony Syme. 2002. *Pattern and Repertoire in History*. Cambridge, MA: Harvard University Press.

Rogers, Mary F. 1974. "Instrumental and Infra-Resources: The Bases of Power." *American Journal of Sociology* 79:1418–33.

Romanelli, Raffaele. 1998. "Electoral Systems and Social Structures. A Comparative Perspective." In *How Did They Become Voters? The History of Franchise in Modern European Representation*, edited by Raffaele Romanelli, 1–36. The Hague: Kluwer Law International.

Rydgren, Jens. 2006. *From Tax Populism to Ethnic Nationalism: Radical Right-Wing Populism in Sweden*. New York: Berghahn.

Sabroso Montoya, Arturo. 1934. *Réplicas Proletarias*. Lima: Editorial Imprenta "Minerva."

Salisbury, Richard V. 1983. "The Middle American Exile of Víctor Raúl Haya de la Torre." *The Americas* 40:1–15.

Sanborn, Cynthia Ann. 1995. "Los obreros textiles de Lima: Redes sociales y organización laboral, 1900–1930." In *Mundos interiores: Lima 1850–1950*, edited by Aldo Panfici H. and Felipe Portocarrero S., 187–215. Lima: Universidad del Pacífico.

Sánchez, Luis Alberto. 1969. *Testimonio personal. Memorias de un peruano del siglo XX*. 4 vols. Lima: Ediciones Villasan.

———. 1982. *Literature and Politics in Latin America: An Annotated Calendar of the Luis Alberto Sánchez Correspondence, 1919–1980*. University Park: Pennsylvania State University Libraries.

———. 1985. *Haya de la Torre y el APRA*. Lima: Editorial Universo S.A.

Sánchez Cerro, Luis. 1931. *Programa del Gobierno del Comandante Luis M. Sánchez Cerro, Candidato a la Presidencia de la República del Perú*. Lima.

Schefler, Israel. 1974. *Four Pragmatists: A Critical Introduction to Peirce, James, Mead, and Dewey*. New York: Humanities Press.

Scheina, Robert L. 1987. *Latin America: A Naval History, 1810–1987*. Annapolis: Naval Institute Press.

Schneiderhan, Erik. 2011. "Pragmatism and Empirical Sociology: The Case of Jane Addams and Hull-House, 1889–1895." *Theory and Society* 40:589–617.

Schwartz, Michael. 1976. *Radical Protest and Social Structure: The Southern Farmers' Alliance and Cotton Tenancy, 1880–1890*. New York: Academic Press.

Seoane, Manuel A. 1931. *Con los trabajadores estamos los Apristas*. Santiago de Chile.

Sewell, William H., Jr. 1996. "Historical Events as Transformations of Structures: Inventing Revolution at the Bastille." *Theory and Society* 25:841–81.

———. 2005. *Logics of History: Social Theory and Social Transformation*. Chicago: University of Chicago Press.

Shook, John R., and Joseph Margolis, eds. 2006. *A Companion to Pragmatism*. Oxford: Blackwell.

Silver, Daniel. 2011. "The Moodiness of Action." *Sociological Theory* 29:199–222.

Skidmore, Thomas E. 1979. "Workers and Soldiers: Urban Labor Movements and Elite Responses in Twentieth-Century Latin America." In *Elites, Masses, and Modernization in Latin America, 1850–1930*, edited by Virginia Bernhard, 79–126. Austin: University of Texas Press.

Skocpol, Theda. 1979. *States and Social Revolutions: A Comparative Analysis of France, Russia, and China*. Cambridge: Cambridge University Press.

Snow, David A., and Robert D. Benford. 1992. "Master Frames and Cycles of Protest." In *Frontiers in Social Movement Theory*, edited by Aldon D. Morris and Carol McClurg Mueller, 133–55. New Haven, CT: Yale University Press.

Snow, David A., E. Burke Rochford, Steven K. Worden, and Robert D. Benford. 1986. "Frame Alignment Processes, Micromobilization, and Movement Participation." *American Sociological Review* 51:464–81.

Soifer, Hillel. 2015. *State Building in Latin America*. Cambridge: Cambridge University Press.

Soifer, Hillel, and Matthias vom Hau. 2008. "Unpacking the Strength of the State: The Utility of State Infrastructural Power." *Studies in Comparative International Development* 43:219–30.

Soule, Sarah A. 1992. "Populism and Black Lynching in Georgia, 1890–1900." *Social Forces* 71:431–49.

Spalding, Hobart A., Jr. 1977. *Organized Labor in Latin America: Historical Case Studies of Workers in Dependent Societies*. New York: New York University Press.

Stark, David. 1996. "Recombinant Property in East European Capitalism." *American Journal of Sociology* 101:993–1027.

Stein, Steve. 1980. *Populism in Peru: The Emergence of the Masses and the Politics of Social Control*. Madison: University of Wisconsin Press.

———. 1982. "Populism in Peru: APRA, the Formative Years." In *Latin American Populism in Comparative Perspective*, edited by Michael L. Conniff, 113–34. Albuquerque: University of New Mexico Press.

———. 1986. *Lima obrera, 1900–1930*. Vol. 1. Lima: El Virrey.

———, ed. 1987. *Lima obrera, 1900–1930*. Vol. 2. Lima: El Virrey.

———. 1999. "The Paths to Populism in Peru." In *Populism in Latin America*, edited by Michael L. Conniff, 97–116. Tuscaloosa: University of Alabama Press.

Steinberg, Marc W. 1995. "The Roar of the Crowd: Repertoires of Discourse and Collective Action among the Spitalfields Silk Weavers in Nineteenth-Century London." In *Repertoires and Cycles of Collective Action*, edited by Mark Traugott, 57–87. Durham, NC: Duke University Press.

Stepan, Alfred. 1978. *The State and Society: Peru in Comparative Perspective*. Princeton, NJ: Princeton University Press.

Stephens, Evelyne Huber. 1989. "Capitalist Development and Democracy in South America." *Politics and Society* 17:281–352.

Swidler, Ann. 1986. "Culture in Action: Symbols and Strategies." *American Sociological Review* 51:273–86.

———. 2001. *Talk of Love: How Culture Matters*. Chicago: University of Chicago Press.

Taggart, Paul. 2004. "Populism and Representative Politics in Contemporary Europe." *Journal of Political Ideologies* 9:269–88.

Tamayo, José. 1980. *Historia del indigenismo cusqueño siglos XVI-XX*. Lima: INC.

Tarrow, Sidney. 1989. *Democracy and Disorder: Protest and Politics in Italy, 1965–1975*. Oxford: Oxford University Press.

———. 1995. "Cycles of Collective Action: Between Moments of Madness and the Repertoire of Contention." In *Repertoires and Cycles of Collective Action*, edited by Mark Traugott, 89–115. Durham, NC: Duke University Press.

———. 1998. *Power in Movement*. New York: Cambridge University Press.

Tauro, Alberto. 1986. *Amauta y su influencia*. Lima: Editorial 'Minerva.'

Tavory, Iddo, and Stefan Timmermans. 2014. *Abductive Analysis: Theorizing Qualitative Research*. Chicago: University of Chicago Press.

REFERENCES

Tejada, Luis. 1985. "La influencia anarquista en el APRA." *Socialismo y participación* 29:97–110.

Thompson, E. P. 1963. *The Making of the English Working Class*. New York: Pantheon.

Thurner, Mark. 1995. "'Republicanos' and 'la Comunidad de Peruanos': Unimagined Political Communities in Postcolonial Andean Peru." *Journal of Latin American Studies* 27:291–318.

Tilly, Charles, ed. 1975. *The Formation of National States in Western Europe*. Princeton, NJ: Princeton University Press.

———. 1976. "Major Forms of Collective Action in Western Europe 1500–1975." *Theory and Society* 3:365–75.

———. 1978. *From Mobilization to Revolution*. New York: McGraw-Hill.

———. 1984. *Big Structures, Large Processes, Huge Comparisons*. New York: Russell Sage Foundation.

———. 1986. *The Contentious French*. Cambridge, MA: Harvard University Press.

———. 1995. *Popular Contention in Great Britain*. Cambridge, MA: Harvard University Press.

———. 2003. *The Politics of Collective Violence*. Cambridge: Cambridge University Press.

———. 2006. *Regimes and Repertoires*. Chicago: University of Chicago Press.

———. 2008. *Contentious Performances*. Cambridge: Cambridge University Press.

Traugott, Marc. 1995. *Repertoires and Cycles of Collective Action*. Durham, NC: Duke University Press.

Trimberger, Ellen Kay. 1978. *Revolution from Above: Military Bureaucrats and Development in Japan, Turkey, Egypt and Peru*. New Brunswick, NJ: Transaction.

Tuesta Soldevilla, Fernando. 2001. *Perú político en cifras, 1821–2001*. Lima: Freidrich Ebert Stiftung.

Učeň, Peter. 2007. "Parties, Populism, and Anti-Establishment Politics in East Central Europe." *SAIS Review* 27:49–62.

Ugarteche, Pedro, ed. 1969–70. *Sánchez Cerro: Papeles y recuerdos de un presidente del Perú*. 4 vols. Lima: Editorial Universitaria.

United Nations (Department of Social Affairs, Population Division). 1952. *Methods of Estimating Total Population for Current Dates*. New York: United Nations (Department of Social Affairs, Population Division).

United States Census Bureau. 2012. "Methodology for the Intercensal Population and Housing Unit Estimates: 2000 to 2010." Accessed June 1, 2016. https://www.census.gov/popest/methodology/index.html.

Valcárcel, Luis E. 1927. *Tempestad en los Andes*. Lima: Editorial Minerva.

van Niekerk, A. E. 1974. *Populism and Political Development in Latin America*. Rotterdam: Rotterdam University Press.

Velázquez, Marcel. 2005. "Notas sobre discursos e imágenes de las elecciones en la República del Guano (1845–1872)." In *Historia de las elecciones en el Perú: Estudios sobre el gobierno representativo*, edited by C. Aljovín de Losada and S. López, 265–99. Lima: Instituto de Estudios Peruanos.

Villanueva Valencia, Víctor. 1962. *El Militarismo en el Perú*. Lima: Empresa Gráfica T. Scheuch S.A.

———. 1973. *El ejército peruano, del caudillaje anárquico al militarismo reformista*. Lima: Librería-Editorial Juan Mejía Baca.

———. 1975. *El APRA en busca del poder*. Lima: Editorial Horizonte.

———. 1977. *Asi cayó Leguía*. Lima: Retama Editorial.

Villarán, Manuel V. 1918. "Costumbres electorales." *Mercurio Peruano* 1:11–19.

Wagner-Pacifici, Robin. 2010. "Theorizing the Restlessness of Events." *American Journal of Sociology* 115:1351–86.

Waisman, Carlos H. 1982. *Modernization and the Working Class: The Politics of Legitimacy.* Austin: University of Texas Press.

———. 1987. *Reversal of Development in Argentina: Postwar Counterrevolutionary Politics and Their Structural Consequences.* Princeton, NJ: Princeton University Press.

Walder, Andrew. 2009. *Fractured Rebellion: The Beijing Red Guard Movement.* Cambridge, MA: Harvard University Press.

Walker, Charles F. 1999. *Smoldering Ashes: Cuzco and the Creation of Republican Peru, 1780–1840.* Durham, NC: Duke University Press.

———. 2014. *The Tupac Amaru Rebellion.* Cambridge, MA: Harvard University Press.

Walker, Edward T., Andrew W. Martin, and John D. McCarthy. 2008. "Confronting the State, the Corporation, and the Academy: The Influence of Institutional Targets on Social Movement Repertoires." *American Journal of Sociology* 114:35–76.

Weber, Max. (1922) 1978. *Economy and Society: An Outline of Interpretive Sociology.* Berkeley: University of California Press.

Weyland, Kurt. 1996. "Neopopulism and Neoliberalism in Latin America: Unexpected Affinities." *Studies in Comparative International Development* 31:3–31.

———. 1999. "Neoliberal Populism in Latin America and Eastern Europe." *Comparative Politics* 31:379–401.

White, James W. 1995. "Cycles and Repertoires of Popular Contention in Early Modern Japan." In *Repertoires and Cycles of Collective Action*, edited by Mark Traugott, 145–71. Durham, NC: Duke University Press.

Whitford, Josh. 2002. "Pragmatism and the Untenable Dualism of Means and Ends: Why Rational Choice Theory Does Not Deserve Paradigmatic Privilege." *Theory and Society* 31: 325–63.

Wickham-Crowley, Timothy P. 1992. *Guerrillas and Revolution in Latin America: A Comparative Study of Insurgents and Regimes Since 1956.* Princeton, NJ: Princeton University Press.

Wolf, E., and E. C. Hanson. 1967. "Caudillo Politics: A Structural Analysis." *Comparative Studies in Society and History* 9:168–79.

Yarlequé de Marquina, Josefa. 1963. *El Maestro, ó democracia en miniatura.* Lima: Librería é Imprenta J. Alvarez A.

Yashar, Deborah J. 2005. *Contesting Citizenship in Latin America: The Rise of Indigenous Movements and the Postliberal Challenge.* Cambridge: Cambridge University Press.

Yepes, Ernesto. 1990. "Comentario." In *Pensamiento político Peruano, 1930–1968*, edited by Alberto Adrianzén, 78–79. Lima: DESCO.

Zald, Mayer N. 2000. "Ideologically Structured Action: An Enlarged Agenda for Social Movement Research." *Mobilization: An International Quarterly* 5:1–16.

Index

Page numbers followed by "f" and "t" refer to figures and tables, respectively.

Alianza Popular Revolucionaria Americana (APRA): allegations of electoral fraud by, 53, 196, 199; Casas del Pueblo, 160–61, 166; endorsement of Sánchez Cerro's coup (1930), 104; founding of, 49, 86, 93–94, 107, 143–44; grassroots incorporative organizing by, 7, 52, 147, 157–62, 170, 177; leadership of, 139, 143–44; middle class support for, 145, 157–58; political persecution of, 108–9, 137, 143–46; political program of, 176, 185–86, 188; and the popular universities, 52, 159–60; propaganda, 107, 161, 199n11; provincial campaigns, 7, 50–52, 145, 162, 170, 173, 176; rallies, 50, 128f, 170, 173–77, 180–82, 188f, 189; and rural schools, 159–60; structure of, 144–45, 147–48, 156–58, 160–61, 170, 177, 197; student support for, 138; women's support for, 158; working class support for, 138, 158, 193. *See also* Haya de la Torre, Víctor Raúl; Partido Aprista Peruano
Amauta, 95–96, 146
Anderson, Benedict, 37
Arequipa, 45; growth of, 64; military garrison, 48, 99–102, 137; politics in, 169, 174f, 220. *See also* Revolution of Arequipa
Argentina, 3, 61n1, 70–74, 76, 94, 202
Aristocratic Republic, 43–45, 81–85
Aspíllaga, Ántero, 85

Barranco, 64, 65f
Basadre, Jorge, 27, 43, 124
Belaúnde Diez-Canseco, Rafael, 88, 124–25, 127
Billinghurst, Guillermo, 45, 67, 84, 100, 126n5, 136n21, 189

Bolivia, 8, 73, 73n18, 94, 202. *See also* War of the Pacific
Brazil, 3, 70–74, 76, 126, 202

Cáceres, Andrés, 82
Cajamarca, 193, 199n10, 200
Callao, 102, 106, 134n18, 183; growth of, 61, 64, 65f, 68, 87; politics in, 160, 168; suffrage in, 114, 116, 117n59, 118; unemployment in, 68
capituleros, 41, 165–66, 195
Cárdenas, Lázaro, 202
Catholic Church, 39, 92
caudillo politics, 44, 47, 59, 109–10, 204
Chávez, Hugo, 8, 57
Chile, 45, 71, 73, 83, 94, 98, 108, 202. *See also* War of the Pacific
Chorrillos, 64, 65f, 99, 168
clientelism: as a feature of popular mobilization, 33, 41–42, 47; as a feature of populist mobilization, 139, 195; under Leguía, 97; in traditional political practice, 8, 38–39, 60, 65, 71, 165n26, 204
Colombia, 72–73, 73n18, 98, 202
Comité de Saneamiento y Consolidación Revolucionaria, 104, 134–35
Communist International, 97, 129–30, 132–33, 151
Concentración Nacional (CN), 125–27, 138, 142
Confederación General de Trabajadores del Perú (CGTP), 108–9, 130
Conscripción Vial, 62, 182–83
Cortes de Cádiz, 38
coup d'état (practice of), 38, 47, 204
Cox, Carlos Manuel, 108, 144

creativity, 3–4, 17–21 passim, 74–75, 122, 133, 206–7
Cuba, 93–94, 202
Cuzco: growth of, 61n1, 64; and Incan Empire, 37; politics in, 39n19, 90, 95, 169; suffrage in, 114, 116

Dewey, John, 19

Ecuador, 72–73, 73n18, 202
Eguiguren, Luis Antonio, 135n20, 165n25, 167
elections: of 1851, 41n24; of 1872, 41, 42, 47; of 1895, 43; of 1908, 84; of 1912, 45; of 1919, 81, 85, 87; of 1924, 86, 88; of 1931, 27–28, 53, 54f, 112, 193, 197–200; practice of, 38–44
electoral reforms: of 1896, 43–44; of 1931 (Estatuto Electoral), 48, 112–13, 115, 117–19
Enríquez, Luis Eduardo, 106–8, 147

fascism: conceptual imprecision of, 213–14; influence on Haya de la Torre, 147–48, 150, 189; influence on Sánchez Cerro, 100n29, 139; in Peru, 6n6, 103, 135
Federación de Estudiantes del Perú (FEP), 89–90
Flores, Lourdes, 56
Flores, Luis A., 167
France, 14–15, 88n8, 210, 213
Fujimori, Alberto, 56

García, Alan, 56
Germany, 94, 107, 162
González Prada, Manuel, 46
grassroots incorporative organizing, 7, 52, 155–57, 169–70, 181, 198; by APRA (*see under* Alianza Popular Revolucionaria Americana); by Unión Revolucionaria (*see under* Unión Revolucionaria)
Great Depression, 48, 68, 88, 123, 130, 145, 194, 205
Gross, Neil, 19, 23n15
guano boom, 39–40, 41n24, 41n25, 44, 60, 71, 72
Guardia Civil, 87, 98, 104
Guatemala, 94, 182

haciendas, 60, 62, 68, 71, 98, 131
Haya de la Torre, Víctor Raúl, 51f, 149f, 178f; biography of, 5, 89–90, 150; exile of, 49, 93–94, 106, 146, 150; and the founding of APRA, 49, 93–94; outsider status of, 6, 49, 79–80, 89; and his Plan de México, 96–97, 106; political disposition of, 5, 79, 90, 96, 133, 143, 146, 149–50; political experience of, 49, 89–94, 144–47, 150; political rhetoric of, 7, 52–53, 146, 149, 181–82, 186–88, 194; and the popular universities, 90, 159, 91f; split from Mariátegui, 96–97, 107n43, 131, 133, 144. *See also* Alianza Popular Revolucionaria Americana
Humala, Ollanta, 57

indigenismo, 34, 46–47, 95–96
innovation, 18–19, 20n14. *See also* political innovation
Italy, 94, 95n21, 100n29, 140, 213

James, William, 19
Jara y Ureta, José María de la, 126, 127, 129
Jiménez, Gustavo, 112, 118n61, 124–25
Joas, Hans, 19

Klarén, Peter, 27–28, 28n1, 35n12

labor movement: and anarcho-syndicalism, 46, 90, 195–96; general strike (1919), 89–90; historical origins of, 66–68, 72, 76; and the PCP, 130–33; protest against consecration of Lima (1923), 91–93; relationship with student movement, 85–86, 89–91, 96–97, 147
La Libertad, 161n12, 162, 193
Lanatta, Francisco, 182
La Tribuna, 145, 162n16
Leguía, Augusto B.: biography of, 83–84; and the consecration of Lima (1923), 92–93; death of, 104–6; elections under, 86; exile of, 84, 87; first presidency of, 84; imprisonment of, 101–2, 104, 106; Leguiístas, 84; modernization under, 5, 61–62, 68, 86–87, 194; overthrow of, 1, 48, 101; political repression by, 5, 46, 86, 93, 98, 123, 143; relationship with the military, 85, 97–98; relationship with the Partido Civil, 84–85, 87–88. *See also Oncenio*
Lima, 179f; civic associations in, 66–67; migration to, 64; modernization of, 61f, 63f, 64, 65f, 71; politics in, 1–2, 6, 45, 103f, 162, 170, 173–74; suffrage in, 114

Magdalena del Mar, 64, 65f, 161, 166–67, 168n31
Manifesto of Arequipa, 101, 104, 137, 139n25, 181, 199
Mariátegui, José Carlos: founding of *Amauta*, 95; founding of the CGTP, 108; founding of the PSP, 96; and the *indigenista* movement, 46–47, 95–96; relationship with Haya de la Torre, 95, 133, 150; split from Haya de la Torre, 96–97, 107n43, 131, 133, 144
Marx, Karl, 10
Marxism, 3, 10, 69, 69n13, 70, 147
Mead, George Herbert, 19
Mexico, 49, 93–94, 143, 202
military: conflicts within, 48, 98, 101–2, 110; professionalization of, 43, 82n2, 97, 99–100, 110, 205; relationship with APRA, 56, 112, 200; relationship with Leguía, 85, 97–98; relationship with Sánchez Cerro, 48–49, 110
Miraflores, 64, 65f, 164, 168
Miró Quesada Laos, Carlos, 126n6, 169, 189

mobilization, 28–29. *See also* political mobilization; popular mobilization; populist mobilization
mobilization, populist. *See* populist mobilization
modernization theory, 69–70
Molinari Morales, Tirso, 27
Morales, Evo, 8

nationalism: conceptual imprecision of, 213–14; in Haya de la Torre's rhetoric, 7–8, 52, 107, 148; in Latin America, 37, 37n14; in Peru, 46–47, 135; and populist mobilization, 31–34; in Sánchez Cerro's rhetoric, 6–8, 52, 100, 129, 137, 141, 181, 184

Odría, Manuel, 56
Oncenio, 46, 86–99 passim, 130. *See also* Leguía, Augusto B.
Osores, Arturo, 126–27, 129

Panama, 93–94, 154t
Paraguay, 202
Pardo, José, 84–85, 89
Pardo, Manuel, 41–42, 83
Partido Aprista Peruano (PAP), 49, 107, 144, 145, 187, 188f. *See also* Alianza Popular Revolucionaria Americana
Partido Civil: adherents of, 53; during the Aristocratic Republic, 43–44, 82–85; founding of, 41–42; internal conflicts within, 82–85; repression by Leguía, 87–88
Partido Comunista del Perú (PCP): alignment with Communist International, 97, 129, 133; and the CGTP, 130; endorsement of Sánchez Cerro's 1930 coup, 104; founding of, 97; increasing militancy of, 121, 129–33, 151, 205
Partido Demócrata, 43–44, 124
Partido Socialista del Perú (PSP), 96, 97, 129
Peirce, Charles Sanders, 19
Perón, Juan Domingo, 70, 72n17, 202, 214
Peru: colonial era, 35, 37; constitution of 1860, 41n24, 42; economic development, 59–60, 86–87, 204–5 (*see also* Great Depression; guano boom); independence, 37–38, 59; modernization of, 60–62, 64–65, 204–5; regionalism, 8, 38–39; state development, 39–40, 41n24, 59, 68, 87; urbanization of, 62–64
Piérola, Nicolás de, 43, 46, 82n2, 88, 97, 124
Plaza de Acho, 1, 176f, 180, 186
Plaza de Armas, 179, 179f
Plaza San Martín, 160, 179, 179f, 180, 182, 184, 186
political culture, 8, 13, 202, 211
political innovation, ix–x, xii, 16, 19–25, 80, 191, 206–10. *See also* innovation
political institutions, 10, 12, 38, 127
political mobilization, 28–29, 30n4

political parties: during the Aristocratic Republic, 43–45, 82–83; in nineteenth century, 39–42; repression by Leguía, 48–49, 87–88
political practice: and contingency, 17–18, 211; and habitual action, ix, 12–13, 20, 121–23, 207; importance of, ix, 11; theories of, 11–12, 17–18, 203, 211. *See also* political innovation; repertoires, political
popular mobilization: definition of, 30–31, 34; as distinct from populist rhetoric, 33, 42; in Latin America, 34–35; in Peru, 41–42, 44–45, 204
popular universities, 46n39, 52, 90–95 passim, 144, 159–60. *See also under* Alianza Popular Revolucionaria Americana; Haya de la Torre, Víctor Raúl
populism: conceptual imprecision of, xii, 35, 213–15; contemporary relevance of, x–xi, 213, 215; structuralist theories of, xi–xii, 3–4, 69–71, 73, 78n22. *See also* populist mobilization
populist mobilization: as conceptually preferable to "populism," xi–xii, 30n4, 213; definition of, 30–34; in Latin America, x–xii, 8–9, 34–35, 201–3; strategic versatility of, xi, 55–57, 213
populist rhetoric: definition of, 31–34, 181; as distinct from popular mobilization, 33, 42; of Haya de la Torre (*see* Haya de la Torre, Víctor Raúl: political rhetoric of); in Latin America, 34–35; in Peru, 38, 44–45, 192–94, 201; of Sánchez Cerro (*see* Sánchez Cerro, Luis M.: political rhetoric of)
pragmatism, 19–23, 74, 77, 206–12
propaganda, 41, 156, 171, 173, 181–82

rallies, 7, 30, 41, 50, 170–73, 180–81, 194; of APRA (*see under* Alianza Popular Revolucionaria Americana); of Unión Revolucionaria (*see under* Unión Revolucionaria)
Ravines, Eudocio, 97, 129, 133
repertoires, political: definition of, 12–13; in Peru, 27–28, 35, 47–48, 55–57, 191–92, 204–6; and political innovation, 15–19, 22–23, 203, 206–10; theories of, 13–16, 210–11. *See also* political practice
República Aristocrática. *See* Aristocratic Republic
Revolution of Arequipa, 48, 103, 103f, 175, 183, 189
rhetoric, populist. *See* populist rhetoric

Samanez Ocampo, David, 112, 124–25; junta headed by, 111–12, 118, 125, 128f, 141–44
Sánchez, Luis Alberto, 108, 108n44, 161, 173
Sánchezcerrista movement: origins of, 103–4; persistence of, 134, 141–42, 197
Sánchez Cerro, Luis M., 51f, 105f, 111f, 140f, 178f, 188f, assassination of, 53n43, 200, biography of, 5–6, 99, 137; coup against Leguía (1930), 1, 48, 99, 100–101, 138; exile of, 48–49, 100, 109–11,

Sánchez Cerro, Luis M. (*cont.*) 118, 138; and the founding of UR, 49; outsider status of, 6, 49, 79–80, 99, 141; political disposition of, 6, 79, 100, 111f, 136–37, 139; political experience of, 100, 136–40; political repression by, 48, 53, 104, 108–9, 200 (*see also* Comité de Saneamiento y Consolidación Revolucionaria); political rhetoric of, 7, 52–53, 181–85, 187–88, 194; popular support for, 99, 102, 109, 137, 138–40, 151, 170, 175; provisional presidency of, 48, 102–4, 109, 136, 143; resignation of (1931), 48, 109–10, 183. *See also* Revolution of Arequipa; Unión Revolucionaria

Sánchez Cerro, Pablo E., 167
Seoane, Manuel, 108–9, 145, 161
Stein, Steve, 27, 28n1
student movement: general strike (1919), 89–90; opposition to Sánchez Cerro, 100; protest against consecration of Lima (1923), 91–93; relationship with labor movement, 85–86, 89–91, 96–97, 147; and university reform, 85, 89. *See also* Federación de Estudiantes del Perú
suffrage: in 1931, 48, 112–18, 193; during the Aristocratic Republic, 44, 82, 135; in nineteenth century, 38–39, 42

Talara, 176
Tarrow, Sidney, 210
Tilly, Charles, 12, 14–16, 23, 29n3, 210
Trujillo: APRA organizing in, 162; APRA regional congress in, 145, 161n12, 162n17; Haya de la Torre's ties to, 89, 150; insurrection in, 198–200; Trujillo Bohemia, 89, 143
Túpac Amaru II, 35, 37

Ugarteche, Pedro, 53, 135, 137n23, 140, 169, 189
Unión Revolucionaria (UR): elite support for, 135, 142, 165; founding of, 49, 134, 162; grassroots incorporative organizing by, 7, 141–42, 157, 163–70, 177, 197; leadership of, 134–35, 139, 141; political program of, 175, 184–85; propaganda, 133n17, 165–67; provincial campaigns, 7, 50–52, 168–70, 173, 177; rallies, 50, 103f, 128f, 170, 173–75, 177–80, 188f, 189; structure of, 156, 163–66, 169–70, 177; women's support for, 167; working class support for, 193. *See also* Sánchez Cerro, Luis M.
Universidades Populares González Prada (UPGP). *See* popular universities
Uruguay, 71, 73, 202

Vallejo, César, 89, 94n17
Vargas, Getúlio, 70, 72n17, 202
Velasco, Juan, 56
Venezuela, 8, 72–73, 182, 202

War of the Pacific, 43, 44n32, 46, 84, 100
Weber, Max, 10